The Public Life of Eugene Semple

Promoter and Politician of the Pacific Northwest

The Public Life of Eugene Semple

Promoter and Politician
of the Pacific Northwest

Alan Hynding

UNIVERSITY OF WASHINGTON PRESS
SEATTLE AND LONDON

This book was published with the assistance of a grant from the Andrew W. Mellon Foundation.

Library of Congress Cataloging in Publication Data

Hynding, Alan, 1936–
   The public life of Eugene Semple.

   Bibliography: p.
   1. Semple, Eugene, 1840-1908. I. Title.
F891.H96 · 1973   979.5'04'0924 [B]
ISBN 0-295-95288-1   73-9903

To my beloved wife, Gayle, and to my mother and father

Contents

Illustrations

All illustrations are reproduced courtesy of the Special Collections Division, University of Washington Libraries

Introduction

At about the same time that Mark Twain made his memorable journey by stagecoach to the Nevada Comstock in 1861, a small army of fortune hunters descended upon the Pacific slope, fleeing Civil War duty and other problems of life in the East. They came by land and sea to the camps and villages that are today the great cities of the Far West. One of these immigrants, somewhat smaller and younger than most, was a twenty-three-year-old prairie-bred lawyer named Eugene Semple, the son of a former United States senator from Illinois. Forsaking the opportunities his family's influence afforded him in St. Louis and southern Illinois, he sailed via Panama to Portland in the summer of 1863. Ostensibly he had come west to practice law, but his real ambitions lay elsewhere. From the year of his arrival until his death in 1908, Semple was engaged in a remarkable variety of pursuits which in one way or another influenced the development of the Pacific Northwest. From the beginning, this wiry, bespectacled man possessed an entrepreneur's instinct about the region's potential for economic development and most of his life was devoted to cashing in on that potential. But Semple also loved the Northwest and, not untypically, combined a promoter's acquisitive drive with a strong sense of civic pride and public responsibility.

Semple's career in the Pacific Northwest paralleled the boom years of the region—and the bust years too. In Oregon he was bankrupted by the Panic of 1873 but was back in business as a sawmill owner in Washington Territory when flush times returned in the eighties. Reminiscent of Twain's Colonel Sellers, the madcap promoter, speculator, and spellbinder of *The Gilded Age*, Semple possessed a charm, glibness, and dedication to endless (and often worthless) financial propositions that made him something of a tragicomic figure.

Opportunities abounded for young men of Semple's disposition in the Northwest during the years after the Civil War. Newspapers and other documents of the period, including Semple's own correspondence, testify that nearly every townsite and hamlet had its flock of boosters, most of whom remained as obscure as the dreams they sought to make realities. Semple was in many respects the typical frontier speculator—imaginative, naively optimistic, a man on the make. Limitless vision, boundless enthusiasm and energy, ingenuity, and resourcefulness—all the characteristics of the species were abundantly evident in him. Typical was his fanciful 1890 prospectus for the Skagit Valley, which even today remains a rather sparsely developed area. "There is nothing in the Arabian nights more astonishing than the growth of this area in the last month," he wrote eastern investors.

The Skagit River is larger and navigable for as great a distance as the Willamette and has a valley much richer and nearly as extensive. Along this river are iron, coal and galena mines and marble quarries besides vast areas of timber. In addition, it affords a low pass through the mountains through which the products of the eastern section of the state can reach the sea by a hundred miles less travel than by way of Tacoma or Seattle.[1]

Semple's greatest fascination was with the bountiful waterways of the Pacific Northwest, so crucial to the commercial and industrial future of the region. Off and on for a quarter of a century he publicized the benefits of various river and harbor improvement projects, from Astoria and Vancouver on the Columbia River to Seattle and Tacoma on Puget Sound.

Semple was also a political figure of some significance in Pacific Northwest history. As territorial governor of Washington during the hectic late 1880s, he advocated greater government concern for the problems of the inrushing waves of settlers. Here his instincts as a promoter came into play once more as he prodded territorial lawmakers to authorize appropriations for hospitals, asylums, and other charitable institutions, and urged the federal government to begin navigation improvements on the Columbia and other watercourses. Later, as the

1. Semple to Lucy Ames, February 13, 1890, Eugene Semple Papers, University of Washington Library, Seattle.

leading member of the Washington State Harbor Line Commission, Semple struggled against private interests to secure valuable public tidelands and harbor areas for the use of future generations.

Throughout his political career Semple was an outspoken supporter of the rights of white workingmen, whom he endeavored to defend against the twin perils of exploitative management and cheap nonwhite labor. During his early stint as editor of the Oregon Democratic party's principal newspaper, the Portland *Herald*, he vehemently denounced both the Chinese "invaders" and powerful capitalists like Ben Holladay. Later, as governor of Washington Territory, he was equally outspoken against the formidable Northern Pacific Coal Company and the Oregon Improvement Company when these firms tried to subvert territorial and federal laws by importing private guards to defeat the union movement in the coal mines of the Cascades.

Semple grew up with the Pacific Northwest. As journalist, printer, lawyer, public official, mill owner, amateur engineer, farmer, and land speculator, he was involved with many of the major issues and personalities of the period. As the center of regional economic power moved north from Portland to Seattle late in the century, so did Semple. For all his timely involvement in those history-making years, however, he had little to show for it in terms of material rewards. He lacked the shrewd business acumen of first rank frontier capitalists like Seattle's Thomas Burke or Oregon's legendary Ben Holladay, both of whom he opposed on several occasions.

As a result, his particular significance to the history of the Northwest is more difficult to assess. Many of his contemporaries had come to the region to recoup lost fortunes in land speculation, or to mine for gold, or to farm or to establish careers. Semple was not inspired by any of these desires, at least not for long. Having arrived in the Northwest, he remained restless and never really settled down. By temperament rather than because of any real lack of ability, he was ill suited for the life of a banker, lawyer, or farmer. His personal affairs were at times in such disorder that he was without the money to pay for even a month's lodging. Semple might have returned to Illinois or St. Louis where relatives continually promised him the economic security he was never able to attain in the West. But having come, he chose to stay, searching for something he perhaps could not define, something he perhaps never found. As a public figure, Semple's life furnishes a case study of a promoter and politician on the Pacific

Northwest frontier. Whether he was a "typical" man of his time in other respects is more difficult to judge.

It should be emphasized at the outset that this study focuses, as the title indicates, on the public life of Semple and not on his private life, in spite of the fact that his personal affairs raise some tantalizing questions for both the author and the reader. I was primarily interested in Semple as a political figure. I was also reluctant to make judgments about his private character in the absence of a fuller understanding of his relations with his family, especially with his wife and children.

This book began as a research paper for a seminar in American history under Professor Arthur E. Bestor, Jr., at the University of Washington a decade ago. It grew into a dissertation under the direction of Professor Vernon Carstensen. I am indebted in various ways to the following people: Professor Bestor and Professor Robert E. Burke for their early encouragement and suggestions; to Thomas J. Pressly for his example as a teacher, scholar, and gentleman; to Semple's granddaughter, Mrs. Lucy Adair of Seattle, who generously donated an indispensable set of papers—a missing link—relating to Semple's early life; to the University of Washington Library while I was conducting my research; to Richard C. Berner, University of Washington Archivist, for his gracious assistance, particularly in obtaining the Adair papers; and to Robert D. Monroe, head of the Special Collections Division, University of Washington Libraries, for his help in finding illustrations. I owe a very special debt to my dissertation supervisor, Vernon Carstensen, for his many insights into Semple, for his guidance, and for his kindness. Lastly, and most importantly, I thank my wife, Gayle, who assisted me in far too many ways to record here, and whose extraordinary patience and understanding were not always adequately appreciated on those many occasions when Semple's ghost intruded on our marriage.

The Public Life of Eugene Semple

Promoter and Politician of the Pacific Northwest

1. The Road West

Eugene Semple's origins were somewhat out of the ordinary when compared to the antecedents of other Pacific Northwest pioneers. Most early white residents of the region came from New England or the upper Midwest. Some had even been born in log cabins—or at least claimed to have been. Semple's beginnings were of a more exotic nature, in the surroundings of his father's consular apartments in Bogota, Colombia, on June 12, 1840. Martin Van Buren had appointed James Semple as United States Minister Plenipotentiary to what was then the young republic of New Granada in 1838, following Semple's active early career in Illinois Democratic politics.[1] Eugene was the only one of James and Mary Semple's children born during the family's four-year residence in the Andean nation; he was also their only son. The sojourn in Colombia appears to have been rather uneventful except for the family's conversion to Roman Catholicism, which seems to have coincided with their infant son's remarkable recovery from a severe illness.

The Semples traced their ancestry back to thirteenth century Scotland. The first of the clan to emigrate to America was Eugene's great-grandfather, John Semple, a parish minister who settled in Virginia in 1752 and eventually served in the legislature.[2] Eugene's

1. Mary S. A. Cushman, "General James Semple," *Transactions of the Illinois State Historical Society,* 1905, pp. 62-74. Information about James Semple contained in this chapter comes from this article unless otherwise noted.
2. A typescript of Eugene Semple's genealogy is in the Eugene Semple Papers, Manuscript Division, University of Washington Library. Hereafter cited as the Semple Papers.

mother, Mary Cairns Semple, was a member of a pioneer Illinois family and a niece of the state's first governor, Shadrach Bond.[3]

In 1842 James Semple resigned his post and returned with his wife, son, and two older daughters, Ada and Lucy, to Illinois. He was soon re-elected to the state legislature where he regained the influence he had wielded as speaker of the house during the 1830s. A year after the elder Semple's return, Governor Thomas Ford appointed him to fill an unexpired term in the United States Senate. In Washington, Semple quickly joined other western lawmakers in demanding American annexation of Oregon and became a prominent spokesman on the issue at lyceums throughout the Midwest. He supported Polk's expansionist platform in 1844, but by the time Oregon was annexed in 1846 Semple's attitude toward political life had soured and he emphatically refused to run for re-election. "I never was so sick of politics in all my life as at present," he told Eugene's mother shortly before the end of his abbreviated three year term in the Senate. "I have seen enough of it," he concluded, and withdrew from public life forever.[4] His Senate successor was Stephen A. Douglas.

In 1853, after several successful years as a land speculator and lawyer in Alton, James Semple purchased several thousand acres of farmland bordering the Mississippi River a few miles below its confluence with the Illinois. The land extended back into Jersey County, Illinois, and much of it was subdivided by Semple and leased to farm tenants. He also laid out a townsite, named it Elsah in honor of an ancestral manor in Scotland, and built a home nearby at Trevue. Eugene attended rural schools in Jersey County during the winters and toiled through the hot prairie summers on his father's estate. Once a week he delivered mail upriver along the banks of the Mississippi between Elsah and Grafton.[5] The great river, with its steady traffic of men and supplies moving upstream for destinations far to the north and west, cast its spell over the boy, much as it captivated his young contemporary, Samuel Clemens.

3. "Journal of the Constitutional Convention," *Journal of the Illinois State Historical Society,* 6 (1913-14): 410-12, 414.

4. Frank S. Stevens, "Life of Stephen Arnold Douglas," *Journal of the Illinois State Historical Society,* 16 (1923-24): 299, 394.

5. "Chronology of Eugene Semple, 1840-1905," Semple Papers. This chronology appears to have been prepared largely, if not entirely, by Semple himself. Information on Eugene Semple in this chapter is from this chronology unless otherwise noted.

During these years of life along the Mississippi, Eugene's curiosity about the Far West deepened. Two relatives were already in California. One, his older half-brother Lansing Mizner, had settled in Benicia near the north end of San Francisco Bay after coming west as an Army private during the Mexican War. Benicia itself owed its beginning to his distinguished uncle, Dr. Robert Semple, who had participated in the Bear Flag Revolt and had published the state's first English language newspaper, the *Californian*, at Monterey, before presiding over the state constitutional convention in 1849.[6] In the spring of 1857, shortly before his seventeenth birthday, Eugene set out for St. Louis hoping to join one of the overland expeditions, but arrived too late in the season to find a westward party.[7]

The next year he entered St. Louis University, where he spent the next two years exposed to higher mathematics, the physical sciences, philosophy, rhetoric, and classical languages.[8] In 1860 he quit school and began to study law under two prominent St. Louis attorneys, John Krum and Chester Harding. Krum and Harding personified the sectional rivalries that divided Missouri on the eve of the Civil War, and both men doubtless impressed their conflicting political views on their young apprentice. Krum was a former mayor of St. Louis and a nationally important Democrat who was soon to serve as chairman of the credentials committee at the ill-fated 1860 convention in Charleston. Harding on the other hand was an avid Republican and a graduate of the Harvard Law School. When the war began in 1861, Harding took a commission in the Union Army and dissolved the partnership, putting an end to Semple's legal studies for the moment.[9]

The events of Semple's life during the first year of the war are

6. Zoe Green Radcliffe, "Robert Baylor Semple, Pioneer," *California Historical Society Quarterly,* 6 (1927): 130-58 passim; Woodrow J. Hansen, "Robert Semple: Pioneer, Promoter, Politician," ibid., 41 (1962): 223-35 passim.

7. Semple recalled this episode in notes for a speech he delivered at Astoria, Oregon, ca. 1900, and in his "Chronology." The notes are in the Semple Papers.

8. The full classical course included "a competent knowledge of the Greek, Latin, and English languages; of geography, use of globes, ancient and modern history, logic and principles of moral philosophy, including ethics and metaphysics; of rhetoric and mathematics, including arithmetic, algebra, plane and solid geometry, trigonometry, surveying, mensuration, conic sections, and the principles of natural philosophy" (Walter H. Hill, *Historical Sketches of St. Louis University,* p. 56). See also Francis P. Cassidy, *Catholic College Foundations and Development in the United States, 1677-1850,* pp. 41, 86-88.

9. William Hyde and Howard L. Conrad, *Encyclopedia of the History of St. Louis,* 2: 1195-96, 989-90.

obscure. He appears to have entered military service, perhaps receiving a commission in one of the opposing armies, but none of this is certain. James Semple's anxious references in a letter to his daughter Lucy, early in 1862, are vague. "What has become of Eugene?" he asked. "Do you ever hear from him? I am told he has received no pay yet. Will he or any of the rest of them ever get any pay? The government seems to have run out of money."[10] Lucy's reply is not available. Whatever the outcome of his government service, Eugene returned to civilian life in the summer of 1862 and enrolled in the law school of Cincinnati College, where he rushed through the curriculum and graduated in April 1863.[11] In May he was admitted to the Missouri bar.[12]

During this time, his family achieved an important position in St. Louis society through Lucy's marriage to Edgar Ames, the junior partner in one of the Midwest's largest wartime meat-packing firms.[13] As a young lawyer, Semple might have capitalized on these fortunate circumstances by remaining in Missouri, but he decided to go west instead. His reasons for leaving are not known, but there are at least two possible explanations. Like thousands of young men during the war, he may have been trying to avoid military service.[14] Or, more likely, as he later said, his restless nature may have prevailed over sounder instincts and propelled him toward the sunset.

At any rate, in late May of 1863, Semple and another young lawyer named Leopold Wolfe departed for New York, where they booked

10. James Semple to Lucy Semple Ames, January 18, 1862, Semple Papers. Several other letters in the Semple Papers, neither written by nor received by Eugene Semple, make vague reference to his whereabouts at this time. See especially one letter from his cousin, Bell Floyd Jones, to an unidentified party, February 10, 1862. Correspondence hereafter cited is in the Semple Papers unless otherwise indicated.

11. Letter from William Jeffrey, Jr., professor of law and law librarian, University of Cincinnati, to the writer, July 16, 1965. See also Reginald C. McGrane, *The University of Cincinnati: A Success Story in Urban Education*, pp. 38-40, 44.

12. Semple "Chronology."

13. Hyde and Conrad, *St. Louis*, pp. 24-25.

14. Many men avoided service through the provision of commutation whereby a man paid another to take his place. Semple may have done this. See Fred A. Shannon, *The Organization and Administration of the Union Army, 1861-1865,* 2:35-38, 57. Despite the commutation provision, evasion was widespread. In June 1863, for example, Lincoln called for 100,000 men from the states of West Virginia, Ohio, Maryland, and Pennsylvania in response to the immediate Confederate threat to those states. Only 8,000 were inducted from the four states; ibid. 1:296.

passage aboard a Panama-bound steamer, the *Northern Light*. They reached Panama safely, crossed the Isthmus to the Pacific by railroad, and continued on to San Francisco by steamer. They visited with the Mizners at Benicia for a while and during the stay they evidently decided to head on for Oregon. In early August they sailed for Portland on the barkentine *Jane Falkinburg* and after twenty-three days at sea landed at the bustling little Willamette River port.[15] Semple's long adventure in the Northwest had begun.

---

15. Semple "Chronology."

2. Establishing the *Herald*

Soon after their arrival in Portland, Semple and Wolfe opened a law partnership, and early in September Semple was admitted to practice before the Oregon Supreme Court at Salem. Lawyers were in short supply in Portland during the Civil War years; as late as 1865 there were only twenty-one attorneys listed in the city—a ratio of one to every five hundred fifty inhabitants.[1] Semple contested a variety of cases ranging from property suits and divorce actions to assaults and murders. Yet he viewed the solemnity of his profession with detachment, noting the foibles of the judicial process in his diary as a reporter might record them in his notebook. "I have seen Deady interrupt counsel in the midst of a speech," he once observed of Circuit Judge Matthew Deady, "to order a spittoon placed in front of a man who spit upon the carpet."[2]

During Semple's first winter in the West big gold strikes were made in Montana and miners streamed into Portland with intoxicating tales of life at the diggings. As Semple recalled it, "Nearly every spirited young man who came to the country was moved to abandon more sober undertakings and hie himself to the mountains in search of sudden wealth and fame. . . . Being not much more than a boy, I yielded to adventurous impulses and started for the . . . mining region."[3] He

1. *Polk's Portland City Directory,* 1865 (published by S. J. McCormick, Portland), passim.
2. Diary, February 1866, Semple Papers. Many of the entries in this diary of 1865-67 are scrawls. It is not an orderly journal and exact dates were not always recorded.
3. Tacoma *Daily Ledger*, August 5, 1892.

departed for Bannack City, Montana, in the spring of 1864, traveling part of the five hundred mile distance alone on foot with a pistol tucked in his belt. Semple arrived at Bannack City as the town was reaching the zenith of its brief period of notoriety. It had already attracted national attention shortly before his arrival when vigilantes had hanged the infamous outlaw-sheriff Henry Plummer and two accomplices. On May 26, 1864, Congress created Montana Territory, with Bannack City as its first capital. In other respects, Bannack was a typical Far Western mining town. Its streets swarmed with miners and camp followers like Semple, whose numbers swelled the population to more than six thousand, making Bannack, temporarily at least, a community larger than Portland.[4] Semple was soon at home in this hectic milieu where, he remarked, "money was easily obtained and much of it spent on cards and whiskey," and where "every night and all day Sunday the saloons were crowded with heavily armed men."[5] He stayed the summer, earning enough in legal fees to make the trip out to Boise and back to Portland in a four-horse wagon before the first snow fell.

After returning to Portland, Semple formed a new law partnership with an obscure attorney named Andrew Lawrence. Lawrence shared Semple's restless ways and, when an extended lull in business set in during the spring of 1866, the pair joined several other men in staking out a mining claim in Washington Territory. The claim, which Semple dubbed "the Washington Nondescript," occupied a two-hundred-foot ledge along a creek bank in Pacific County. Work at the diggings was harder than anticipated, or, as Semple put it, "tough as a boarding house beefsteak."[6] It soon became obvious that the claim was worthless and the partners abandoned it.

Semple's life as a young bachelor on the frontier was predictably an exciting one. Portland had become the winter refuge of hundreds of miners from the Idaho and Montana gold fields and the city catered to a wide variety of vices. "It was a very lively place," Semple reminisced years later. "Many of the men," he noted, "were veritable Counts of Monte Cristo, who spent their money with a princely hand."[7] He

4. Rodman W. Paul, *Mining Frontiers of the Far West, 1848-1880,* p. 140; Hubert Howe Bancroft, *History of Washington, Idaho, and Montana, 1845-1889,* p. 407; Thomas J. Dimsdale, *Vigilantes of Montana* (New York, 1882), passim.
5. Tacoma *Ledger,* August 5, 1892.
6. Semple Diary, April 1866.
7. Tacoma *Ledger,* August 5, 1892.

emulated them, gambling compulsively, drinking and smoking excessively—all to the detriment of his health. By 1866 he had contracted gout and was complaining of failing eyesight. The entries in his diary reveal a troubled conscience:

February 11, 1866:	"Agree to play no more cards for three months."
March 23, 1867:	"Quit drinking whiskey, brandy, gin, rum for one year."
April 22, 1867:	"Play no more cards from this time for three years."
May 7, 1867:	"Quit smoking and chewing for one year."
June 19, 1867:	"If I ever commit either of these faults again I hope God will curse me for it and make his curse felt."
December 24, 1867:	"Quit absolutely and imperitively [sic] under penalty of dishonor from playing any kind of a game of cards for drinks or money in any public place—this for three years from this date."[8]

Quite a bit of the money he lost gambling came from his father, who found it increasingly difficult to finance his son's indulgences, as Eugene's younger sister Julia pointed out to him on one occasion: "Pa received your letter last night asking him to send you more money. He says he will send you fifty dollars a month and my dear Eugene that ought to be enough. . . . Pa has not got much money."[9]

These remittances ended in December 1886 when James Semple died, leaving no will. At the time of his death he had been trying to recover some of the land that had been seized from him for back taxes during the Civil War. Part of his legacy to Eugene and the rest of the family was a legal snarl of tax suits requiring prompt attention. Lucy pleaded with Eugene to come home as soon as possible to settle the estate since he was the only direct male heir. It was clear, however, that her aim was also to coax him back to Elsah to manage the family's affairs. She made her arguments as persuasive as possible: "The land is almost all under cultivation and requires a man's constant attention to see after the ground rents and town rents. . . . If the place were attended to well it ought to bring in a very handsome income . . . and besides I

8. Diary, Semple Papers.

9. Julia Semple Scott to Semple, March 28, 1864. (Correspondence cited is in the Semple Papers unless otherwise noted.) Semple was also borrowing money from Lucy.

think you ought to get plenty of [law] practice in the state where your father filled so many important offices."[10]

But Eugene refused to return. Instead, he directed Lucy's husband, Edgar Ames, to act for him regarding his share of the estate, telling him to yield to the interests of the rest of the heirs wherever necessary. All he wanted, he told his wealthy brother-in-law, were his father's private papers.[11]

A year later Edgar himself died, intestate. Lucy, who was high strung by nature and already several months pregnant at the time of her husband's death, was on the verge of a nervous collapse. Edgar had directed the huge meat-packing business since his older brother Henry's death in 1862 and apparently had groomed no successor. In near desperation Julia wrote to Lansing Mizner in California, pleading with him to persuade Eugene to return immediately to aid the family. Lansing, who was involved in state politics at the time, relayed the message to Portland after adding his own opinion that Eugene ought to terminate his career in Oregon and return to Illinois. [12]

Semple hesitated. Although Ames had left no will, it was likely that most of his fortune would go to Lucy and her three children. It was also possible that, as an inducement to return, Lucy might offer him an important position in Ames's meat-packing business. He weighed the alternatives in a letter to Lansing. There was an excellent chance to save the business, he told him, if the two of them were allowed to take over the management on lucrative terms. Otherwise he could see no point in coming home simply for the sake of uniting the family and comforting Lucy's troubled mind.[13] But in the months that followed, no offer materialized and the meat-packing firm stayed in the hands of Ames subordinates while Lansing and Eugene remained in the West. Lucy herself eventually assumed control of the business and later passed the responsibility on to her sons, Edgar and Henry.

A major reason for Semple's decision to stay in Oregon was his growing involvement in the affairs of the state's war-torn Democratic party. Even before coming west he had developed a strong dislike for the Republican party. He had attended the Republican national

10. Lucy Ames to Semple, January 9, 1867.
11. Semple to Edgar Ames, January 22, 1867.
12. Julia Semple Scott to Lansing Mizner, December 13, 1867; Lansing Mizner to Semple, January 16, 1868.
13. Semple to Lansing Mizner, February 22, 1868.

convention at Chicago in 1860 and later related his political conversion in a letter to Lansing's wife Ella:

> I was delighted . . . with being informed of Lansing's disgust at the fanatical crew of disturbance breeders and cowardly slanderers who invariably constitute a majority of every Yankee Puritan assemblage . . . . Lan was led astray at the start and parted company with his friends. The very same warm blood and reverence for the Union made me at the outset do the same thing. But I was at Chicago and could see the hypocrites work while Lan was on this coast where all that the people were allowed to read were the lies brought across the continent by a Union League telegraph. I was cured in a few months; Lan is being cured now.[14]

Semple's attachment to the Democratic party remained unshaken by the changing views of his family. Even James Semple, who shared his son's apprehension about Lincoln's nomination in 1860, supported the President in 1864 against the Democratic candidate, General George B. McClellan.[15]

Early in 1865 Semple became acquainted with Lafayette Lane, the son of former Oregon Senator Joseph Lane, John C. Breckenridge's vice-presidential running mate on the Southern Democratic ticket in 1860. The younger Lane was a member of the Knights of the Golden Circle, an organization of Confederate sympathizers who were active in Oregon.[16] Through his contact with Lane, Semple joined a nucleus of men dedicated to rebuilding the state Democratic party and removing those who had championed it as a pro-Lincoln war party. "The next fight," Semple told Lane before the 1865 state elections,

> must be on the open issue of war to the knife against abolitionism and usurpation [of American liberties] and we must place vigorous men . . . before the people . . . . These are revolutionary times and the programe for the next campaign must be made to suit them. Cautious non-combative men must be kept out of the canvass on our side and the most inflammatory mode of speaking adopted by our candidates. [17]

At the time of Semple's arrival in Oregon in 1863 the once powerful state Democratic party was in decline, divided like Democrats elsewhere by the issues of the Civil War. In Oregon the dissolution of old party

14. Semple to Ella Mizner, December 24, 1868.   Lansing was in Washington, D.C., on political business at the time. Semple refers here to the 1860 Republican convention at Chicago.

15. James Semple to Eugene Semple, May 15, 1865; Lucy Ames to Eugene Semple, March 2, 1864.

16. Sister Mary Kelly, *The Career of Joseph Lane, Frontier Politician*, p. 189.

17. Semple to Lafayette Lane, February 20, 1865.

lines at the beginning of the war had led to the ascendancy of a Republican-dominated Union League coalition which drew many Democrats temporarily into its ranks. Many others chose to remain silent or became outright Confederate supporters, or, as the Republican Jacksonville *Oregon Sentinel* called them, "whiskey-soaked, taunting traitors."[18] In the meantime, other prowar and antiwar Democrats fought for control of what was left of their party, focusing on the unresolved issues of slavery and reconstruction. The Polk County Democrats of western Oregon, for example, favored the Union cause "for the purpose of suppressing rebellion," but denounced "any war for the abolition of slavery."[19] Opposing this faction were militant Secessionists like James O'Meara, a veteran Oregon newspaper editor who decried what he called "the present unnatural, unjust, savage abolition war." There was, he said, "no such thing as a prosecution of this war for the restoration of the Union and the supremacy of the Constitution."[20] Southern independence, he insisted, must be recognized.

The division within the weakened party was implicit in the platform adopted by the state convention in April 1864. O'Meara's faction extracted a pledge of endorsement for its states' rights sentiments, as expressed in the Virginia and Kentucky resolutions of 1798 and 1799. For the sake of party unity, however, the convention felt obliged to add to the O'Meara plank a contradictory resolution condemning the rebellious southern states.[21]

During the campaign the Union League press branded the Democrats traitors for their endorsement of the nullification doctrine. The Democrats countered by bringing Joseph Lane out of semiretirement and onto the stump in an unsuccessful effort to revive the prewar party unity. But the election result confirmed Semple's fear that the party could not yet accommodate its present factions. Out of fifty-six seats in the legislature, Democrats won seven—two out of eighteen in the senate and five of thirty-eight in the house.[22]

18. Jacksonville *Oregon Sentinel,* March 12, 1863.

19. Walter Carleton Woodward, "The Rise and Early History of Political Parties in Oregon," *Oregon Historical Quarterly,* 13 (1912): 30-31. This is the best account of the internal party squabbles in the state during the 1860s.

20. Ibid., p. 31. O'Meara was the leading Oregon Copperhead editor, described by one writer as "an old fire eating secession advocate." George S. Turnbull, *History of Oregon Newspapers,* p. 173.

21. Salem *Oregon Statesman,* April 18, 1864.

22. Ibid., July 18, 1864.

One prerequisite for the return of the Democrats to power in Oregon politics was the establishment of a strong party newspaper, preferably in Portland. To this goal Semple dedicated most of his energies during the next several years. By 1864 he had already become an active participant in Portland's editorial wars by concentrating his political idealism and exuberance into the writing of lively partisan editorials which gained him a reputation as a vigorous spokesman for local party causes.

Western journalism in the 1860s had a distinctly personal quality unknown in today's large newspapers which are, at least nominally, politically independent. As often as not, frontier newspapers were adjuncts to job-printing enterprises. Wherever a frontier settlement sprang up, a printer with a crude hand-press and "a shirt-tail-full of type" was sure to appear before long.[23] The tiny weekly and daily publications that came to life in the West often played an important part in promoting or demolishing the political factions of their communities and they welcomed pungent contributions from nearly any source. Almost every shade of political persuasion had its organ somewhere, and the close alliance between the local press and local politics usually extended to financial support and patronage. Even within a party, as schisms developed, papers lined up quickly on one side or the other and became spokesmen of the contending groups. Although the newspaper profession at large often attracted men of high literary qualifications, frontier journals were frequently the creations of semi-literate printers who had a penchant for politics and a desire to capitalize on the local craving for gossip. Mid-nineteenth century American journalism, as Horace Greeley observed, was a profession apart; its ranks were filled by ministers and merchants, and by young men like Semple who had been "brought up to the bar."[24] Indeed a vocation that combined the three arts of law, politics, and journalism was an ideal avenue to fame and success.

The task of launching a successful Democratic paper in Portland was formidable. By 1865 the Republican Portland *Oregonian* had become the strongest newspaper in the state, having surpassed the Salem *Statesman,* the former voice of the once dominant Democrats, at the outset of the war.[25] During 1865 Semple began making inquiries

23. Frank Luther Mott, *American Journalism,* p. 282.
24. Ibid., p. 311.
25. Leslie M. Scott, "The Oregonian Newspaper in Oregon History," *Oregon*

among friends in the newspaper profession about the possibility of starting a Democratic daily in Portland. One of his contacts was Urban E. Hicks, a seasoned member of the Oregon·journalistic fraternity. Hicks had managed several papers in the state and at one time had been city editor of the *Oregonian* itself before souring on its politics.[26] At the time, he was associated with the Salem *Democratic Review,* which had been started by C. B. Bellinger and Anthony Noltner. Hicks informed Semple that Noltner was anxious to move the *Review* to Eugene but would consider Portland instead if some loyal Democrat made him a liberal offer. Semple replied that he had heard of Corvallis investors who might help finance a Portland paper and suggested that Hicks and Noltner contact them.[27] The Corvallis group was not interested, however, and Semple turned elsewhere for support.

In December, following more inquiries and disappointments, Semple met M. H. Abbott, a journeyman printer and editor with a long and interesting background. Abbott introduced himself as soon as he heard Semple was trying to start a paper in Multnomah County. He had arrived in Oregon in October after 20 years of newspaper editing in Minnesota and Illinois. A steadfast Democrat, Abbott boasted to Semple, "In my time I have killed six opposition papers; I would like to kill the Oregonian and then quit."[28] For an unemployed printer recently arrived, this was quite an ambition. The fact remained, however, that Portlanders had no daily alternative to the *Oregonian* and might well support a second paper. For that matter, the entire state had only two or three solidly Democratic newspapers in 1865 and none of these was a regularly published daily. Semple mentioned these facts to Abbott, who then persuaded J. B. Butler, a Monmouth merchant, to loan him fifteen thousand dollars on condition that Abbot share management of the proposed paper with Butler's son Nehemiah. He also got a promise of financial help from Ben Hayden, a rising figure in Oregon politics who later became speaker of the state house of representatives.[29]

*Historical Quarterly,*29 (1928): 225-41.

26. According to Turnbull, Hicks had worked in the composing room of the Hannibal (Missouri) *Journal* where he had taught young Mark Twain to set type! (Turnbull, *Oregon Newspapers,* pp. 19, 141, 168).

27. Hicks to Semple, July 21, 30, 1865.

28. Abbott to Semple, December 4, 1865.

29. Abbott to Semple, December 14, 27, 1865.

Meanwhile, Semple exerted his own influence in Portland in hopes of borrowing the remainder of the necessary funds. He did not have much luck. "The banks and capitalists have all they can do in the money loaning business with merchants who borrow for sixty to ninety days on personal security," he explained to Abbott. He tried other sources, including the Bank of British Columbia but again without success. Still, he was optimistic. "I have begun inquiries among the small fry hereabouts in hopes of securing the amount in small sums from different men and may succeed," he told Abbott. But this also proved fruitless and he next explored the faint possibility that they might get press equipment and other materials on credit in San Francisco and "depend on friends for current expenses."[30] Once again his hopes were disappointed; for the moment his sources of support seemed to be nonexistent.

In the meantime Abbott had decided to plunge into politics in quest of the 1866 Democratic nomination for state printer. By winning the nomination and then the election Abbott reasoned that he could guarantee the success of a daily newspaper in Portland with lucrative state printing contracts. But these plans took for granted that he and Semple could launch at least some semblance of a daily there beforehand. Semple endorsed the strategy: "I think if you start here you would be entitled to the nomination on account of your greater chance to render aid to the party at large."[31] Unfortunately, Abbott lost the nomination to James O'Meara, editor of the Albany *States Rights Democrat.* In March of 1866, however, he did scrape together enough capital to start Portland's first Democratic daily paper, the *Oregon Daily Herald.* Hicks joined the staff of the new journal as city editor and compositor and on March 17 the first issue of the *Herald* appeared on the streets of Portland.[32]

Abbott may have been chiefly responsible for founding the *Herald,* but Semple also deserved some of the credit. Despite a lack of funds or journalistic experience, he was instrumental in calling the attention of veteran editors like Hicks and Abbott to the opportunities at Portland. As midwife to the birth of the partisan daily, he had done the Democrats of Oregon an important service. For Semple, the first edition of the *Herald* signaled the beginning of a seven year association

30. Semple to Abbott, December 30, 1865.
31. Semple to Abbott, January 16, 1866.
32. Turnbull, *Oregon Newspapers*, p. 168.

with the paper. With little prospect of a regular income in or out of journalism, he hired on as a reporter for the fledgling daily. Abbott himself stayed only briefly before moving on to Baker in eastern Oregon. There he started another newspaper and later took a hand in the beginning of other publications in Albany, LaGrande, and Pendleton.[33]

The main task facing the *Herald* staff in the spring of 1866—aside from keeping the newspaper alive—was to rally squabbling Democrats from the debacle of 1864 in time for the June elections. With the Civil War over, transcending feelings toward the Union subsided and a drift back to the pre-war political alignments began. Optimism ran high in the ranks as the minority party awaited the campaign. "Democrats look ahead with great expectations of beating the Blacks," a friend wrote to Semple from southern Oregon. "Don't forget to come out south . . . lectioneering," he added.[34] From other points in the state the news was also encouraging. In Umatilla and adjacent counties in the northeast, settlers with Democratic loyalties from southern and border states were taking up land in increasing numbers.[35] Against this backdrop of shifting political allegiances the *Herald* struggled to win a readership for the Democratic party in Portland.

Semple took a lively part in the pre-election activity, writing editorials and canvassing opinion. He was especially hopeful of seeing the party revived under the leadership of younger men. "The work must be done by the young men of the Country," he told Lafayette Lane. "I have no confidence in the integrity and courage of the older men who are conspicuous in this state now."[36] But even more important to Semple than the ascendancy of younger party leaders was party unity. For this reason his personal choice to head the ticket as candidate for governor was Judge William Strong, one of the Northwest's older Democrats. Strong had been one of President Zachary Taylor's three original appointees to the supreme court of Oregon Territory in 1849 and had more recently become chief council for the Oregon Railway and Navigation Company.[37] "As to the old man's disposition to help us," Semple wrote to Salem Democratic

33. Ibid., pp. 151, 285.
34. T. H. B. Shipley to Semple, December 5, 1865.
35. Portland *Oregonian,* June 9, 1866; Salem *Statesman,* June 18, 1866.
36. Semple to Lafayette Lane, February 20, 1865.
37. Sidney Teiser, "William Strong, Associate Judge of the Territorial Courts," *Oregon Historical Quarterly,* 64 (1963): 293, 303-4.

leader C. G. Curl, referring to Strong, "I think that matter could be arranged satisfactorily . . . .Besides he is not under the influence of anyone. We could 'see' that he went right."[38]

Semple's greatest fear, which was shared by many other Democrats, was that James O'Meara would again split the party on the states' rights issue as he had done in 1864. Rumors circulated that O'Meara's group planned to disrupt the convention by demanding that the party denounce the Reconstruction policies of the federal government in the Southern states. "If they do," Semple told Curl, "I want to see such a combination on the floor as will enable the true men to destroy at once and forever these men and their miserably presumptuous policy." "Our plan," he wrote to another party official, "is to get the balance of power in the convention and compromise with the anti-Jimmy men."[39]

The state convention opened in Portland on April 5 and adopted a compromise slate that made no one particularly happy. To Semple's disgust O'Meara defeated Abbott for the nomination for state printer, and James K. Kelly of The Dalles was nominated for governor over several other aspirants, including Strong. On the other hand, the party drafted a platform which angered the O'Meara faction by including a strong endorsement of the Johnson administration's Reconstruction program for the South.[40]

The election campaign which followed centered on two closely related national issues: readmission of the former Confederate states, and Nego equality. Waving the bloody shirt, the *Oregonian* urged all good Unionists to "give the old traitor, Jo Lane, another kick," claiming that a Democratic victory would send Lane back to the Senate. The Democratic press also played upon popular fears. "Shall negroes be placed upon the same social and political footing with white men?" asked the *Herald* in an editorial Semple himself may have written.[41]

After a campaign which the *Oregonian* asserted was "the severest . . . ever known in the state," the Union coalition again elected its entire slate. George L. Woods of The Dalles defeated Kelly, his crosstown opponent, for governor, and Samual E. May collected the biggest

38. Semple to C. G. Curl, February 9, 1866.
39. Ibid.; Semple to N. T. Caton, February 13, 1866.
40. Salem *Statesman*, April 23, 1866.
41. Portland *Oregonian*, May 16, 1866; Portland *Daily Oregon Herald*, April 5, 1866 (hereafter cited as the *Herald*).

majority, six hundred votes, in defeating Lafayette Lane for secretary of state.[42] Meanwhile O'Meara's Albany rival, W. A. McPherson of the *Journal,* defeated him in the contest for state printer. The Union party triumph, however, was to be its last. An indication of resurging Democratic strength was the increase in its number of legislators from seven to twenty-eight, although the opposition still controlled both houses.[43] There seemed to be justification for Semple's pre-election forecast that "in two years we can have all the show if the cards are played right."[44]

During the next year or so Semple continued to supplement the uncertain income from his dwindling law practice by writing editorials for the Democratic press. He supported Clement Vallandigham's controversial election in the Ohio race for the United States Senate, and railed against radical Republican efforts to impeach President Johnson. Closer to home he endorsed several schemes for the construction of a railroad from California into the Willamette Valley.[45]

Toward the end of 1867, a group of prominent Democrats headed by Lafayette Grover and James Kelly purchased the *Herald* and early in 1868 they hired Semple as city editor. Grover was state party chairman and considered the *Herald* an important asset for the next campaign. "I wish we had one good paper here and that you had charge of it as editor," he wrote to Semple from Salem on February 5. Grover placed him in control of the paper's editorial strategy for the 1868 election and pried loose funds from the party treasury for publishing costs. That spring they began issuing a special four-page Saturday tabloid under the banner, *The Campaign Herald.*[46]

The Oregon Democratic platform of 1868 reflected the changing political and economic interests of the postwar era. The party repudiated Andrew Johnson's leadership by endorsing George H. Pendleton of Ohio for President and advocated large federal appropriations for railroad construction in Oregon. But far more significant locally was the resolution which opposed "sharing with servile races the priceless political heritage achieved alone by white men."[47] The reference here was to the Chinese rather than to blacks

42. *Oregonian,* June 30, September 15, 1866.
43. Salem *Statesman,* July 30, 1866.
44. Semple to Curl, February 9, 1866.
45. Semple Diary, jottings for editorials, July, 1867.
46. Turnbull, *Oregon Newspapers,* p. 152.
47. *Oregonian,* March 21, 1868.

and it was a prejudice Semple enthusiastically shared. As a self-appointed spokesman for the white workingman he wrote a series of strong anti-Chinese resolutions which were adopted by the influential First Ward Democratic Club of Portland shortly before the state convention.[48] Even the *Oregonian,* which had once ignored the issue in deference to Republican business interests, expressed fear "that the long-tailed, moon-eyed nuisances from China were about to take Oregon."[49] In both 1868 and 1870 the Chinese "question" probably generated more newsprint than any other issue in Oregon politics.

The state elections of June 1868 brought the Democrats a decisive victory—their first in a decade. Joseph S. Smith, one of the owners of the *Herald,* was elected to Congress by a twelve hundred vote majority and the Democrats won forty-three of the sixty-nine seats in the legislature to gain a majority in both houses.[50] Republicans blamed the result on an influx of southern settlers to northeastern Oregon. The *Oregonian* went so far as to suggest that followers of Confederate General Sterling Price, some of whom had fled West after his unsuccessful invasion of Missouri in 1864, had determined the outcome of the balloting. "It appears," said the *Oregonian,* "that Price's boys in Eastern Oregon can be relied on to give any required majority for the restoration of 'The Lost Cause.' "[51] Despite these partisan allegations, the election demonstrated that Oregon's antebellum political balance had been substantially restored. The November election furnished further proof of this as the Democrats carried Oregon for Horatio Seymour over Ulysses S. Grant.

Following the state elections, the editorship of the *Herald* became vacant when Beriah Brown, who had refused to renounce President Johnson during the state convention, quit the paper to edit the Salem *Press,* a competing Democratic journal. Semple was a logical replacement and asked for Grover's backing,[52] but other influences prevailed and the job went instead to Sylvester Pennoyer, a future governor of Oregon. At that point, with the election won, the *Herald* had served its purpose for the party leaders who had purchased it the

48. Semple "Chronology." Numerous resolutions were passed throughout the state urging federal action to remove all Orientals. See Robert Arden Wilson, "A History of the Chinese Question in Early Oregon, 1850-1886" (master's thesis, University of Washington, 1942), p. 22.

49. *Oregonian,* July 10, 1866.

50. Hubert Howe Bancroft, *History of Oregon, 1848-1888,* 2: 667, 669.

51. *Oregonian,* November 10, 1868.

52. Semple to Grover, June 25, 1868.

year before. In November they dissolved their organization and sold the paper to a member of their group, William Weatherford, who retained Pennoyer as editor.[53] Semple resigned as city editor the following January, 1869.

His resignation coincided with his decision to buy the *Herald* in partnership with Thomas Patterson, former business secretary of the paper. Patterson had reliable information about the *Herald*'s financial status and had already made an unsuccessful offer to buy the paper from Weatherford in December 1868. Semple was determined to gain control of the *Herald* and early in 1869 he left Oregon to seek financial backers in St. Louis.[54]

The proposition he carried with him sounded attractive. Because of the *Herald*'s usefulness during the recent campaign, the paper stood an excellent chance of being awarded substantial state printing contracts (including a large backlog) if the Democrats elected the governor in 1870, which appeared likely. Moreover, an increase in population and newspaper circulation in the Portland area seemed inevitable as railroad construction proceeded up the Willamette Valley, linking the country with California and the East. By Patterson's estimate, the *Herald* would soon be worth at least fifteen thousand dollars![55]

While Semple traveled east, Patterson resumed his negotiations with Weatherford in Portland. Soon afterward, Weatherford suddenly became seriously ill. Fearing he would lose his entire investment before he could regain his health, he hastily sold the paper to Pennoyer for five thousand dollars before Patterson could make an offer. Pennoyer's enthusiasm for the publication soon cooled, however, and he too decided to sell. "His desire to sell has not been made known to anyone except myself," Patterson wrote to Semple in May. "He approached me first . . . and expressed an earnest desire that the concern should go into our hands," Patterson continued. "He says no two persons in the state can run the paper more satisfactorily than you and I and says you are the only person he knows who he would be willing to have take charge of the political columns."[56]

To Patterson's chagrin, however, Pennoyer had also received a tentative offer from J. V. Butler, the Monmouth merchant who had

53. Flora Belle Ludington, "The Newspapers of Oregon, 1846-1870," *Oregon Historical Quarterly,* 26 (1925): 249.
54. Patterson to Semple, December 10, 1868.
55. Patterson to Semple, May 14, 1869.
56. Ibid.

been financially involved with the start of the *Herald* three years earlier under Abbott. As a result of Butler's offer, Pennoyer's opening price to Patterson was seventy-five hundred dollars. This was one-third more than Pennoyer had recently paid Weatherford for the paper but it represented only half the potential value, according to Patterson's own calculations.[57] After some hard bargaining, Patterson persuaded Pennoyer to accept an offer of seven thousand dollars. He then cabled Semple in St. Louis to "raise seven thousand, telegraph fifty-five hundred and come soon." Semple had trouble getting the money, however, and after more haggling Pennoyer agreed to take the fifty-five hundred and wait two years for the remaining fifteen hundred. On these terms Semple was able to raise the amount, with his wealthy sister Lucy's help, and returned to Portland. On July 1, 1869, the new owners took possession of the *Herald,* with Patterson as business manager and Semple as editor.[58] Emblazoned across the top of the editorial page was the paper's new motto, Semple's inspiration: "In all discussions of American policy, with us liberty goes first." [59]

Ahead loomed the problem of survival against two formidable rivals. One was the *Oregonian* which, under the editorship of Harvey Scott, had risen to the first rank among newspapers of the Northwest. The other was the *Daily Bulletin,* a newly established voice for the interests of Ben Holladay, the transportation titan who was to dominate the business and political life of Oregon for the next several years. Holladay had recently amassed a fortune through the sale of his extensive stagecoach and freight-carrying enterprise and was now determined to gain control of Oregon's rail and navigation lines. To publicize his interests he spared no expense, importing the finest press equipment and hiring what he considered to be a peerless editorial staff—headed by none other than James O'Meara.[60] Holladay's opulently outfitted publication and the solidly established *Oregonian* afforded Patterson and Semple all the competition they could handle. Their hopes for survival depended heavily on government printing accruing from Democratic patronage. With this in mind they made ready for the political battles of 1870 and beyond.

57. Ibid.

58. Patterson to Semple, telegrams, May 18, May 19, June 5, 1869.

59. Portland *Herald,* July 3, 1869; and Semple "Chronology."

60. James V. Frederick, *Ben Holladay,* p. 272; Turnbull, *Oregon Newspapers,* pp. 153-54.

3. The Holladay Era—and After

In the spring of 1870 Semple was married to Ruth Adelaide Lownsdale of Portland. Addie, as her friends called her, was the attractive seventeen-year-old daughter of the late Daniel H. Lownsdale, one of the first landholders of the city.[1] The couple had become engaged in December 1869, following a short courtship which Semple did little to publicize. Eugene's mother, to whom news of the engagement came as a complete surprise, gave her son her blessing: "I think as you have made up your mind to make Oregon your permanent home it is the best thing you can do. If you get a good sensible wife it will be the making of you."[2] The wedding, on May 17, was a special Catholic ceremony in the Portland home of Dr. John A. Blanchard, a former friend of Semple's father in Illinois.[3] For her new daughter-in-law, Mary Semple had some timely advice about her son. "With judicious management he will make his mark in whatever he undertakes," she predicted. "But," she added, "Eugene was always inclined to be a little extravagant. If he is so now you must admonish him not to go beyond his income."[4]

The change in Semple's domestic life did not alter his relationship with the *Herald*. And while he and Patterson remained occupied with the management of their newspaper, Ben Holladay was engrossed in much larger undertakings that were soon to involve Semple and the

1. Oregon Historical Records Survey, vol. 1, *Multnomah County,* pp. 6, 7, 9, 14, 15, 17; Harvey W. Scott, *History of Portland,* pp. 98, 497; Percy Maddux, *City on the Willamette,* p. 195.
2. Mary Semple to Eugene Semple, January 9, 1870.
3. *Oregonian,* May 18, 1870; and Semple Genealogy.
4. Mary Semple to Ruth Adelaide Semple, May 20, 1871.

Herald. Holladay's goal was to acquire nothing less than a monopoly of Oregon rail and water traffic and, in the process, build a railroad to link the Willamette Valley with the markets of California. In 1868, after arriving in Oregon with the capital obtained from the sale of his stage and freight lines, he had begun to buy control of the Oregon Central Railroad, which held a federal right of way through the lower Willamette Valley. By May 1870, Holladay had absorbed the Oregon Central into his own Oregon and California Railroad Company, which had gained right of way between Portland and the southern Willamette Valley. By a variety of methods, including bribery, he also extended his influence deep into the Republican party and the legislature.[5]

Even more controversial was his importation of hundreds of Chinese laborers from California to help build his railroad. The presence of large numbers of Orientals angered white workingmen who had anticipated plenty of jobs at good wages on Holladay's road gangs. Such activities made Holladay a prime target for the broadsides of ambitious editors like Semple. It was no surprise that the state election campaign of 1870 developed into a contest between Holladay's supporters and his enemies, in which the Chinese question became a central issue.

The arrival of Ben Holladay and the railroad dramatically altered the political relationships within the state. Farmers, politicians, newspaper editors, and the public generally reassessed the issues, the candidates, and the parties in terms of the progress Holladay's railroad was making up the Willamette Valley. The weekly *Oregon State Journal* of Eugene furnished an illustration of this tendency in its changing editorial policy. Originally a vigorous Democratic opponent of Holladay, the paper became increasingly friendly as the railroad approached the city and local real estate values climbed. The *Oregonian* was proof of the opposite tendency. Whereas it had cautiously supported some of Holladay's early activities, it became one of his strongest critics, editorializing against his real estate promotions in newly incorporated

5. A detailed account of this period is contained in ~~Bancroft~~, *History of Oregon,* 2:695-706. Joseph Gaston, Holladay's opponent, is heard from in "The Oregon Central Railroad," *Oregon Historical Quarterly,* 3 (1903): 315-26. More objective is John Tilson Ganoe's "History of the Oregon and California Railroad," ibid., 25 (1924): 273-83; and Randall V. Mills's "History of Transportation in the Pacific Northwest," ibid., 47 (1946): 289-90. See also the *Senate Journal of the State of Oregon,* 1872, p. 529, and Ellis Lucia's *Ben Holladay,* pp. 261, 299. This colorful but cliché-ridden account is the only book devoted to Holladay's activities in Oregon. James Vincent Frederick's *Ben Holladay,* cited earlier, is a scholarly biography but ignores almost completely his career in Oregon.

East Portland and denouncing his efforts to bankrupt the Oregon Steam Navigation Company.[6]

The *Herald* became a leader of the anti-Holladay chorus, which grew to include newspapers in dozens of communities where residents were fearful Holladay would decide to bypass them with his railway, or swindle them, or both. The controversy surrounding his operations boosted newspaper circulation in many parts of western Oregon and helped insure the initial success of the *Herald*. In the process, Semple acquired a reputation as a lively and effective editorial crusader against the Holladay empire and the Chinese "menace." "It is very flattering to receive so many complimentary notices of you in all the other papers," his sister Julia wrote to him from St. Louis. In an effort to increase circulation, Semple introduced changes in the makeup and typography of the paper and contracted for daily wireless dispatches from the East, claiming (dubiously) that the *Herald* was the first Democratic daily west of the Rockies to subscribe to a regular news service.[7] Meanwhile, he remained busy in politics. T. H. B. Shipley, who had first met Semple in the Boise Basin in 1864 during his own "wild goose chase through Idaho," invested him with his proxy as Jackson County representative on the 1870 Oregon Democratic Central Committee.[8] Semple thus became, simultaneously, spokesman of the party's strongest southern county and its editorial voice in populous Multnomah County.

With Democrats already in control of the legislature, party leaders concentrated on winning the top administrative offices when the state convention met at Albany in late March. A spirit of compromise prevailed among the various factions. Lafayette Grover, who represented the powerful Salem clique and chaired the convention, received the nomination for governor. The Democrats of eastern Oregon were placated with the nomination of James H. Slater of Baker for Congress. Then, in recognition of the *Herald*'s pre-eminence among Oregon Democratic newspapers, the convention caucus nominated Patterson for state printer.[9] The choice seemed to be a popular one:

6. Dorothy O. Johansen, "Capitalism on the Far Western Frontier: The Oregon Steam Navigation Company" (Ph.D. diss., University of Washington, 1941), pp. 259-60.

7. Julia Scott Semple to Semple, August 1, 1869; William F. Prosser, *A History of the Puget Sound Country*, 2:535; Turnbull, *Oregon Newspapers*, pp. 151-52.

8. Shipley to Semple, December 5, 25, 1869.

9. Portland *Herald*, March 25, 1870.

soon after the convention, James D. Fay, president of the state senate, informed Semple that "the position assumed by the *Herald* is heartily endorsed by the rank and file of the Democracy everywhere; and also by very many republicans who have had their eyes opened to the corruptions of their party." [10]

The Republicans, with Holladay's support, chose General Joel Palmer to oppose Grover in the race for governor. Palmer was an aging Indian fighter whose exploits fifteen years earlier had made him a minor legend, at least in parts of southern Oregon. His reputation was not unassailable, however, and Fay advised Semple to "indulge in some reminiscences during the campaign of . . . Palmer's conduct when Superintendent of Indian Affairs at the outbreak of the Indian war of 1855-56." According to Fay, Palmer's nomination had been "received with huge disgust by the Republicans . . . who were participants in that war. Many of them swear they will not support him." Grover, through the *Herald,* wasted little time before challenging his Republican rival to a series of public debates. Palmer accepted but only on the condition that he be assisted by incumbent Governor George Woods. When Woods subsequently boasted in a Portland speech that he had held the Democratic party of Oregon by the throat for four years, Semple had an appropriate editorial reply: "He was somewhat mistaken as to where his grasp was fixed. It was not the Democracy, but the State, that he was holding by the throat. He has almost squeezed the life out of her with his clutch. . . . Her industries have shriveled and fallen away and her financial prosperity has been literally paralyzed by the stoppage of her circulation which has resulted from that clutch." [11]

Repeatedly, the *Herald* denounced Holladay's association with the Republican party. In particular, it assailed his influence in Congress through Senator George Williams. Semple's editorials accused the "Holladay-Williams alliance" of selling out Oregon railroad interests to Holladay's own monopoly. Even more unsavory were Holladay's alleged dealings with San Francisco's notorious Tongs for the importation of Chinese "coolies" into Oregon. In short, said Semple, Holladay had retarded the state's economic growth by establishing a railroad monopoly through his corruption of the Republican party and his exploitation of Oriental "wage slaves." For the young editor, the sides were clearly drawn. "There is no Republican Ticket in the field, either

10. Fay to Semple, April 7, 1870.
11. Ibid.; *Herald,* May 25, 26, 1870.

for the state, or any county that we have heard of," he editorialized. "The contest is between Ben Holladay and the Democracy. The first aims to get control of the entire railway system of the state and oppress the people as heretofore with exhorbitant [sic] rates of transportation, while the latter aims to protect citizens from the evil designs of a foreign monopolist who has always accomplished his ends by unfair means." [12]

The outcome of the election was gratifying to most Democrats. Grover defeated Palmer for governor and Patterson was elected state printer. Democrats also returned majorities to both houses of the legislature. In Multnomah County and especially in Portland, however, Holladay men won many offices. [13] The *Herald*'s part in the Democratic victories was acknowledged even by the *Oregonian*, which attempted to take credit for the result after belatedly lining up with the Democracy against Holladay: "Could we have had the assistance of a Democratic paper of the stamp of the *Herald* in every county we could have made a clean sweep . . . . We thank the *Herald* for the assistance it has given us, and can only regret that it did not circulate more extensively during the campaign in distant parts of the state." [14]

The rivalry among the three Portland dailies—the *Herald, Oregonian,* and *Bulletin*—remained intense even after the election. Each fancied itself the eventual lone survivor; in truth each lost heavily and Patterson and Semple were forced to depend increasingly on state printing contracts and other official patronage for income. These public beneficences were often enacted especially to insure the solvency of the party press. Typical was a law passed by the Democrats in October 1870 which permitted the state printer to choose, with the governor's consent, one general circulation newspaper in the state to publish the laws of each legislative session. [15] Predictably, Patterson awarded the lucrative work to his own newspaper.

Another rewarding piece of legislation was the controversial litigant printing act of 1870. Under this statute the governor was allowed to designate one newspaper in each county to publish all judicial and legal advertisements for that county. [16] Such laws tended to strengthen the partisan loyalties of the press, especially in underpopulated or highly

12. *Herald,* June 2, May 28, June 2, 1870.
13. Ibid., June 9, September 13, 1870.
14. *Oregonian,* June 8, 1870.
15. *Oregon Laws, 1843-1872,* p. 715.
16. Ibid., p. 716.

competitive areas where struggling rival editors counted on this kind of political patronage to keep their respective newspapers alive. In Eugene, where Noltner's Democratic *Review* enjoyed Grover's favor, the competing *Oregon State Journal* called the litigant printing law an "act of tyranny" under which "every person in every county in the state must publish all legal advertisements in the paper named by this petty despot styled by courtesy a Governor."[17] Loyal party men like Semple were not disturbed by such charges: the litigant printing for Multnomah County and for *three* other counties as well (which for some reason failed to produce any qualified publications) went to the *Herald.*[18] To sweeten these contracts, the Democratic legislature then passed a law which increased the fee paid per line of government printing done. [19]

Under the original legislation enacted in 1859, Patterson as state printer was authorized to print a thousand copies of the acts and resolutions passed at each legislative session and to do all printing required by other branches of the state government. He was also empowered to print the journals of both houses of the legislature, the reports of committees, and any codifications of the law.[20] In order to expedite this work and the large backlog from previous sessions, Semple eventually assumed most of the printer's duties while Patterson took up the problems of managing the *Herald.* Accordingly, Patterson resigned as state printer in March 1872, and in June, Grover appointed Semple to fill out the term.[21]

Soon after Semple took office, Grover vetoed a bill to repeal the litigant printing act. When an insurgent legislature then demanded an investigation of the state .printer's work, the governor appointed Semple's old friend Urban Hicks as official examiner. The Hicks report heaped praise on Semple's work, calling it the best ever turned out by an Oregon state printer.[22] The integrity of the report was not challenged, but in October 1872 the legislators passed a bill authorizing a new codification and printing of Oregon laws under *private* contract. The act was unconstitutional in its provisions for the private printing because Article Twelve of the Oregon Constitution authorized only the

17. Eugene *Oregon State Journal*, September 5, 1874.
18. Grover to Semple, December 23, 1870.
19. *Oregon Laws*, pp. 599-612.
20. Ibid., pp. 714-16.
21. A copy of Patterson's resignation, dated March 29, 1872, is in the Semple Papers; see also Grover to Semple, June 17, 1872.
22. A copy of the Hicks report, dated October 16, 1872, is in the Semple Papers.

state printer to do the work. With several thousand dollars in potential printing profits at stake, Semple called Grover's attention to the error. Since the governor had already called for bids on the contract, however, he advised Semple to file a complaint in Marion County Circuit Court against the state on grounds of the new law's unconstitutionality. The court subsequently ruled in Semple's favor, declaring the contested parts of the statute void and awarding the contract to the state printer.[23]

Having won the prize, Semple now faced the fact that the job was too big for the *Herald*'s facilities to undertake alone. With insufficient equipment and funds at his disposal and no hope of reimbursement from the state until the entire code was printed, delivered, and approved, he decided to sublet the work to the A. L. Bancroft Company of San Francisco, the largest publishing firm on the West Coast. In August 1874, after several delays, the complete edition of more than thirteen hundred finely bound and elaborately indexed and annotated volumes of the new code rolled off the Bancroft presses.[24] Semple had spared the taxpayer no expense; each volume contained a thousand pages and included copies of the Declaration of Independence and the United States Constitution, with an index to each. This evidently was stretching the intent of the codification act and Semple tried to conceal the fine points of the contract from suspicious eyes. With a tidy profit in sight for themselves, the Bancroft people cooperated. "We will not divulge the contents of the contract until you are willing," the company agent assured Semple.[25] Grover received and accepted the code on September 19 and the lawmakers subsequently approved it, apparently without complaint. With the publication of the new code, Semple's term as printer expired and he relinquished the office to his elected successor, another Democrat, M. V. Brown.[26]

Back in Portland, Ben Holladay continued to extend his influence

23. A transcript of the case is in the Semple Papers; see also Grover to Semple, January 19, 1874.

24. A. L. Bancroft to Semple, August 22, 1874. One side light was a controversy over the spelling of "Willamette," which some, led by Judge Matthew Deady, wanted spelled "Willamet." Semple insisted upon the former spelling, which prevailed. See Eugene *Oregon State Journal,* October 24, 1874; Semple to Deady, February 4, 1874; Grover to Semple, February 26, 1874; and *Oregon Laws,* p. 919.

25. F. P. Stone to Semple, June 13, 1874.

26. Grover to Semple, September 19, 1874; Eugene *Oregon State Journal,* June 27, 1874, and April 3, 1875.

into the political life of the city. Municipal elections became thinly disguised contests between pro-Holladay and anti-Holladay forces. The 1873 city election exemplified the situation and, in particular, the weakened position of the local Democracy, which the *Oregonian* claimed had "definitely resolved not to run a party ticket."[27] The Republicans, although much stronger, were also in trouble from internal strife as Holladay battled for control of the party organization. Through his influence over the majority party he hoped to induce the city to sell him cut-rate franchises for the municipal water works, a street railway, and numerous other concessions.[28] The local party structure buckled under the strain and broke into two factions. Holladay's men gained control of what was left of the regular party organization while a new wing calling itself "The Committee of Twenty Seven" won support from the *Oregonian* and nominated the popular Henry Failing for mayor.[29] As if to confirm allegations that Holladay planned to buy Democratic support in order to win the election, his "regular" Republicans nominated a former Democratic officeholder, John McCracken, for mayor.[30]

The leaders of the Portland Democracy, including Semple, did not acknowledge their impotence without first putting up some semblance of a fight. A small but respectable group of delegates filed into Philharmonic Hall on June 9 to choose a slate of candidates and to adopt resolutions condemning Chinese labor, further city indebtedness, monopolies in general, and Ben Holladay in particular. Semple was elected chairman of the convention and had no sooner called the meeting to order than the legality of the proceedings was challenged by former *Herald* publisher Sylvester Pennoyer. Pennoyer charged that Semple and Urban Hicks, who represented the second ward, had not been properly selected by their constituents. (There is some question as to whether Semple, as state printer in Salem, was a valid resident of Portland at the time.) Semple, instead of vacating the chair until the matter was decided, ruled him out of order and the convention proceeded to the job of choosing a candidate for mayor. A member of the first ward delegation nominated Semple but the chairman declined. Then Hicks nominated Colonel A. P. Dennison, a former member of the

27. *Oregonian*, June 9, 1873.
28. Ibid., June 17, 1873; Lucia, *Holladay*, p. 300.
29. *Oregonian*, June 5, 1873. Failing had already served as mayor for two terms, in 1864 and 1865 (Maddux, *Willamette*, p. 214).
30. Bancroft, *History of Oregon*, 2:323, 325, 698.

legislature, who also declined. Former Governor George L. Curry was the next nominee. Since Curry was not present, he might conceivably have been drafted, but there was evidently so much noise on the floor by this time that Semple failed to hear his name advanced and Curry escaped the nomination. Growing somewhat desperate now, the delegates agreed to instruct the secretary to cast the vote of the convention for Semple. This time he accepted. The delegates departed a short time later without much enthusiasm. It was, said the *Oregonian,* "a little spartan band with little hope of success."[31]

The election was no contest as far as the Democratic candidates were concerned. Semple had been drafted into the race under circumstances which at best suggested apathy and at worst hinted that the convention may have been rigged, possibly to suit Holladay's purposes. Henry Failing, representing the anti-Holladay Republicans, ran a very close race with McCracken but won by 40 votes, 1,038 to 998. Semple, who ran slightly behind his ticket, polled 148 votes, only 34 of which came from his own second ward. The overall result, amid charges of bought votes and other corruption, was a standoff between the two Republican factions. Holladay's proposal to buy the city water facilities was turned down by the voters, but four of the nine city councilmen elected, as well as the city treasurer and the police judge, were Holladay men.[32]

One reason for the Democratic setbacks in Portland was the personal feuding among state and local party leaders in which Semple became involved. These squabbles probably stemmed from lingering animosities caused by the divisive events of the sixties as well as from disputes over patronage and the betrayals of party officials to the Holladay interests. At one point during the legislative session of 1872 this discord erupted into a brawl at Salem, with Semple in the middle of it. Although the specific cause of the fracas is not known, several newspapers gave similar accounts of the action. On the evening of October 9, as Semple walked from the Chemaketa Hotel towards State Street, he was confronted by James Fay, president of the state senate, and James Lappeus, Portland police chief. Some harsh words were exchanged and then Lappeus hit Semple with his fist. Semple retaliated by pulling a pistol and clubbing Lappeus to the ground with several sharp blows to the head. Fay then joined the fight, striking Semple with a metal-tipped cane. Seeking refuge from his assailants, Semple darted into a nearby

31. *Oregonian,* June 10, 1873.
32. Ibid., June 17, 1873.

saloon and was nursing his wounds when Victor Trevitt, a former state senator from Wasco County, entered and, according to the Salem *Mercury* account, "began abusing Semple." This time using his fists, Semple landed some telling blows and Trevitt cried out for help. Lappeus and Fay soon reappeared and rescued Trevitt. The three of them then began to beat Semple with their canes until, in the words of the *Mercury*, "he was covered with blood from head to foot." Semple finally managed to break free and stumbled out of the saloon to safety.

The Salem *Statesman* and the *Mercury* later contended that Lappeus had struck the first blow. None of the other papers disputed this, but Holladay's Portland *Bulletin* asserted that Semple had been the only participant to use anything but his fists. Unaccountably the *Herald*, far from vindicating Semple, did its best to portray Fay as a peacemaker. The *Oregonian* scoffed at the whole episode under the headline "Battle of the Giants."[33]

The fight, whatever its antecedents, was indicative of Oregon's volatile politics during the Holladay era. In the wake of changing economic and social conditions brought about in part by Holladay's manipulation, party loyalties became correspondingly flexible. As a result, Portland Democrats crossed party lines to vote for Holladay men while many Republicans abandoned their party to oppose Holladay as independents, and, in some cases, as Democrats. Such conditions did not strengthen any of Portland's daily newspapers financially. The *Herald, Oregonian,* and *Bulletin* all lost money as circulation and advertising fluctuated, and much of the profit Semple and Patterson obtained from government printing went into unsuccessful efforts to keep the *Herald* in business against its competitors. By 1874, according to one estimate, the paper had lost $150,000.[34] The *Oregonian* also faced trouble and, according to its editor, Harvey Scott, was on the verge of bankruptcy on at least one occasion.[35] But the biggest loser

33. Ibid., October 11, 1872. Accounts appeared in the Portland *Daily Bulletin,* the Portland *Herald,* and the Salem *Statesman* on October 10, 1872, as well as the Salem *Mercury,* October 10 and 12. Fay represented Jackson County in the senate and was president of the upper house in 1870 and 1872 (*Senate Journal, Oregon,* 1870, p. 4; and ibid., 1872, p. 7). Lappeus had been Portland city marshal before becoming the city's first police chief in 1872 under a reorganized city-charter (Maddux, *Willamette,* pp. 23, 76, 88; *Samuel's Directory of Portland,* 1873-1874, p. 209; George H. Williams, "Political History of Oregon, 1853-65," *Oregon Historical Quarterly,* 2 [1901]:29). Trevitt served in the legislature from 1870 to 1872 (*Senate Journal, Oregon,* 1870, p. 5).

34. Scott, "The Oregonian Newspaper," p. 232.

35. Ibid., p. 233.

was Holladay himself. The *Bulletin,* in view of his lavish expenditures for equipment and personnel, was probably the greatest newspaper debacle in the history of Oregon journalism. Although the paper generated sporadic support for some of his business undertakings, Holladay lost an estimated quarter of a million dollars on it, and finally stopped regular publication in 1875.[36]

As early as 1871 Semple and Patterson had attempted to sell their own debt-ridden publication. In September of that year the *Herald* was incorporated as the Portland Printing and Publishing Company. The object was to sell enough stock in the enterprise to prevent the paper from going bankrupt and to enable Patterson and Semple eventually to sell out.[37] This scheme collapsed, however, and Patterson appealed to Grover and others in Salem for help, proposing that another corporation be formed through the sale of a new issue of stock in Salem and elsewhere. A new corporation, the Herald Printing Company, was quickly created and capitalized at thirty thousand dollars for the purpose of buying the *Herald* in order to continue its publication and expand its facilities for job printing.[38] Patterson and Semple subscribed much of the stock, with Grover and several other Salem men purchasing smaller amounts, but the number of shares sold fell short of the amount needed.

Unloading their white elephant on a suspicious market was no easy task for the two proprietors. Potential investors seemed altogether too scarce, or perhaps too well aware of the paper's shaky fiscal status to risk their money. Nevertheless, in late November 1871, Semple wrote to Grover, setting forth a third plan. This involved employees of the paper, including a print shop foreman, reporters, and compositors, who had been persuaded to join Semple and Patterson in subscribing enough stock to enable the Herald Printing Company to buy the paper. The plan was contingent on Grover's appointment of the company as litigant printer for the counties already represented by Patterson and Semple.[39] Persuaded by Semple's confident prospectus, Grover cooperated and on December 1, Semple and Patterson "sold" the *Herald* to the new firm.[40]

36. Turnbull, *Oregon Newspapers*, p. 154.
37. A copy of the corporate agreement, dated October 25, 1871, is in the Semple Papers.
38. A copy of the proposal and a duplicate of the agreement are in the Semple Papers.
39. Semple to Grover, November 20, 1871.
40. Turnbull, *Oregon Newspapers,* p. 151.

With the litigant printing to sustain it, the Herald Printing Company figured to be a more attractive property to prospective investors, to whom Semple and Patterson might finally sell their stock and be done with the paper. "We can now sell the concern without endangering the official patronage," Semple wrote Lucy, his most understanding creditor. Then, with bitterness, he reviewed the situation for her more fully.

If we cannot dispose of it to members of the party it represents we will be compelled ... to sell it to the other side .... We have stood by the party so far ... to our great damage pecuniarily for we have had to fight Holladay and every other monopolist in the state and we have been most seriously injured by such a course. If we had gone in with the monopolists and rings instead of opposing them with bitterness, we would today have been worth many thousands of dollars more and would have been at the head of a printing house free of debt and declaring large dividends .... If the Democratic politicians do not "come to time" with sufficient money we will endeavor to sell the Herald stock to whoever may apply. The main chance is to sell to Holladay and we will follow that chance using every means to make our design a success.[41]

Semple reiterated these sentiments to Grover early in January 1872. He and Patterson were willing to accept an offer from investors headed by the governor, he said, but only if the deal took place by January 15. Meanwhile Semple did not rule out the possibility of doing business with Holladay and arranged a meeting with the latter to talk about "business matters."[42] But Holladay already had one sick paper on his hands and was evidently not interested in acquiring another. Nor did Grover and his colleagues "come to time." As a consequence, Semple and Patterson reluctantly held on to the paper for another year and a half while they hunted without success for a buyer. Funds from state printing afforded temporary relief, but in May 1873 the *Herald* was finally forced to suspend publication.[43] Late in August, soon after the Portland fire (which did only moderate damage to the *Herald* offices), the two partners silenced the presses and their newspaper passed into history.[44]

While the *Herald* was struggling for survival, a railroad boom swept western Oregon in the early seventies, sending property values soaring

41. Semple to Lucy Ames, December 9, 1871.
42. Semple to Grover, January 12, 1872; Semple to Holladay, January 13, 1872.
43. Turnbull, *Oregon Newspapers,* p. 151.
44. A copy of a statement of closure, August 24, 1873, is in the Semple Papers.

and afflicting Semple with an acute case of speculative fever. Failing to heed the wedding advice of Eugene's mother to curb her husband's tendency toward "extravagance," Addie meekly allowed Semple to use her inherited property as his chief source of investment collateral. In 1872 he mortgaged seventeen hundred acres of her land in Columbia County to the Bank of British Columbia for a $14,500 loan to expand the *Herald* printing operations and to invest in East Portland real estate.[45] As the boom continued into 1873 he went on borrowing money at inflated interest in order to finance new and more dubious enterprises. One such venture was a $2,500 quarter interest in a self-adjusting balance wrench developed by a California engineer named H. R. Leonard. The wrench patent was still pending at the time, but Patterson, who had already purchased a quarter interest for himself, enticed Semple to do likewise. The patent was delayed, however, and by the time it was awarded, the wrench had lost much of its novelty and marketable value and the two partners were left virtually empty-handed.[46] Undaunted by such reversals, Semple continued to speculate recklessly, borrowing money by mortgaging Addie's inheritance, including several blocks of choice Portland real estate. Much of the money went into small land and building investments, particularly in East Portland. During 1872 and 1873 he borrowed more than $50,000 from more than two dozen creditors, including Ben Holladay.[47] His biggest source of credit was Lucy, with whom he accumulated a debt of more than $20,000.

As the effects of the financial panic of 1873 began to grip the Pacific Northwest, Semple's position with his lenders worsened. The impact of the depression hit Portland at a time when many of his mortgages were falling due. To add to his plight, fire swept the city in August, doing more than a million dollars' damage and leveling more than 250 buildings. Semple's own loss was not more than two thousand dollars, but the immediate effect of the fire on the community at large was to depress land values even further at the very moment when he had

45. See documents (1872) and title abstract and mortgage (August 24, 1872) in Semple Papers.

46. Documents on patent wrench (1872), Semple Papers.

47. Holladay loaned him $700 in January 1872 and $700 in April 1873; both were 60-day loans. Addie's brother, J. P. O. Lownsdale, loaned him more than $1,000 in December 1872 and smaller amounts in April 1873 and January 1874. See promissory notes (1872-74), Semple Papers.

hoped to capitalize on his investments.[48] In the meantime, the land he had inherited from his father in Illinois had also declined in value, from twenty thousand to twelve thousand dollars, depriving him of another badly needed source of income.[49] Facing bankruptcy, Semple tried to persuade his creditors early in 1874 to put his property in the hands of their trustees in order to dispose of it for payment of debts out of court. His lenders had grown impatient, however, and filed suit against him in March. Multnomah County assessed his liabilities at forty thousand dollars against assets of more than thirty-five thousand dollars in cash and securities. Semple managed to repay most of the debt within a few months by selling or mortgaging his Illinois land and more than eighteen thousand dollars' worth of Addie's property. On December 2, 1874, he received a discharge of bankruptcy from Judge Matthew Deady.[50]

Semple was not the only one facing hard times. Patterson, according to a friend, was also "in a pretty rough row of stumps" and had fled Portland, leaving an ailing wife to face his angry creditors.[51] Ben Holladay, too, had been brought to the end of his financial tether. Having overextended himself with foreign bankers at the onset of the slump, he was eventually forced to surrender his Oregon holdings to Henry Villard, his successor as the leading figure in the transportation history of the Pacific Northwest.

By the winter of 1874-75, Semple's career in Portland was in a shambles. Early in 1875 he left the city and relocated his growing family (which by now included two daughters, Maude and Zoe) on a small rented stock ranch by the McKenzie River near Eugene. Like Portland earlier, the area seemed destined for rapid development. The Oregon and California Railroad was already making twice-daily runs through Eugene between Portland and the line's southern terminus at Roseburg and in 1872 the legislature had selected Eugene as the site for the new state university.[52] The countryside, however, was still thinly

48. Lansing Mizner to Semple, August 17, 1873, January 1, 1874; Bancroft, *History of Oregon,* 2: 718.

49. Lansing Mizner to Semple, March 23, June 12, and August 17, 1873.

50. A copy of the warrant in bankruptcy against the estate of Eugene Semple, filed in U. S. District Court, Oregon, April 23, 1874, is in the bankruptcy documents, Semple Papers, as are a copy of the certificate of final discharge of bankruptcy, issued December 2, 1874, and a statement of assets and liabilities, April 23, 1874.

51. N. T. Bingham to Semple, July 9, 1875.

52. Holladay's railroad reached Roseburg by November 1872 (Lucia, *Holladay,*

populated and cheap land was plentiful. Lansing Mizner was more than delighted with his stepbrother's new location and offered an optimistic if naive appraisal of the region, hinting that he too might come to the area: "Sooner or later railroads will increase the value of land very much . . . . Give me a description of the country near you, value of land, timber, rainfall, etc . . . and where the railroad from Winnemuca if built will strike the Willamet [sic]."[53]

Whether he shared Lansing's enthusiasm or not, Semple was in no position financially to engage in any more property speculation at the moment. Political opportunities also seemed limited by local anti-Catholic prejudice. His friend Lafayette Lane, who had been godfather at the Catholic baptism of Semple's daughter Zoe in 1873, was victimized by this intolerance when he ran for a vacated congressional seat in the fall of 1875. Despite the fact that Lane County, of which Eugene was the county seat, had been named for his illustrious father, Joseph Lane, the son's Catholicism became the main issue. The Eugene *Oregon State Journal* speculated that his nomination by the Democrats as "the 'Pope's Candidate' [was] doubtless part of the same general plan to bring our government under the control of the Catholic church."[54] Lane won in spite of such opposition but was unseated in the regular election in 1876. Semple himself became active only in minor party affairs, serving in 1875 as a delegate to the county convention where he chaired the committee on resolutions. It was clear that Lane County held little future for him, and in June 1876 he ended his sojourn in the Willamette Valley and moved his family north again, this time to Columbia County.

The new home was a small farm at Scappoose Bay along the Columbia River on land Addie had inherited. To supplement the farm's meager yield, Semple and Thomas Stewart, a Columbia County physician, scraped together enough capital to build a small cedar shingle mill on Cedar Mountain in adjacent Washington County. The mill operated sporadically for a year or two, but despite Semple's usual

p. 308; Bancroft, *History of Oregon,* 2:671-72).

53. Lansing Mizner to Semple, March 1, 1875. Railroad promoter Joe Gaston had been trying to interest the owners of the Central Pacific in extending their line from Winnemucca, Nevada, to Oregon, thus providing the latter state with a direct transcontinental link and Holladay with a competitor. It was rumored that the connection would be made at Eugene (Bancroft, *History of Oregon,* 2:703).

54. Eugene *Oregon State Journal,* November 20, 1875.

optimism it failed to prosper and he and Stewart finally abandoned it.[55]

Although still comparatively poor, Semple soon became a familiar figure in county affairs. Voters elected him to the first of three terms as county school clerk in 1877 and in 1878 he was selected to preside as grand marshal during the annual Fourth of July celebration at St. Helens.[56] He was also a Democratic candidate for state representative in 1878 but lost the election by fifty votes to his Republican opponent, Nelson Cole, as Columbia County voters went against the statewide Democratic trend.[57] At the county convention that year, as chairman of the resolutions committee, Semple drafted a majority proposal that the government regulate the Oregon Railway and Navigation Company and other transportation monopolies along the Columbia River and aid in building locks to bypass the rapids at Cascades and The Dalles.[58] The proposal aroused controversy at the state Democratic convention later in the year and, although defeated, was one of the early organized protests from constituencies along the lower Columbia against the exorbitant charges imposed on local commerce by the railroad and navigation companies. It was also a prelude to the formation of the Columbia Waterway Convention, an organization created six years later, partly through Semple's efforts, to secure unimpeded navigation.

Semple remained active in Columbia County politics for several more years. In 1880 he filled an unexpired term as county clerk and in 1882, while serving as chairman of the county Democratic convention, won the nomination for county clerk but lost the election. Outside of local politics, however, there was little to cheer him. By 1882, in his forty-second year, he was the father of four children for whom he had been, at best, only a modest provider. As journalist, politician, and businessman, his life so far had been highlighted by setbacks and disappointments. And while he erratically pursued various interests, the

55. Little is known of this mill operation. That it existed is indicated by a letterhead used by Semple during these years, and by miscellaneous receipts in the Semple Papers. Semple reminisced about the mill to a reporter years later, claiming it was the first of its kind in the region (Seattle *Post-Intelligencer,* February 1, 1894). Actually, cedar milling had been going on at nearby Cedar Creek in Washington County since at least 1848 when Elam Young built a mill there. See Oregon Historical Records Survey, vol. 34, *Washington County,* p. 25.

56. Columbia County Courthouse Records (Deeds, 1878-82), Vols. F and G; St. Helens *Mist,* July 6, 1878.

57. Election returns are from the *Oregonian,* June 5, 7, 18, 1878.

58. A copy of the resolution is in the Semple Papers.

more immediate and obvious needs of his family often escaped his attention. Addie had already suggested their deteriorating domestic situation in a pathetic letter to her wandering husband shortly before the family left Lane County.

How I wish I could be with you instead of having to write to you. We all want to see you awfully bad . . . . You do not know how lonely I feel at night. I never in my life before missed you as I do this time . . . . It would make you laugh to see the sitting room after we are ready to go to bed at night. We put the machine against the outside door, high chairs against the bedroom and kitchen doors and the big rocking chair against the parlor door, and against the stair door I put Maude and Zoe's little trunks. We lean them up so that if anyone would open the door they would fall and awaken us, and I keep buck-shot in your gun. It lays by my bed . . . . I do hope you won't get this letter for I want you to come home before it can reach you.[59]

Semple seemed indifferent to such entreaties, as well as to pleas from relatives in the East to exploit the opportunities that supposedly awaited him in Illinois and St. Louis. The appeals became more earnest after Mary Semple died in December of 1875, leaving her three-hundred-acre share of the family estate in Illinois to Eugene and his family. The land was fenced and under cultivation and, as his sister Julia reminded him, "If you have any political ambitions, Illinois is the place to come where the name of Semple is well known and honored."[60] But cousin Oscar Bradford in Springfield, Illinois, was not so encouraging. When Semple inquired about the possibility of selling his mother's estate for badly needed cash, Bradford replied that there was no market. The only thing to do, he counseled, was "to await the 'good times coming.' We are all plodding along making a living but not much more."[61]

Semple may have been inclined to "await the good times coming," but Addie was not. Her marriage to Semple had been filled with drudgery and loneliness in the later years. As time passed and the

59. Ruth Adelaide Semple to Semple, April 29, 1876. In addition to Maude (born in the family residence at Yamhill and Lownsdale Streets in Portland on January 14, 1872) and Zoe (born at the family home in Portland on April 1, 1873), there were Mary Ethel (born in Portland on December 30, 1875) and their only son, Eugene Lownsdale Semple, born in Portland in 1877 (no date).

60. Julia Semple Scott to Semple, January 28, 1876. According to Lucy, the best farming land from James Semple's estate had been given to their mother (Lucy Ames to Semple, January 24, 1876).

61. Bradford to Semple, April 3, 1879. Bradford and Semple corresponded periodically from 1876 onward regarding the latter's Illinois holdings.

burdens of raising a family increased, her sense of security must have diminished as she watched her husband flitting from one undertaking to another. Had she been older, she might have resigned herself to a spouse who persistently neglected to establish a sound livelihood in any of the professions for which he was qualified. But Addie was not yet thirty years old as the summer of 1882 approached and she had lost only a little of the youthful beauty that had first attracted Semple. In June 1882 she sued for and got a divorce without opposition on Semple's part—with the provision that he be awarded custody of all four children. Addie's subsequent actions reveal another reason for the separation. Eleven days after the divorce was granted in Multnomah County Circuit Court, she remarried. Her new husband was Frank M. Hoyt, a young St. Helens businessman.[62] The romance had evidently been blooming for some time, and it was with a sense of relief that Semple poured out his feelings in a letter to Lansing shortly after the remarriage.

When I wrote you last matters were not in good shape, but now the last act in the drama has occurred and while I cannot now find heart to write you an extended account I will give you the main facts. Mrs. Semple obtained a divorce without resistence [sic] on my part upon condition that the custody of all the children should be awarded to me. July 9, she was again married to a boy of the neighborhood and is living near his mother's house.

Then, looking to the future, he added:

I will take the children and put them to school and then take up the threads of life where I dropped them 12 years ago. Let all those years of doubt and dread and paralyzed energies be stricken from my record. Send this to Lucy and Julia. I will write you and my sisters oftener after this and hope our old relations may be restored.[63]

Semple's career in Oregon was nearing an end. Before the year expired he yielded to insistent appeals from Lucy and sent his three daughters East for what she considered "a proper education." The

62. Interview with Mrs. Lucy Adair of Seattle (Semple's granddaughter), April 1965; and Semple Genealogy.
63. Semple to Mizner, July 12, 1882. The latter part of the letter to Lansing seems to hint that the marriage had somehow led to an estrangement between Semple and his sisters. If so, it was primarily because of Semple's neglect. As for the "paralyzed energies," it is hard to tell just whom he is blaming; at the moment he wrote the letter, he was probably not in the most rational of moods. In later years, as Semple's fortunes improved, he tried to conceal news of the divorce. Several brief biographical accounts of his life assert that Addie died in 1883. See, for example, Prosser, *History of Puget Sound,* 2:534-37.

youngest child, five-year-old Eugene, remained with his father in Oregon as Semple prepared to make a fresh start. [64]

64. Lansing Mizner to Semple, August 15, 1883. Addie evidently lived on in St. Helens and Portland until at least the early 1900s when the infrequent references to her in the Semple Papers end. If there were other women in Semple's life after his separation from Addie, there is no mention of it in his papers. Their son apparently lived with Semple for a year or two and then went to stay with his mother, but there is virtually no mention of him in Semple's correspondence after 1885.

4. "An Open Waterway"

Semple had scarcely settled his personal affairs in Oregon when he embarked on a new business venture, the construction of a sawmill across the Columbia River in Vancouver, Washington Territory. Thus began his experience with the headaches of operating a lumber mill and the related problems of overcoming the obstructions to commerce—natural and man-made—common to mill owners along the Columbia during the 1880s.

Early in 1883 Semple persuaded Lucy to lend him fifteen thousand dollars with which he began to buy land and equipment for the mill. His first purchase in Vancouver was a suitable piece of waterfront property at the lower end of town on a five-thousand-dollar quit-claim deed from a local couple, William and Kate Ranck. He then ordered a new seventy-five horsepower engine and boiler from a firm in Indianapolis, Indiana.[1] His activities soon attracted the attention of a number of local businessmen who were eager to cooperate in the establishment of a new sawmill which, according to the Vancouver *Weekly Independent,* would represent "a big industrial addition to our city." When Semple appeared before the Vancouver Board of Trade in July, its members welcomed him warmly and appointed a committee to help raise the additional sums needed to complete the mill.[2] Within a short time the committee secured a four-thousand-dollar loan from the

1. Miscellaneous receipts, July 27, 1883, and Semple to H. G. Knapp and Company, September 14, 1884, Semple Papers; Vancouver (weekly) *Independent,* August 16, 1883.
2. *Independent,* August 16, August 2, 1883.

Vancouver First National Bank.[3] Although construction of the mill did not begin until early August, Semple confidently predicted it would be operating in September. As late as mid-November, however, the *Independent* was still promising its readers that the mill would "start cutting in a few days." To the relief of local boosters, the plant finally did open on December 10.[4]

In honor of his generous sister Lucy, Semple named his fledgling enterprise the Lucia Mills. The new mill was the largest in Clark County. Running at full capacity it could employ thirty men and cut thirty thousand feet of timber a day—figures reportedly equalled in the area only by one mill in St. Helens. Abundant nearby forests of pine, cedar, and fir furnished a reliable source of logs at moderate cost. The Lucia Mills, according to advertisements in the *Independent,* could supply on short notice not only planed lumber, but shingles and lath, using one of the six steam-powered engines in the county. Semple's sole competitor in Vancouver was Loring Palmer, an experienced lumberman whose mill had a sawing capacity barely half as large as Semple's.[5]

As owner of the largest mill in the vicinity, Semple confidently anticipated success. The city of Vancouver, although it contained only three thousand inhabitants, was growing steadily, while adjacent Fort Vancouver and nearby Portland offered additional markets for lumber. Furthermore, an economic boom in Washington, Idaho, and Oregon had created a demand for lumber far beyond the locale of Vancouver. During the decade, as railroads penetrated the territory and brought settlers, the population of Washington increased five fold, from 75,000 to more than 350,000. Railroads were built along the Columbia River and through the Walla Walla and Palouse country, opening up two and one-half million acres of new agricultural land. Almost fifteen thousand new farms were established and most of the settlers prospered as the value of their produce increased from five million to fourteen million dollars.[6]

In order to penetrate this market Semple and other lumbermen along the lower Columbia had to deal with the Oregon Railway and

3. Miscellaneous receipts, November 16, 1883, Semple Papers.
4. *Independent,* August 16, November 15, December 10, 1883.
5. Ibid., August 16, 1883; and *Report of the Governor of Washington Territory to the Secretary of the Interior, 1885,* pp. 49-51.
6. *Tenth Census (1880),* 1:75, 83, 116; *Eleventh Census (1890),* Pt. 1, p. 45; and Dorothy O. Johansen and Charles M. Gates, *Empire of the Columbia,* p. 385.

Navigation Company. By 1884 the ORNC was a subsidiary of the Union Pacific Railroad and exercised a veritable monopoly of rail and water traffic eastward through the Columbia Gorge to the inland markets.[7] The rough water and the terrain along this stretch of the river virtually forced mill men and other shippers to do business with the company, which exploited the situation through high freight charges, load regulations, and price manipulations. These circumstances frequently made it unprofitable for lumbermen on the lower parts of the river to ship to points east. Semple and other mill operators were especially irritated by the ORNC refusal to construct sidings at landings along the Columbia to enable them to reach inland customers. The lumbermen often had neither the capital nor the right of way to build such facilities for themselves. The Bonneville Rapids posed another barrier to commerce that Semple and others sought to overcome with the help of the ORNC, which operated a siding around the rapids. "It is practically impossible for loaded barges to reach the inclines at Bonneville during high water," Semple told H. S. Rowe, a company official in Portland.[8] But Rowe had undoubtedly heard such complaints before and took no action.

The ORNC worried Semple more than it might have bothered other mill men. As a novice in the lumber business he had saddled himself with a large mill operation which could survive only by selling to outside markets. In his quest for distant customers he turned early in 1884 to the California trade. In March he approached the managers of the Muckle Brothers' mills at St. Helens with a scheme for combining operations in order to win a competitive position in the San Francisco market. The Muckle brothers, who had been exporting lumber since 1868 and possessed the experience and contacts Semple needed in order to deal with the far-off California buyers, declined his proposition.[9] Semple's hope of acquiring California clients five times

7. "Joint Ownership of the Oregon Railway and Navigation Company," *Northwest Magazine,* 15 (March 1897): 24-25. The Oregon Railway and Navigation Company had been created by Henry Villard in 1879 through the merger of several smaller companies, including the Oregon Steam Navigation Company. Later, by merging the O.R.&N. with the Northern Pacific Railroad, he obtained a federal government right of way on both sides of the Columbia River. See *Memoirs of Henry Villard, Journalist and Financier, 1835-1900,* vol. 2, chap. 10, *passim.*

8. Semple to Rowe, May 2, 1884.

9. Semple to Muckle Brothers, March 29, 1884; and John S. Hittel, *The Commerce and Industries of the Pacific Coast,* p. 594.

more distant than those he was already losing in the Columbia Basin stemmed in part from stepbrother Lansing Mizner's influence as a California legislator. By June, Mizner, a state senator, had arranged for shipments of Lucia Mills lumber to several Bay Area firms. Encouraged by this development, Semple made plans to expand into the San Diego and Los Angeles markets.[10] As weeks passed, however, the anticipated demand for Lucia Mills lumber in California failed to develop. One reason was competition from larger Puget Sound lumber companies which exercised monopolies in California ports through price fixing and transportation agreements. Eventually realizing the futility of his efforts, Semple abandoned his California hopes and redirected his efforts to the interior markets of the Northwest and to the Vancouver-Portland area.

While lumbermen along the lower Columbia haggled with the ORNC for lower rates, inland orders for Lucia Mills products accumulated and many impatient buyers were forced to look elsewhere for their supplies, or do without. Semple reluctantly cautioned his customers not to request any short notice orders until the ORNC came to terms with the mill men. At the same time, however, he had to anticipate a brisk rise in trade when transportation eventually did become more readily available. As a result, the Lucia Mills kept on sawing logs and piling up inventory. During the summer of 1884, Semple relied heavily on local orders to keep his mill running, with most of his business coming from the army detachment at Fort Vancouver.[11] Despite the army trade, more than half his bills remained unpaid in late July and he was forced to beg his creditors for more time in hopes of winning some new orders from the fort.[12] Meanwhile, many retail lumber dealers with whom he did business in the vicinity faced the same problems he did and could not pay immediately for their orders. Many of *their* customers were farmers who depended on the seasonal harvest and could pay their bills only at certain times of the year. Similarly, the transportation problem that caused delays in shipments for the mill operators downstream was just as irritating to inland buyers upriver. In August, Semple's business picked up. Besides obtaining new orders from the fort, he received several overdue payments from inland customers. "The money," he remarked, "could not have been received at a more favorable time."[13]

10. Semple to Mizner, June 12, June 22, 1884.
11. Semple to A. O. Ankeny, September 5, 1884.
12. Semple to H. P. Gregory and Company, July 23, 1884.
13. Semple to Reese and Redman, August 8, 1884.

But as winter approached, the Lucia Mills was still operating at a deficit and at low capacity.

In 1885 Semple became active in a movement of mill owners and other businessmen of the region to remove the obstacles, natural and corporate, that impeded river traffic between the interior and the coast. One outcome of the movement was the formation of the Columbia Waterway Convention, an association devoted to improving navigation and commerce on the river. The first session of the convention met at The Dalles on December 2, 1885. Semple had been one of the delegates chosen by the board of trade to represent Vancouver. Late in the year, however, he was called East to attend his daughter Maude who had been stricken with typhoid fever.[14] As a result he was unable to attend the initial meeting.

With the exception of Portland, the communities represented at the first session were small river or farming towns like Dayton, Goldendale, Vancouver, and Walla Walla in Washington Territory and Astoria, The Dalles, and Waitsburg in Oregon.[15] They constituted an important political bloc whose representatives at the meeting (predominantly delegates of local chambers of commerce and boards of trade) spoke for a growing number of citizens who favored an "open" river. The convention adopted resolutions asking Congress for aid to build canals and locks at The Dalles and Cascade City, for improvements at the mouth of the Columbia, and for the regulation of transportation corporations operating in the region. Having stated their grievances and suggested some remedies, the delegates adjourned, agreeing to hold a second meeting at Vancouver the following year.[16]

In April 1886, several months before the second session, Semple, Loring Palmer, and several other Columbia River lumbermen met in Portland to discuss further the ORNC's intransigence on rates and access routes and to otherwise publicize their predicament.[17] One of their chief complaints was against the Pacific Pine Lumber Company, a combine of Puget Sound mills which provided its members with a common lumber yard in San Francisco. As Semple already knew, the combine had for several years regulated prices and production quotas so

14. Vancouver *Independent,* December 17, 1885.

15. *Official Proceedings of the Columbia Waterway Convention* (1st sess., 1885), p. 2. A copy of the proceedings is in the Northwest Collection of the University of Washington Library.

16. Ibid., pp. 10-12.

17. Portland *Oregonian,* May 2, 1886.

as to exclude most Columbia River mills from the California markets.[18] The mill men also spoke out against the high pilotage fees charged by licensed navigators who guided traffic past the river's numerous bars and shoals. In an open letter to their fellow lumbermen, published in the *Oregonian,* Semple and Palmer complained bitterly that the mills of the Portland-Vancouver area were being "shut out of the ocean trade by the San Francisco combine . . . [and] restricted to supplying a country within the sound of their steam whistles."[19] Except as a recitation of grievances, however, the Portland meeting was an exercise in futility.

The second session of the Columbia Waterway Convention began on October 14, 1886, at Vancouver. This time Semple was on hand as a member of the host delegation. In the months preceding the second meeting he had made an extensive study of the problems of navigation on the Columbia. The result was a rather remarkable series of ambitious and elaborately detailed proposals publicized beforehand and submitted to the convention for inclusion in the published report of the second session. The most striking of these proposals was a plan for a canal to connect Young's Bay near Astoria with the Pacific Ocean. With completion of such a waterway, Semple argued, seagoing vessels could bypass the hazardous sand bars and currents at the mouth of the Columbia with safety. A second proposal dealt with the rapids upstream at The Dalles. To overcome them, he urged the installment of a "vertical lift" (not specifying exactly what he meant) to raise boats from below the rapids to a point upriver above the obstructions at Celilo Falls. His final recommendation related to navigation of the upper Columbia from Celilo Falls to the Canadian border. To enable shippers to reach grain growers in the region beyond, he suggested installation of a series of firmly anchored steel cables reaching from above the head of each rapid to the foot of the rapid, with the lower end of each cable supported by a buoy. "With the cable occupying a position in the middle of the channel," he explained, "a steamer approaching from below would touch the bouy, and being supplied with a steam windlass suitable for the purpose, would pick up the cable and warp over the swift water."[20] The response from the other

18. *Oregonian,* January 1, 1882; *West Shore Magazine* (Portland), 13 (October 1882): 183, and 16 (March 8, 1890): 311; Edwin T. Coman, Jr., and Helen M. Gibbs, *Time, Tide and Timber: A Century of Pope and Talbot,* pp. 409-13.

19. *Oregonian,* April 28, 1886.

20. The above proposals are included in the *Official Proceedings of the*

delegates to these surprising (and perhaps impractical) recommendations is not recorded.

Semple concluded with words that undoubtedly struck a responsive note with the gathering. "The only hope of the people of the interior for cheap transportation to the sea board," he said, "lies in the opening of our waterways. The opening of the Columbia river," he predicted, "will have the effect of emancipating the people of its valley from the thraldom of railway domination. I therefore urge this convention to maintain its organization and keep the main idea of an open waterway constantly before its eyes."[21] In line with these remarks the convention adopted new resolutions asking Congress for internal improvements and stiffer regulation of transportation companies. A committee was also formed to solicit financial support for the organization. The delegates then adjourned, agreeing to meet a third time in August of the following year at Astoria.

Enthusiasm waned after the Vancouver meeting as community leaders became discouraged with the convention's inability to influence Congress or the ORNC. Semple and other founders of the organization withdrew from participation in later sessions and by 1890 the short-lived movement had passed into history. Despite its ineffectiveness, the Columbia Waterway Convention had helped to focus attention on the region's growing need for adequate transportation. In this work, Semple had played an active part.

The futile battle for an open river and free trade typified the struggles of local groups around the country against corporate monopolies at the time. Nor did the situation along the lower Columbia improve noticeably during the next several years. Semple managed to do enough business to keep his mill running, but there were no profits and his initial debts remained unpaid, gathering interest.[22] He had seen the shape of things to come during his first year at Vancouver and had decided by the end of 1884 to entrust the daily management of his enterprise to more qualified hands. Early in 1885 he leased the mill to Loring Palmer, his chief local competitor, thus creating what amounted to a local lumber monopoly, the very type of evil they both so vehemently denounced. Under the terms of the agreement Semple received a thousand dollars in annual rent but retained the use of part

Columbia Waterway Convention (2d sess., 1886), Appendix, pp. iii, iv, v.
21. Ibid., p. 17.
22. Semple still owed Lucy the fifteen thousand dollars.

of the facilities to cut lumber for export outside the Columbia Basin. Palmer meanwhile got Semple's trade with Fort Vancouver and other local buyers.[23] The arrangement seemed to satisfy both men. Palmer, a sound businessman who was anxious to expand from his own small operations, became manager of the largest mill in Clark County while Semple received an annual income and retained ownership of the mill. But even under Palmer's experienced management the Lucia Mills could not turn a profit. In the years ahead he was forced into costly competition against newer, bigger, and more resourceful rivals along the Columbia and on Puget Sound.[24]

Semple's experiences as a lumberman must have typified those of many ambitious men in the Northwest at the time—men without much experience or financial backing who rushed into the business and failed in spite of growing markets and abundant timber. In Semple's case, however, these shortcomings did not entirely explain his unwillingness to remain a mill operator. The agreement with Palmer, besides freeing Semple from a frustrating situation, enabled him to turn his restless energies once again to the more intriguing business of politics.

23. Information on the transaction is in the miscellaneous items and business receipts (February 25, 1885), Semple Papers.

24. Semple and Lucy maintained ownership of the mill until Semple's death in 1908. There is much correspondence relating to the mill affairs after 1887 in the Semple Papers.

5. Scrambling for Governor

Semple did not lose interest in the Lucia Mills simply because the business was floundering. During his sojourn as a Clark County lumberman his desire for public office had returned. In fact, politics had probably been uppermost in his plans since November of 1884 when the election of Grover Cleveland returned control of the national government to the Democratic Party for the first time in twenty-four years. As a loyal and popular Democrat Semple cheered his party's triumph, lifting its banner proudly as he led a Vancouver delegation in the Portland victory parade.[1] It was not a complete surprise to some people when, shortly before Cleveland's inauguration, Semple announced his candidacy for the appointment to the governorship of Washington Territory.

Semple was only one of at least a dozen applicants, most of them relatively unknown, who sent lists of endorsements to the new administration calling attention to their unique qualifications for the governorship. To most of the applicants the job was probably well worth seeking in spite of the modest annual salary of $2,600. The governor's patronage had increased substantially during the early 1880s as the bureaucracy of the territory proliferated. He appointed scores of inspectors, surveyors, and revenue officers, as well as members of commissions created by the legislature to direct tasks ranging from artesian well drilling to prison construction. In consequence, the

1. Semple was grand marshal in the Vancouver contingent at the parade (Vancouver *Independent,* November 27, 1884).

governor's influence in many areas rivaled that of the legislature.[2]

Even more important than Cleveland's victory, as far as office seekers in the territory were concerned, was the election of a Democrat as territorial delegate to Congress. While Cleveland outpolled James Blaine for the presidency, Charles Stewart Voorhees narrowly defeated his Republican rival James Armstrong to become the territory's first Democratic delegate in a decade.[3] Voorhees, who resided at Colfax in eastern Washington, was the son of Indiana Senator Daniel Voorhees. The new delegate's endorsement would carry considerable weight with the President in his choice of a new governor.

During the early months of 1885 Semple and the other gubernatorial candidates waited anxiously for Cleveland to make up his mind on a successor to Republican incumbent Watson C. Squire, who had been appointed only the previous July by President Chester Arthur. The new chief executive was not about to be rushed into any hasty decision on the matter of a territorial governorship. His campaign pledge to end the patronage scramble by broadening civil service reform made it unlikely that he would act hastily and risk the appointment of incompetent Democrats. Caution would be particularly necessary in filling offices in a territory like Washington where Republicans had dominated politics for more than twenty years.

As for the residents of the territory, they had exhibited an open-minded independence on the issues of the recent election and were consequently unpredictable at the moment as far as political loyalties were concerned. The refusal of the Northern Pacific Railroad to extend its line north from Tacoma to Seattle, for example, had created a widespread suspicion among the voters that collusion existed between the railroad and the Republican majority in the capital at Olympia. This suspicion, mistaken though it may have been, had cost the Republicans considerable support in the Puget Sound country. At Seattle and elsewhere during the 1884 campaign Voorhees had pledged to fight in Congress for forfeiture of the remaining Northern Pacific land grants in the territory. This promise alone had probably secured him enough Republican votes to win the election. Another potent issue

2. Wilfred J. Airey, "A History of the Constitution and Government of Washington Territory" (Ph.D. dissertation, University of Washington, 1945), p. 124.

3. Edmond S. Meany, *History of the State of Washington,* p. 371. See also Jonathan Edwards, *Illustrated History of Spokane County,* p. 309, for a biographical sketch of the younger Voorhees.

in the territory was statehood. Most residents wanted Washington admitted to the Union, viewing it as inevitable in light of the territory's rapid growth in population during the eighties.[4] But leaders of both major political parties were reluctant to act. This was especially true of the Democrats. Cleveland and his Mugwump supporters held an insecure grasp on the Congress and could not be expected to give active support to statehood for a territory which, if admitted, might revert to its traditional Republican voting habits and possibly upset the President's slim advantage on Capitol Hill. Cautious Democrats noted that the territorial legislature still had a Republican majority and that Voorhees had been elected by a paper-thin margin of 146 votes.[5]

With this confused situation prevailing, Semple's sources of support for the appointment were uncertain. It is likely his name was unknown to the vast majority of residents of the territory. Outside the territory, potential backing seemed more certain, especially among influential Oregon Democrats like Lafayette Grover and Sylvester Pennoyer. Semple's family influence was also important. Charles S. Beardsley, a well-known New York Democrat whose wife Ellen was Semple's first cousin, was a friend of President Cleveland.[6] James Semple's career in the Senate was yet another consideration. Lansing Mizner reminded the President of the elder Semple's service to the country in an early letter of recommendation: "His [Eugene's] selection would be a graceful recognition of the distinguished services of his father, who in the Senate of the United States first moved to abrogate the treaty of joint occupancy of Oregon with England and who contended to the last with President Polk that 'our title to 54-40 was clear and unquestionable.' "[7]

Semple's first public endorsement came from the Vancouver Board of Trade. In late February 1885 the board sent a petition to the President urging Cleveland to appoint Semple governor when and if the chief executive replaced Squire.[8] The qualifying "if" in the board's

---

4. Meany, *History of Washington,* p. 277.

5. The legislature, composed of a Council of twelve and a House of Representatives numbering thirty, still gave the Republicans an overall majority of nine. Election returns from Olympia *Washington Standard,* November 28, 1884.

6. Beardsley to Cleveland, May 21, 1885, Department of Interior Appointment File (Eugene Semple). A microfilm copy of Semple's appointment file, reproduced by the National Archives and Records Service, is in the Newspaper and Microcopy Center, University of Washington Library. The file lists letters of endorsement, petitions, etc., relating to Semple's campaign for the appointment. Hereafter cited as Appointment File.

7. Lansing Mizner to Grover Cleveland, September 9, 1885, Semple Papers.

8. Appointment File. Squire was evidently a competent chief executive. He

resolution was significant. Customarily, a changeover in national administrations meant prompt appointment of members of the party in power to high territorial offices. Such was not to be the case this time. Cleveland's intention of reducing if not halting the traditional clamor for spoils had been clearly spelled out.[9] The territorial governorship was not, however, an appointment strictly governed by the rules of civil service. Semple pointed this out to H. T.Crowley, editor of the Spokane Falls *Chronicle,* who had attacked him for office seeking: "The position of governor of a territory is one where it is important that the policy of the dominant party should be represented. The status is the same as in diplomatic and consular positions. A change, if made, will be upon that ground alone. The Civil Service rules apply only to minor offices, which do not reflect the policy of the administration." Another argument in Semple's favor, as Beardsley reminded the President, was the party's campaign promise ·to select territorial officers only from among inhabitants of the territory.[10]

Cleveland's early reluctance to distribute the fruits of victory did not dampen Semple's enthusiasm for the governor's office; nor did many of the other candidates lose heart. More than a dozen nominees received endorsement, although half of the aspirants were definite "outsiders" who soon faded from the political picture. These included George Crosette of Chico, California, H. Clay Conde of St. Louis, Charles R. Buckalew of Pennsylvania, Dr. Henry Plummer of Kentucky, and William P. Bently of St. Louis. Within the territory several other candidates besides Semple emerged in the early months of 1885, although most of them soon threw their support to more powerful contenders. One early favorite was Benjamin L. Sharpstein of Walla Walla, a former legislator and candidate for territorial delegate. Thomas Carroll, a Tacoma lawyer, also got some influential initial backing. A more significant candidate was Henry L. Blanchard of Irondale who

---

came West from New York in 1879, a college graduate with service in the Civil War. He was wealthy, having married Ida Remington, granddaughter of the founder of the firearms company, in 1868. Despite dealings with Henry Villard, he urged forfeiture of Northern Pacific land grants in his reports to the Interior Department in 1886. See *Seattle and Environs,* 3:340-53.

9. Allan Nevins, *Grover Clevel d: A Study in Courage,* p. 200.

10. Semple to Crowley, printed in the Spokane Falls *Chronicle,* June 11, 1885 (Semple had written the reply to the paper on May 28 from Washington, D.C., at Crowley's request); Beardsley to Cleveland, May 21, 1885, Appointment File.

received praise from prominent Seattle Democrats including Thomas Burke. Even more popular was J. B. Reavis, a North Yakima member of the legislature who had been elected by the biggest majority in the history of the territory, according to his sponsors. Finally there was Thomas R. Tammatt, a colorful army engineer and pioneer railroad builder in the region but a man allegedly tainted by too much Republican support.[11]

Nowhere was interest in the appointment more keen than at Seattle. The Republican *Post-Intelligencer* observed that no sooner had Squire taken office than a new Democratic administration was ready to kick him out. The paper endorsed J. R. McDonald, a wealthy lumberman who had recently come to Seattle from Michigan and was reportedly about to do big things for the city.[12] Burke, who had been offered early support for the governorship by Voorhees but had declined, was now backing McDonald.[13] Probably the strongest candidate in the Puget Sound country, however, was Semple's former boss on the *Herald,* Beriah Brown. By June, McDonald had withdrawn from the race and given his support to Brown, mainly because of the latter's greater popularity.[14]

Brown was an interesting fellow. He had spent his early years in Wisconsin politics before coming West to make a reputation in journalism. He was also an old Wisconsin friend of William Vilas, Cleveland's close adviser and postmaster-general. Brown was seventy years old—one objection to his appointment was his age—and had already edited several Pacific Coast newspapers. In 1865 he had supposedly been chased north from San Francisco by a mob that had objected to his editorial support of Andrew Johnson. From Oregon he had eventually moved on to Seattle to establish the *Daily Dispatch* in the 1870s, and to become mayor and a member of the University of Washington Board of Regents.[15] Brown received what proved to be

11. Information on all the above candidates is taken from Semple's Appointment File.

12. Seattle *Post-Intelligencer,* February 24, 1885. President Chester Arthur had appointed Squire governor only the previous summer.

13. Ibid., and Robert C. Nesbit, *He Built Seattle: A Biography of Judge Thomas Burke,* p. 89.

14. *Post-Intelligencer,* March 5, 1885; Portland *Sunday Welcome,* June 27, 1885.

15. Clarence B. Bagley Scrapbook No. 8, p. 26, Northwest Collection, University of Washington Library; Edmond S. Meany Pioneer File (s.v. Beriah Brown, Sr.), Northwest Collection.

Eugene Semple as a young man

James Semple

Lansing B. Mizner, 1879

very important backing from William H. White of Seattle, a Cleveland favorite who was soon to be appointed United States attorney for the territory. Even more important, Brown won endorsement from Voorhees, quite possibly because Brown's son had established a Democratic newspaper, the *Weekly Commoner,* in Colfax, the delegate's home town.

Brown revealed his ambitions in February 1885 when he asked Vilas to "have a word [with the President] in behalf of an old Wisconsin laborer." According to Brown, the Puget Sound newspapers had already endorsed him "spontaneously," virtually forcing him into the race. "My name," he told Vilas, "will be presented to the President for the appointment of Governor of Washington Territory and if the popular expression, public and private, is a criterion, I have abundant cause to believe it meets the approval of a large majority of the people of all political parties and I have not yet heard or learned of a single adverse expression."[16]

Brown's position on the important political issues was orthodox. He denounced the activities of the Northern Pacific Railroad and the incompetence of Republican appointees sent in from outside the territory. He recommended the wholesale removal of these "carpetbaggers" in what, despite the spirit of civil service reform, he avowed were the best interests of the Democrats of Washington Territory. The Seattle editor's supporters painted his portrait in the most glowing colors while discrediting Semple. Brown, they claimed, was the only candidate who had been active in the politics of the territory before 1884. By comparison, Semple was an interloper with little apparent support from Democrats in the region. Brown's backers charged falsely that Semple owed what small appeal he enjoyed to family money and influence and that he had "bought" his job as Oregon state printer from Patterson while hiring a more skilled journalist to write his editorials in the *Herald.*[17]

Brown was not the only formidable candidate with whom Semple had to contend for the appointment. The Democratic central committee of the territory had already met at Wallula near Pasco in January to endorse a slate of appointments.[18] The committee's choice

16. Beriah Brown, Sr., to William Vilas, February 9, 1885, William F. Vilas Papers, Wisconsin Historical Society. A microcopy of the letter is in the Manuscripts Division, University of Washington Library.

17. Appointment File.

18. *Post-Intelligencer,* September 10, 1885.

for governor (although by no means the favorite of the entire party) was Dr. Nathaniel Ostrander, a leader in Olympia politics. Unlike Semple or Brown, Ostrander could boast of being an authentic pioneer of the territory, having settled in the Cowlitz River Valley with his family in 1852 when that area was still a part of Oregon. Ostrander was one of the forty-four men who had unsuccessfully petitioned Congress that year for the creation of a Columbia Territory. He was also Washington Territory's first probate judge under Governor Isaac Stevens. Ostrander had settled in Olympia in 1879, had been twice elected mayor and had also served in the legislature.[19] His appeal was obviously more than local, but, like most of the candidates, he was not well known everywhere in the territory. His bailiwick, Cowlitz and Thurston counties, bordered Semple's own Clark County on the north—an indication that the two men might eventually have to share regional support. Apparently Ostrander's main liability was that he was not widely known in the Puget Sound country north of the capital. As the months passed his appeal waned. By September no action had been taken by the federal government on the Wallula nominations and Ostrander's candidacy had gathered few new supporters, perhaps due in part to his own reluctance to campaign strenuously.[20]

While gubernatorial aspirants continued to come forth, Cleveland's inauguration day arrived and passed into history. The pages of the *Post-Intelligencer* teemed with hearsay from such sources as the "Grapevine Special" concerning the President's plans for Washington Territory. One rumor had it that Cleveland favored Brown but feared local repercussions and the wrath of the territorial central committee which had endorsed Ostrander. Another *Post-Intelligencer* item claimed from good sources that Cleveland had already signed an executive message to the senate nominating Ostrander. Meanwhile, Semple was not totally ignored; the paper commented that his absence at the inauguration had been noted with dismay by his supporters.[21]

Such reports had little credibility and at any rate were of local interest only. As gossip circulated, Semple prepared to travel East in an effort to win support from influential congressmen and government officials. A testimonial dinner in his honor brought more than two

19. For more information on Ostrander, see Meany Pioneer File (s.v. Nathaniel Ostrander); *Cowlitz County Historical Quarterly*, August 1959, p. 1; and Bancroft, *History of Washington, Idaho, and Montana, 1845-1889*, pp. 53, 58.

20. *Post-Intelligencer*, September 10, 1885.

21. Ibid., March 5, 6, 1885.

hundred Vancouver citizens, including Mayor J. Randolph Smith, together at Marsh's Hall. The *Independent* probably expressed local sentiment accurately when it wished him success and affirmed that his candidacy "meets with approval here [because of] his business energy and active public spirit."[22]

In Washington, D.C., Semple's main task was to gain some backing from Voorhees. This was no easy objective. Like most territorial delegates, Voorhees exercised considerable influence over federal appointments in his constituency and did not want to jeopardize that influence by bestowing his endorsements indiscriminately.[23] In Semple's case, the delegate was especially wary, it seemed, because of the former's political connections in Oregon and elsewhere outside the territory. He may also have been ruffled that Semple had announced his candidacy without first consulting him, or, as Semple phrased it, without showing "sufficient deference to your prerogative as Delegate to Congress."[24] Some time before April 1885, Semple had written to Voorhees, pointing out that he had already received support from several Congressmen and would now like his backing as well. Voorhees politely replied that he did not want to be compelled to choose between friends—a possible reference to pressures exerted on him by Brown supporters. Semple then asked if he would at least remain neutral and allow a canvass of territorial voters to determine the candidate. Voorhees balked. While he hesitated, Semple won endorsements from congressmen and senators from Missouri, Alabama, Texas, Kentucky, Louisiana, Georgia, Nevada, South Carolina, Mississippi, and Tennessee. This new support, particularly from the South, evidently impressed Voorhees who now promised to remain neutral, as Semple had initially requested.[25]

Voorhees did not maintain his neutrality for long. Three months later, without bothering to tell Semple, he gave his endorsement to Brown, alleging that he had been forced to do so by "pressures from the territory."[26] This change in plans was somewhat embarrassing to

22. Vancouver *Independent,* March 12, 1885.
23. Earl S. Pomeroy, *The Territories and the United States, 1861-1890,* p. 80.
24. Semple to Voorhees, April 2, 1885, Appointment File. Voorhees' attitude toward Semple is hard to determine since there is no known collection of his papers, and no evidence of correspondence between Voorhees and Cleveland, or with Brown, or others, concerning Semple.
25. Ibid.
26. "Statement of Eugene Semple to the President of the United States," n.d., Semple Papers.

Voorhees' father, Senator Daniel Voorhees of Indiana, who had written to Alabama Democratic committeeman Henry C. Semple, one of Eugene's numerous cousins, earlier that year to say, "I have talked freely and fully with my son on the subject and he shares with me the appreciation and esteem which I entertain for Mr. Eugene Semple." [27]

The delegate's advocacy of Brown was a hard blow to Semple. In September the Vancouver *Independent* asserted that the younger Voorhees was now so strongly behind Brown that the commission of appointment was expected in a matter of days. "Eugene Semple would make a much better governor than [that] ancient sample from Wisconsin secession sympathy. . . ," the paper noted regretfully. But Semple had no intention of conceding defeat to Brown or any other candidate. He wrote to Secretary of the Interior Lucius Lamar, asking him to delay the appointment until October 1, by which time Semple hoped to have a mandate from the people by means of the canvass he had proposed to Voorhees earlier in the year. [28]

The result of that canvass is not known (if indeed one was even taken). Semple's insistence on a survey of opinion may simply have been a ruse with which to buy time. At any rate, he wasted no time getting in touch with William White, the influential Seattle attorney whose endorsement he needed in order to diminish Brown's prestige among Puget Sound Democrats. Semple's trip to Seattle was a success. On October 3, White notified him that he had changed his mind.

Since I saw you in Seattle last and more particularly since coming to Portland, and inquiring about you, I have changed my views somewhat concerning your appointment as Governor. . . . You know I have stood by Mr. Brown in this matter. The only reason for so doing was that I wished to see someone appointed who was sound on the issues between the people and the Northern Pacific Railroad corporation. I am assured by persons in Portland in whom I can place confidence, that you are a person beyond the control of such influences. Colonel Teal, a friend of yours and myself, will call upon Delegate Voorhees this afternoon relative to your appointment. If you think a letter from Teal to the President necessary for your success, he says he will gladly write it. You can show this letter to Delegate Voorhees. [29]

White's decision helped keep the contest open. At about the same time, but probably independent of White's decision, Voorhees also

27. Daniel W. Voorhees to Henry C. Semple, May 20, 1885.
28. Vancouver *Independent,* September 17, 1885; Semple to Lamar, September 9, 1885, Appointment File.
29. White to Semple, October 3, 1885.

dropped his sponsorship of Brown. Instead of endorsing Semple, however, he switched his favor to J. B. Reavis, the popular territorial legislative leader from North Yakima. [30]

Despite Voorhees' refusal to endorse him, Semple's support in the territory continued to grow during 1885. In September Colonel Frank J. Parker, the editor of the Walla Walla *Statesman,* offered his support to the Vancouver candidate. [31] Parker was thoroughly disillusioned with Voorhees and had criticized his activities in Congress at length during a recent editorial series. According to Parker, Voorhees had retaliated by spreading malicious rumors about him which had reached Secretary Lamar and even the President. The Walla Walla editor appealed to Semple to help him redeem his good name in the high circles of government. In return he promised political backing. Parker was a very useful ally. As a pioneer of the Walla Walla country and owner of the largest newspaper in southeastern Washington, he wielded a substantial influence. [32] Semple welcomed his help. In addition to Parker, two other prominent Walla Walla Democrats became Semple supporters: Ben Sharpstein, an early aspirant for the governorship himself, and N. T. Caton, former Democratic delegate and ex-speaker of the territorial house of representatives. [33]

In Seattle, several others joined White to espouse Semple's candidacy, including C. D. Emery, George Venable Smith, and T. H. Cann. Emery had at first supported Brown but advised Cleveland that he and his friends had decided Semple would be the best choice. Smith, an attorney who was soon to play an important part in Seattle's anti-Chinese troubles, also backed Semple, claiming that in spite of his own Republican leanings, he could think of no better man for the job. The third supporter, T. H. Cann, was "an old Oregon friend" of Semple's who had since become active in Seattle politics. Such endorsement in the heart of Brown's constituency was encouraging, although it did not by any means indicate a majority sentiment in King County. [34]

An example of the influence such local endorsements occasionally

30. Appointment File.
31. Parker to Semple, September 19, 1885.
32. "Colonel Frank J. Parker," *Washington Historical Quarterly,* 19 (1928): 159-60.
33. Appointment File.
34. See ibid.: C. D. Emery to Cleveland, January 20, 1886; Smith to Semple, June 23, 1885; T. H. Cann to Congressman William R. Morrison of Illinois, September 4, 1885.

had on political figures of national prominence was provided by Robert Williams, a retired Iowan living in Vancouver. Williams wrote to Iowa Senator William B. Allison, describing Semple's political qualifications in lavish phrases.[35] It mattered little that Williams and Allison were both Republicans. Allison gave his endorsement.

Along the Columbia River and especially in Oregon, Semple gained some extensive backing. Resolutions urging his appointment were passed by the bar associations of Pendleton, Astoria, The Dalles, and St. Helens. Thirty-six Portland lawyers also gave their support, as did four ex-senators, two former governors, and the poet Joaquin Miller. Typical was the letter of endorsement from W. W. Thayer, former governor and chief justice of the Oregon supreme court, who told Lamar that Semple was not only a bona fide resident of the territory but was "promoting and developing the land."[36]

Various newspapers of the region also began beating the drum for Semple's appointment. The editor of the Tacoma *News,* H. C. Patrick, told Cleveland in no uncertain terms that his city was strongly behind the Vancouver aspirant. Some of this boosting was exaggerated. At Seattle, Cann stretched the truth considerably when he told Congressman William R. Morrison of Illinois that three-fourths of the local residents and most of the newspapers backed Semple. The Portland *Mercury* went even further by asserting that at least two-thirds of the newspapers of the country favored Semple—although it is more likely that most of them had never heard of him.[37]

Semple's far-flung relatives also lent their support to his candidacy. In California, Lansing Mizner and another kinsman, cousin William Semple Green, the editor of the Colusa *Sun* in the Sacramento Valley, helped Semple garner the backing of prominent San Francisco attorney Samuel Wilson, to whom Cleveland had offered ambassadorial posts in Spain and in China.[38] R. F. Morrison, the chief justice of the California supreme court, also came forward. In the South, Henry Semple gave influential backing to his distant Vancouver cousin. A widely known figure in the legal circles of Dixie, Henry was an Alabama member of the national Democratic committee.[39] His influence was probably

35. Williams to Allison, March 11, 1885, ibid.

36. Ibid., and Semple Papers.

37. Appointment File: Patrick to Cleveland, October 1, 1885, and Cann to Morrison, September 4, 1885; Portland *Oregon Mercury,* n.d., 1885, news clipping in Semple Papers.

38. Wilson to Cleveland, September 14, 1885, Appointment File.

39. *National Cyclopedia of Biography,* 17:223.

responsible for winning the support of Senator John T. Morgan of Alabama and Congressman John Floyd King of Louisiana.[40] King, who was serving his fourth term in the lower house, became one of Semple's most ardent sponsors in Congress.

Although he had succeeded in gaining what was probably enough national and regional support to prevent Cleveland and Voorhees from uniting for the moment on any other candidate, Semple had by no means yet insured his own nomination. Early in 1886 he jeopardized his chances by speaking out on the most volatile issue in the territory, the Chinese labor problem. On February 7, the day after his return to Vancouver from a trip to the East, growing anti-Chinese sentiment in Seattle erupted in violence. Semple's attitude toward the event could easily have been predicted. On the editorial pages of the *Herald* more than a decade earlier he had directed some of his sharpest attacks against what he termed "the Mongolian Menace, the heathen horde." His Sinophobia, like that of so many of his contemporaries, was associated with hostility toward the railroads, which had been among the first to undercut the wages of white workingmen by employing large numbers of Chinese.

In Seattle the hatred was fanned by worsening business conditions during 1885. In September, while Semple solicited support for his candidacy back East, Seattle residents began taking sides on the Chinese question. Sinophobes, represented by the Knights of Labor and other organizations of white workingmen, held several mass meetings. Among their chief spokesmen was George Venable Smith, one of Semple's most recent and enthusiastic backers. Smith's inflammatory rhetoric helped to raise tensions to an intolerable level.[41]

On the morning of February 7, 1886, a mob burst into the Chinese quarter at the south end of town and ordered the terrified inhabitants down to the wharf and aboard a San Francisco bound vessel. At that point William White, the recently appointed U. S. attorney for the territory, appeared before the crowd and told it to disperse. When his command was ignored, Governor Squire, who was in town at the time,

40. *Biographical Directory of the American Congress, 1774-1961*, p. 1216.
41. Jules A. Karlin, "The Anti-Chinese Outbreaks in Seattle, 1885-1886," *Pacific Northwest Quarterly*, 39 (1948): 105; Nesbit, *Burke*, pp. 174, 177, 178-79. Smith claimed to have known Semple for twenty years although Semple did not acknowledge this and there is no evidence of Smith in Semple's correspondence. See Smith endorsement letter, March 6, 1885, and Smith to Semple, June 25, 1885, Appointment File.

issued a similar proclamation. This order was also ignored. By now the mob was threatening several of Sheriff John McGraw's deputies who had reached the beleaguered Asians and were trying to escort some of them to safety. Seeing the turn of events, Squire decided to declare martial law. Moving quickly he telegraphed his decision to Secretary Lamar and then activated territorial units of the National Guard, meanwhile requesting federal troop reinforcements from the Fort Vancouver Barracks.

The next morning, as some of the Chinese, escorted by McGraw's men, attempted to return from the wharf, an angry mob met them at Main and Commercial streets. Both sides exchanged insults and soon hand to hand fighting broke out. In the confused moments that followed, shots rang out from the ranks of McGraw's deputies and their supporters, the self-styled "law and order" forces, whose numbers included some of Seattle's most respectable citizens. Several rioters were wounded and one of them, an unemployed woodsman named Charles Stewart, died the next day. By then, reinforcements had arrived and an uneasy peace was restored. While the city stopped to catch its breath, President Cleveland declared a state of emergency and Squire suspended the writ of habeas corpus, thereby nullifying attempts by the anti-Chinese group to bring legal action against the "law and order" faction for the shooting. [42]

The crisis passed but the political repercussions continued. At Vancouver, city officials and community leaders met to organize a home guard in case the wave of strong feeling against the Chinese swept south. At one gathering, on February 22, Semple was called upon to express his opinions on the Seattle trouble. In the course of what the Portland *Oregonian* described as a tirade, he criticized Squire's conduct during the disorder. Following the speech, Semple introduced a series of resolutions condemning the governor's actions. To his considerable dismay, the majority waved aside his proposals and voted instead by an overwhelming margin to commend Squire's conduct. Nor did his remarks endear him to the powerful *Oregonian,* which asserted that "Mr. Semple's attitude shows how fortunate a thing it is that he is not the governor of the territory." [43]

Semple was clearly alarmed by these negative reactions and feared

42. Karlin, "Anti-Chinese Outbreaks," pp. 120-30, is the source of the above information.
43. Portland *Oregonian,* February 24, 1886.

they might bring retaliation against him from the national party, as well as a critical loss of support in the territory. His fears were at least partly confirmed when one of his leading local backers, Louis Sohns, a Republican and the president of the Vancouver Board of Trade, withdrew his endorsement. "Mr. Sohns . . . was very much in my favor last spring," Semple told Congressman King, "when it was supposed that a change would undoubtedly be made. Now," he asserted, "when there appears to be a chance to keep a Republican in office he is ready to oppose me and seized upon the incident of my speech as a pretext for telegraphing to Washington withdrawing his support. He has been working hard against me with the army officers here and has doubtless written to Washington. . . . If you could find out the nature of the communication made by Sohns to the President it would be of great value to me." Semple had given the recent events at Seattle considerable thought and explained to King his motives for speaking out, along with his assessment of the political significance of the riot:

This question will decide the election in Washington Territory next fall and will carry the Pacific Coast at the next presidential election. If the present administration retains Squire and thus endorses his course at Seattle, it will be useless for our party to make nominations for elections on this coast. I knew that my speech would endanger my appointment but I had to choose between that and the danger of destroying my future chances at home which I would have done by keeping silence on the occasion referred to.[44]

Semple publicly responded to local critics like Sohns and the *Oregonian* by publishing a nineteen-page pamphlet stating the reasons for his attack on Squire. Entitled *Martial Law at Seattle: An Inquiry into the Necessity Therefor,* it equated Squire's use of martial law with tyranny. Semple's purpose, he said,

is not to defend or excuse the actions of these citizens of Seattle who attempted to drive out the Chinese residents. . . . On the contrary, I am of those who believe in the rigid endorsement of all the laws of the country, at all times and at every hazard. My object is to show: that no necessity existed for declaring martial law; that the law abiding people of Seattle were numerous enough, vigilant enough, and brave enough, to enforce the processes of the courts, and that this fact had been demonstrated before the governor's proclamation was issued.[45]

According to Semple, the riot had been ignited by an "excited and

44. Semple to King, March 11, 1886.
45. Eugene Semple, *Martial Law at Seattle: An Inquiry into the Necessity Therefor,* p. 2.

nervous officer," who had provoked the firing on a small, outnumbered, unarmed, and peaceable group of curious bystanders. Obviously, he said, this was no occasion for a declaration of martial law and a suspension of the writ of habeas corpus. Such action was all the more unjustifiable, he contended, since in other parts of the territory worse disorders had recently occurred in connection with the Chinese and martial law had not been invoked. Relying on *Oregonian* accounts of the Seattle misfortune, he argued that only a few persons had actually threatened violence, and then only after being provoked.[46]

Although eyewitness accounts of an event are often notoriously inaccurate, the testimony of George Kinnear, captain of the Seattle Home Guard at the time of the outbreak, sharply contradicts Semple's own secondhand observations. According to Kinnear, who wrote an account of the trouble twenty-five years later, the city was completely in the hands of the mob. Far from being a harmless minority, the rioters, he maintained, had enlisted the support of the acting chief of police and nearly the entire city police force in perpetrating acts of lawlessness.[47]

Semple, however, was convinced that his pamphlet would set matters straight with his detractors. In a long-winded conclusion he sanctimoniously linked his defense of the rioters with his loyalty to the Democratic party and to the principles of justice:

> The duty of making such a speech devolved upon some member of the great Democratic Party that has steadfastly adhered to the vital principles of Magna Charta and the habeas corpus act through 28 years of continuous defeat. . . . To have done less than I did in the emergency which presented itself would have been to descend from the position which I am proud to believe I hold in the esteem of my fellow Democrats of the great territory of Washington, as a consistent defender of their faith. I will not pay such a price as that for any promotion but will go to the people on the issues that have been made and continue to hope that "the right will come uppermost."[48]

These statements ignored the more crucial fact that nonpartisan Chinese as well as Caucasian Democrats were entitled to the protection of the law. But Semple's biases were shared by numerous public officials, including Voorhees, who called the Seattle disturbance a manifestation of the growing national resentment toward the "pauper

46. Ibid., pp. 12-14.
47. George Kinnear, *The Anti-Chinese Riots at Seattle*, p. 6.
48. Semple, *Martial Law*, pp. 18-19.

labor of the Chinese."[49] Despite the prevalence of such feelings, most people appeared to be willing to put the matter to rest in the interest of peace. The newspapers, the President, and most Seattle residents agreed that Squire's course of action had been the correct one.[50] Semple for his part had overreacted to the whole situation, first in his speech at Vancouver and then in his blustering pamphlet. As it turned out, there was no political gain in it for him, but neither did it seem to be any lasting liability in the hurly-burly of territorial politics.

Racial tensions subsided in the months that followed as the questions of railroad regulation and land grant forfeiture re-emerged as paramount issues in the territory with the approach of the elections of 1886. In Congress Voorhees had made little progress against the Northern Pacific, in part because effective regulation hinged upon nullification of the railroad's original 1864 land grant. This huge subsidy had legally expired in 1879 after several questionable extensions of the building time limit had been granted by Congress under pressure from the powerful railroad lobby. During the 1880s, however, court cases and legislative debate over the matter dragged on and land along the projected routes in the Northwest was withheld from settlement.[51] Voorhees pointed out to his fellow Congressmen the consequences of continued government subsidization of the railroad: "Such contracts have resulted in checking the tide of immigration into Washington Territory and are of themselves, entirely sufficient to justify the restoration of the unearned grant to the public domain. . . . The multitude is patient to a certain point. The American people after years of lethargy and indifference have reached that point, and refuse longer to enact the role of pack-horses for the corporations of this country."[52] Despite his efforts and those of other western lawmakers, Congress remained deadlocked on the forfeiture issue. The stalemate did nothing to help Voorhees' chances for re-election.

Meanwhile, Colonel Frank Parker of Walla Walla had begun to groom Semple to replace Voorhees as the Democratic candidate for territorial delegate in the November election. "Your name meets with great favor," he told Semple in June, predicting that "the Spokane people will go for you solid but will drop Voorhees to a man. Tell me what

49. *Oregonian,* February 11, 1886.
50. Karlin, "Anti-Chinese Outbreaks," pp. 129-30.
51. David Ellis, "The Forfeiture of Railroad Land Grants, 1867-94," *Mississippi Valley Historical Review,* 33 (1946): 30, 49.
52. *Congressional Record,* 40th Cong., 1st sess., p. 7567.

you are doing in the down counties. If the primaries are well looked after and they send anti-Voorhees men to the convention we can beat them with you. No more of the forfeiture business as the people will have none of it. If you can bring in the down counties and the river counties you are all right."[53]

But presumably Semple still sought the governorship. If so, why antagonize Voorhees by challenging him for the party nomination simply because Parker thought he could win it? Semple's position became even more uncomfortable when others began speculating on his availability for Congress. The Portland *Sunday Welcome* mentioned him as a prominent candidate, as did the Vancouver *Independent,* which was glad to see him have any office and pronounced the local mill owner "a man of ability and a real nail driver." As if to entice him further, King reported that congressional sentiment against Voorhees was growing because of the delegate's alleged unfriendliness toward some of the other representatives.[54] In spite of the apparent trend against Voorhees, however, Semple evidently made no attempt to incur his displeasure by seeking the nomination for himself.

Ultimately the Seattle *Post-Intelligencer* proved to be a more accurate forecaster of the political winds than Parker. The paper predicted a party landslide for Voorhees "despite the efforts of many distinguished Democrats months ago to stop his renomination." At the state party convention in Tacoma, Voorhees won renomination on the first ballot by a 114-10 margin over Frank Henry of Seattle.[55] Much to Parker's chagrin, Semple's name was hardly mentioned. Voorhees then went on to defeat the Republican candidate, Charles M. Bradshaw, in November, again campaigning successfully on the forfeiture issue.[56]

By the time of Voorhees' re-election nearly two years had elapsed since Semple and the other office seekers had entered the contest for the appointment. During that time Cleveland had remained silent, evidently satisfied with Squire's performance and aware that Democrats in the territory were not united behind a candidate of their own party. Under these circumstances, rumors continued to circulate about the President's intentions, the political backing of the various candidates still in the race, and the prospects of Squire continuing in office until

53. Parker to Semple, June 6, 1886.
54. Vancouver *Independent,* August 5, 1886; King to Semple, April 21, 1886.
55. Seattle *Post Intelligencer,* August 14, 1886. Semple evidently had not tried, as Parker had hoped, to seek the nomination.
56. Olympia *Washington Standard,* November 28, 1886.

the next presidential election. King was as uncertain of Cleveland's intentions as anyone else. Although he reported to Semple that he had heard talk that Squire would be removed before 1887, he also noted that the governor's friend, Senator Warner Miller of New York, was influential with Cleveland and would urge the President to retain Squire. Squire's retention was also urged in the territory. The Spokane Falls *Chronicle* claimed that the incumbent Republican's good record as well as Cleveland's pledge not to remove capable officeholders were sufficient reasons not to endorse Semple, even though the paper admitted he was probably a qualified applicant.[57]

By early 1887 it began to appear that the *Chronicle* had spoken correctly. Semple's petition was now two years old and presumably gathering dust with the dossiers of scores of other job hunters in the cluttered appointment files of the Interior Department. The voters' apparent contentment with the status quo (i.e., Voorhees and Squire) was working to defeat Semple's gubernatorial ambitions. However, while some Democrats began to reconcile themselves to Squire as a permanent fixture at Olympia, Semple redoubled his efforts to secure the appointment early in 1887. He may have reasoned that, because of Voorhees' impressive re-election, the President was now ready to name Squire's Democratic successor. But this was still only speculation. Furthermore, Voorhees himself had yet to be heard from.

Then, rather suddenly, almost mysteriously it seemed, after two years of inaction, the situation began to change. In January and February Semple began to receive reports that Cleveland was ready to appoint him—*if* Voorhees would agree to drop his rather lukewarm support of Reavis. Accordingly, Semple informed O. F. Wegener, one of his backers in the capital, to keep on friendly terms with the delegate at all cost.

I have received several letters from Washington regarding my appointment in a favorable light as Voorhees was disposed to favor it in case he could not get Reavis appointed. . . . I am satisfied that my case does not need further attention at the White House or the Interior Department but that the matter is entirely in the hands of Mr. Voorhees. Send my kindest regards to Voorhees and tell him I never had the idea of disregarding his prerogatives in the premises.[58]

Whether his case needed further attention or not, Semple partisans continued to send letters to the White House. T. W. Padden, a territorial

57. King to Semple, May 8, 1886; Spokane Falls *Chronicle,* May 21, 1885.
58. Semple to Wegener, February 23, 1887.

legislator from Vancouver, told Cleveland that his city had given Voorhees a 550-vote majority in the last election, "mainly due to the efforts of Mr. Semple and at his own expense." Former governor Lafayette Grover of Oregon, now a United States senator, also wrote to the President, saying that he had lately met a number of prominent Washington Territory Democrats who wanted Semple appointed.[59]

In the meantime Voorhees continued to block Semple's appointment with silence. On March 17, Wegener reported that the delegate was now urging that Squire be retained. "Your chances look doubtful," Wegener wrote, adding that William Sparks, commissioner of the General Land Office, also endorsed Squire. But Semple had evidently heard different tidings. That same day he wrote to Parker, asking for renewed support, for "by telegram from Washington D.C. today I am informed that a change in the governorship will be certainly affected very soon. The issue is between someone recommended by Voorhees and myself. . . . The letters you promised to send from Columbia and Walla Walla counties would be effective if they get to Washington soon. Simply recommend me and don't mention anyone else."[60]

Obviously, not everyone was certain exactly which candidate Voorhees was sponsoring. Voorhees was probably also in an awkward position. As Semple's letters indicate, Cleveland had left the appointment largely in the delegate's hands. Although Voorhees was opposed to Semple, he had evidently exhausted his own list of likely candidates. Consequently, when Semple's spokesmen accosted him, he wavered. On March 21, King announced to the President that Voorhees had finally consented to endorse the Vancouver lumberman. According to King, the delegate had told Lamar in King's presence that Semple would "reflect credit upon the office."[61]

With the Voorhees endorsement finally obtained, it was only a matter of days until Cleveland recommended Semple to the Senate for the appointment as governor of Washington Territory. Early in April

59. Padden to Cleveland, March 15, 1887, and Lafayette Grover to Cleveland, March 18, 1887, Appointment File.

60. Wegener to Semple, and Semple to Parker, March 17, 1887. Parker later (April 17, 1887) told Semple he had learned Voorhees had briefly switched his support to Chester H. Warner of Colfax just before deciding, finally, to support Semple. Warner, who a few years later became a Democratic nominee for Congress, had not officially sought the appointment to the governorship.

61. King to Cleveland, March 21, 1887, Appointment File.

the President indicated his choice and conveyed his nomination to Lamar, who issued Semple's commission, subject to the formality of Senate approval.[62]

Several possible reasons for Cleveland's course of action suggest themselves. Voorhees' re-election in November appeared to demonstrate growing support for the Democratic Party in the territory. As Seattle Democrats had pointed out to Cleveland just before Semple's nomination, the territorial legislature was now only two members short of obtaining a Democratic majority.[63] Moreover, expediency may have restrained the President from removing Squire earlier, for Cleveland realized the need for experience and continuity in major territorial offices.[64] In addition, there was the ever-increasing pressure from job-hungry Democrats for patronage—a pressure to which Cleveland eventually yielded. Semple's own candidacy amply illustrated this fact. By 1887 he had received endorsements from Democrats in twenty of the thirty-eight states, from thirteen senators, an equal number of congressmen, and dozens of other individuals of local or national political importance. Such support, although much of it came from outside the territory, could hardly be ignored.[65] And yet, ultimately, it appears to have been neither Cleveland's executive authority nor Semple's connections, but Voorhees' own indecisiveness that most determined the choice. Taking all of these circumstances into consideration, the lateness of Semple's nomination becomes more understandable.

News of his appointment reached Semple in Vancouver on the evening of April 8, a Saturday. A torchlight parade serpentined through

62. Lamar to Cleveland, April 8, 1887, Grover Cleveland Papers. Microcopy of the Cleveland Papers is in the Newspaper and Microcopy Center, University of Washington Library.

63. A letter from Seattle Democrats to Cleveland, March 22, 1887 (Cleveland Papers), urged the President to appoint a Democratic governor quickly.

64. In his first year in office, Cleveland removed only seven officials from the territories, usually waiting for vacancies to occur naturally and making removals only for unfitness (Pomeroy, *Territories*, pp. 70-71).

65. Semple's support was indeed varied. Among his endorsers were Seattle attorney John B. Allen, who in 1888 became Voorhees' Republican successor as delegate, and Joaquin Miller, the renowned "poet of the American West," whose days as an Oregon journalist had probably placed him in contact with Semple. He wrote: "Certainly! And with all my heart I ask the President to appoint you to the great little post of governor of Washington Territory. . . . Side by side in the dark days we stood as boys together, and now at last, if you will have this place, or even a better one, I say it is yours by right" (Miller to Semple, April 8, 1885, Appointment File).

the streets to his door. The new governor came out to greet the crowd and to express his gratitude to the local citizens. His first reaction to the news of the nomination, he said, was one of surprise since he had heard nothing about his candidacy for several days.[66] Celebrations were also organized in Olympia, Tacoma, and Walla Walla. Newspaper reaction was mixed. The *Oregonian,* which a year earlier, on the occasion of the Seattle riot, had given thanks that Semple was not governor then, was brief and factual: "No doubt the appointment of Eugene Semple as governor of Washington Territory will be a surprise to many. It was known long since that he was an applicant but the appointment had been delayed so long it was scarcely supposed it would be made."[67] The Seattle *Post-Intelligencer* also expressed surprise and stated that the Voorhees supporters were not happy with the choice. According to the newspaper, Cleveland had made a last minute decision between Semple and Pierce Young of Georgia, who was then serving as American consul-general at St. Petersburg, Russia, having been appointed to that post by Cleveland a year and a half before.[68] The *Palouse Gazette,* representative of eastern Washington, was relieved at the selection, noting that Semple had "no taint of 'Mugwumpism' like many Cleveland appointments." [69]

Some reactions were openly hostile. The Seattle *Republican* called the new governor "a failure who has never succeeded in anything."[70] A more violent blast came from Daniel H. Gilman, president of the Seattle Puget Sound Construction Company, in a letter to Augustus Schoonmaker, Cleveland's Civil Service commissioner. Gilman was a leading promoter of outside capital in Seattle and one of the most prominent Democrats in the territory—a man who was soon to become chairman of the party's territorial central committee. Gilman slanderously characterized Semple as a "dangerously incompetent, weak and foolish demagogue . . . a drunken, drooling fool without the capacity for office above that of a poundmaster . . . another Oregon tramp." In Gilman's opinion, the President had been "grievously deceived" and should "instantly revoke" the appointment since most of

66. Vancouver *Independent,* April 13, 1887.
67. Portland *Oregonian,* April 10, 1887.
68. *Post-Intelligencer,* April 10, 1887; *Journal of the Executive Proceedings of the Senate of the United States,* 25 (1885-87): 100, 284.
69. Colfax *Palouse Gazette,* n.d., 1887, news clipping, Semple Papers.
70. Governors Pamphlet File (s.v. Semple), news clipping in Northwest Collection.

the new governor's sponsors "don't know Semple from Adam." If it was any consolation to Semple, Gilman also held Voorhees in contempt for his "all-sufficient, overweaning egotism."[71] Fortunately for both men, Gilman's attitude was not typical of the average Democrat.

Thus, with opinion divided on his qualifications, Semple traveled north to Olympia in April 1887 to take his oath of office while people in the territorial capital made ready to greet their first Democratic governor in twenty years. Some of Semple's harsher critics saw a drifter, a political hack who had wandered seemingly without purpose from job to job since coming West in 1863. He was indeed, by 1887, a man with a varied past: lawyer, editor, printer, lumberman, and now governor. Yet his rivals for the appointment were also men of diverse callings. Nathaniel Ostrander, his early opponent for the appointment, was a physician, land speculator, sometime farmer, and mayor of Olympia, as well as a territorial legislator; Beriah Brown had at one time or another found employment as printer, farmer, editor, and mayor of Seattle. Whatever the merits or faults of his background, Semple had managed to climb in less than two years from political obscurity to the highest appointive office in a territory of nearly 200,000 inhabitants—an administrative unit larger in population and area than several states. Admittedly, outside influence, particularly from relatives, had been important in Semple's success. But his personal handling of a delicate relationship with Voorhees, as well as his management of his own supporters, demonstrated political savvy. There was, finally, and perhaps most importantly, his dogged persistence in seeking the nomination long after most of his rivals had abandoned the chase.

The office Semple had attained was habitually viewed by territorial residents as a prize granted to some unknown (and perhaps none too successful) but loyal servant of the party in power. This stereotype of the political hack, more than Gilman's invective or the coolness of Voorhees, was Semple's real liability as he stood on the verge of becoming, at the age of forty-six, an important political figure.

---

71. Gilman to Schoonmaker, April 10, 1887, Cleveland Papers. Gilman was also a business partner of prominent Seattle promoter Thomas Burke.

6. Governing the Territory

Semple arrived in Olympia to begin his term as governor amid an aura of change and expectation. The time was one of rapid growth and economic development for Washington Territory. The Northern Pacific Railroad had at last linked the region to the rest of the continent and settlers migrated into the area in ever-increasing numbers. At the time Semple took office on April 23, 1887, the population of the territory approached 200,000. This was twice the number of inhabitants recorded in the 1880 census; and yet the figure would nearly double again during Semple's term of office.[1] Behind the façade of prosperity ushered in by the completion of the railroad, problems existed which were related to this growth and development. In Seattle agitation of the Chinese question had been revived, as Semple would soon discover. In Walla Walla and Olympia women were waging spirited campaigns for equal suffrage.[2] Labor troubles also made news. Along the Columbia River and at Grays Harbor, Washington salmon fishermen fought off union organizers from Oregon with loaded guns in a series of night skirmishes. Similar violence was about to occur in the coal mines at Roslyn and Newcastle. Meanwhile, the territorial government acted to meet the needs of change. Within a fortnight of Semple's inauguration a new territorial penitentiary opened at Walla Walla amid charges of land

1. *Report of the Governor of Washington Territory to the Secretary of the Interior, 1887,* p. 6 (hereafter cited as *Report of the Governor, 1887*).
2. Nelson A. Ault, "The Earnest Ladies: The Walla Walla Women's Club and the Equal Suffrage League of 1886-1889," *Pacific Northwest Quarterly,* 42 (1951): 123-37; and Stella E. Pearce, "Suffrage in the Pacific Northwest," *Washington Historical Quarterly,* 3 (1912): 106-14.

grabbing and outrageous building costs.[3] In eastern Washington work began on a second territorial hospital for the insane, and at Vancouver construction had already started on a school for handicapped youth.

In this setting, Washington's last Democratic territorial governor stepped to the rostrum in the capitol council chambers at Olympia on his inauguration day to take the oath of office from Territorial Supreme Court Justice Frank Allyn, while outgoing Republican Governor Watson Squire looked on. A correspondent from Seattle watched the ceremony, then commented to his editor: "The governor is a rather spare man, of medium height, who is pleasant in appearance and wears eyeglasses."[4] To most of the crowd on hand for the ceremonies that April afternoon, the speaker who addressed them as their new chief executive was a stranger, the survivor of an unpublicized two-year political struggle that had led to the event they were now witnessing. As if anticipating accusations, Semple delivered a defensively worded inaugural message which stressed his desire for law and order and his hope for integrity in his administration. The speech was brief and humble in tone. The new governor, emphasizing that he was "a servant of the people," urged his listeners to "take it out on me later," if they found fault with the President's appointment, adding, "I may have deceived him, but I cannot deceive you." He hoped, he said, "to dispel, with the help of God and your cooperation, whatever grave doubts may arise in regard to my abilities."[5] The press reacted to the speech favorably. "Governor Semple's strong accent on enforcement of the law has greatly strengthened our confidence in the man," the Seattle *Post-Intelligencer* noted, perhaps recalling Semple's denunciation of Squire during the Seattle disorder a year earlier.[6]

The duties of the new chief executive were not elaborately defined by law, nor were they extensive. The Organic Act of 1853, which established the government of Washington Territory, specified that the territorial executive was to hold office for four years "unless sooner removed by the president."[7] He was designated commander-in-chief of the militia and was empowered to "grant pardons and remit fines and forfeitures for offences against the laws of the United States, until the

3. Frank Parker to Semple, April 28, 30, 1887.
4. Seattle *Post-Intelligencer,* April 24, 1887.
5. Ibid.
6. Ibid.
7. "Organic Act of Washington Territory," Section 2, *Statutes of the Territory of Washington,* 1st sess. (Olympia, 1854), pp. 31-42.

decision of the president can be made known thereon." He shared with the secretary of the territory the responsibility for disbursement of funds "to defray the contingent expenses of the territory."[8] In addition to the duties specified in. the Organic Act, the governor by 1887 had acquired other functions. He could veto laws passed by the legislature and recommend legislation to it. The remuneration for these and other services was an annual salary of $2,600.

In the history of the United States, the territorial governor has been compared to the colonial governor serving in the far-flung dominions of the British Empire. The comparison seems apt. As an appointed executive, Semple had no direct responsibility to the Democrats of the territory, nor did he represent the choice of territorial voters, as did their delegate to Congress. Instead he exercised a stewardship of sorts, supervising the conduct of affairs in the territory and usually acting with minimal guidance from the national government. For instruction there were the confusing and often unavailable federal *Revised Statutes* and *Statutes at Large* to which puzzled territorial governors were often referred by perplexed secretaries of the interior.[9]

These problems of defining authority did not prevent the legislature or the governor from responding to a variety of public needs ranging from cattle quarantine to the licensing of dentists. When the eleventh biennial session convened in October 1887, there was bipartisan support for the legislation Semple urged. In line with his recommendation for higher corporate taxes, for example, the lawmakers levied new assessments against railroad property.[10] In the realm of regulatory law, the legislature enacted several statutes. In response to reports of deaths in the coal mines of the territory, resulting from the use of faulty equipment and inadequate ventilation, it authorized grand juries to inspect mines and report on their operation. In addition, it created a six-member joint legislative committee to compile a code of territorial mining statutes, as Semple had requested.[11] The legislature also amended fish and game laws to protect endangered species of migratory water fowl and wild animals. It

8. Ibid., Section 11.

9. Pomeroy, *Territories*, pp. 24, 153.

10. Charles M. Gates, ed., *Messages of the Governors of Washington Territory to the Legislative Assembly, 1854-1889*, pp. 271, 274; *Report of the Governor, 1888*, p. 33; *Laws of Washington Territory, 1887-1888*, pp. 63-64, 191, 220.

11. *Messages of the Governors*, p. 270; *Laws of Washington, 1887-88*, pp. 32-43.

confronted the problem of liquor control by delegating to county commissions the power to regulate the sale of alcoholic beverages.[12] The legislators also enacted regulations governing the operations of the first telegraph and telephone companies in the territory, and, with local needs increasing, bestowed charters of incorporation on many smaller communities, allowing them to undertake bonded indebtedness for civic improvements.[13]

This growing interest of the territorial government in the public welfare during Semple's administration was also evident in an extensive program of construction of new educational, eleemosynary, and correctional institutions. The first hospital for the insane was completed at Steilacoom, southwest of Tacoma, at a cost of nearly $100,000 with another $90,000 allocated for future maintenance and improvements.[14]   Meanwhile, at Medical Lake near Spokane work began on another mental asylum. Early in 1888 Semple signed an appropriation of $80,000 for this project and $12,000 for support of the new territorial School for Defective Youth at Vancouver.[15] The biggest appropriation went to the recently finished territorial penitentiary at Walla Walla. Work had been completed and the first inmates transferred to the new prison from makeshift quarters near Seattle shortly after Semple took office. Later in the year Walla Walla businessmen persuaded the legislature to grant $180,000 more for a new cell wing, work shops, and heating facilities.[16]

A lot of this spending may have seemed imprudent to some, in view of the territory's dwindling treasury reserves. Indeed, an $80,000 surplus at the start of Semple's administration had become a deficit of $75,000 by the time the lawmakers adjourned in 1888.[17] Defenders of the deficit pointed out, however, that the value of taxable property in Washington had increased from $19 million in 1878 to $85 million by 1887, thus providing an ample tax base for future needs.[18] Semple

12. *Laws of Washington, 1887-88,* pp. 87-88, 97-100, 124-26.

13. Ibid., pp. 65-68.

14. Ibid., pp. 111-13.

15. Ibid., pp. 82-85, 108-111.

16. Ibid., pp. 164-68; *Report of the Penitentiary Building Commissioners to the Governor and Legislative Assembly of Washington Territory,* pp. 3-4.

17. *Messages of the Governors,* p. 267.

18. Territorial Treasurer William McMicken claimed, however, that despite a sharp increase in the value of taxable property, only 75 percent of the revenues due the territory were being regularly collected and paid by the counties (*Report of the Territorial Treasurer to the Legislative Assembly of Washington, 1885-1887,*) pp. 49-51.

condoned the expenditures for simple humanitarian reasons. "The territory," he told the legislators, "should always deal liberally with the unfortunate." [19]

The enactments of the 1887-88 legislative session provided solutions to only a few of the problems confronting the territory. Other dilemmas remained for time or the federal government to resolve. One was the continuing scarcity of surveyed public land, which disturbed local authorities and prospective settlers alike. Although more than twelve million acres were available, exclusive of Indian allotments, no federal surveys had been made since 1885.[20] The need for surveys was acute, and Semple, in his annual report to the Secretary of the Interior, pleaded the case of the settler:

> The need of surveys in various portions of the territory is now so great that almost any one who wanders to the limits of the older settlements will be immediately struck by it. . . . Many refrain from selecting homes on the unsurveyed lands. . . . Others have taken their chances. . . have gone on the unsurveyed land, have made bold enough to add this improvement, then that improvement, in the hope of a speedy survey, until to-day these have enough at stake to be ill at ease.[21]

The main cause of complaint about unsurveyed lands was the remarkable growth in the population of the territory. During the eighties the number of inhabitants increased from scarcely 75,000 to nearly 360,000—a population more than four times as large as that of the *state* of Nevada.[22] And only half of this increase had occured when Semple came into office. The land problem was also related to the quandary over federal Indian policy. Shortly before Semple became governor, Congress had passed the Indian Allotment Act of 1887, the Dawes Severalty Act. The new law authorized the division of certain reservation lands into individual holdings which the Indians could sell.[23] Under the severalty act and by various other means, two million acres of Indian lands in Stevens County in eastern Washington passed into the hands of white speculators and settlers. Still residents hungered

19. *Messages of the Governors*, p. 268.
20. *Report of the Surveyor General of Washington Territory to the Legislative Assembly, 1887*, passim.
21. *Report of the Governor, 1887*, p. 9.
22. U.S. Bureau of the Census, *Tenth Census (1880)*, 1:75, 83, 116, *Eleventh Census (1890)*, Pt. 1, p. 45.
23. Paul Wallace Gates, "The Homestead Act in an Incongruous Land System," *American Historical Review*, 41 (1936): 652-81.

for more, eyeing especially some 800,000 acres of choice reservation land in the Yakima Valley. Semple tried to justify this land hunger to Secretary of the Interior Lamar. Most settlers, he asserted, did not object to Indians retaining large amounts of land, "but all condemn a policy that gives this idle people immense tracts of the finest soil that they may let it grow up in weeds." But the governor had not run out of hope for the Indians. Unlike the Chinese, they might be assimilated. As he explained to Lamar, "They are not a dull or an unreasonably obstinate race, and recognizing the march of events, they perceive that the choice for them is to adapt themselves to the ways of the white man or fade from the face of the earth."[24]

Accordingly, Semple urged the government to "encourage the abandonment of the tribal relation, and to turn the ambition of the individual Indian from feats of arms and daring to the attainment of distinction in the walks of civilized life." The resultant benefits, he maintained, would be two-fold: a transfer to the public domain of surplus reservation land, and an end to hostilities between whites and Indians.[25] The provisions of the Dawes Act reflected the same view.

The settlers' clamor for real estate abated when railroad land sales increased after the completion of the Northern Pacific's line up the Yakima Valley and across the Cascades into Tacoma and Puget Sound in 1887. During the year ending in June 1888 the railroad sold nearly 270,000 acres of its domain to more than sixteen hundred purchasers.[26] For a time, the Northern Pacific was doing more land business in the territory than the General Land Office.[27]

Having suffered at the hands of outfits like the Oregon Railway and Navigation Company (a Northern Pacific subsidiary) as a Vancouver lumberman, Semple, as governor, at last was in a position to influence their regulation and taxation in order to alleviate some of the inequities of commerce and transportation in the territory. In his annual report to the secretary of the interior he urged the federal government to expedite the forfeiture of railroad land grants along uncompleted routes.[28] He also sought new taxes on land held outright by the railroads. In his message to the legislature in October 1887 he

24. *Report of the Governor, 1887,* pp. 34, 34.
25. Ibid., pp. 37-38.
26. Ibid., p. 13.
27. Roy M. Robbins, "The Federal Land System in an Embryo State," *Pacific Historical Review,* 4 (1935): 368.
28. *Report of the Governor, 1887,* p. 37.

recommended higher levies on railway property in order to create a more equitable distribution of the tax burden between the corporations and individual taxpayers. The legislators the next year enacted new taxes affecting railroad property in or near incorporated areas,[29] but they failed to devise any truly fair system of taxation. While advocating stiffer taxes on railroad property, Semple also sought federal laws to improve public access to the territorial waterways, notably the Columbia. It was urgent, he said, that the government make "large appropriations so as to emancipate the people of the interior from the tyrannical exactions of the railway companies."[30]

Although the eleventh biennial session of the Washington territorial legislature was, in Semple's words, "a pleasant and profitable one,"[31] it left many issues unresolved. One of the most controversial was woman suffrage. Women had been fighting for the right to vote in the territory since 1854 when the first legislature had nearly enacted an equal suffrage law, although there was no provision for it in the Organic Act.[32] In 1883 the legislature did pass a law giving women the ballot but its legality was challenged in February 1887, two months before Semple took office, when the territorial supreme court ruled that women could not serve as jurors. The wording of the decision strongly implied that woman suffrage was also contrary to the intent of the Organic Act. [33]

The court's action created a furor which cut across regional and party lines. When the legislature defiantly began drafting a new suffrage bill early in 1888, Semple found himself deluged with petitions, pleas, and dire warnings from suffragettes and their opponents. A majority of the business community seemed to oppose any extension of the voting franchise. Thomas Burke led a prominent group of Seattle petitioners who urged Semple to veto any new suffrage law or jeopardize the movement for statehood. From Spokane, A. H. Clarke, the president of the city board of trade, also pleaded with the governor to block passage of any new measure. Other members of the board, however, were divided on the issue. In Walla Walla former legislator W. T. Asbury

29. *Messages of the Governors,* pp. 271, 274; *Report of the Governor, 1888,* p. 33; *Laws of Washington, 1887-88,* pp. 63-64, 191, 220.

30. *Report of the Governor, 1887,* p. 37.

31. *Report of the Governor, 1888,* p. 33

32. Ault, "The Earnest Ladies," p. 127.

33. Claudius O. Johnson, "George Turner of the Supreme Court of Washington Territory," *Oregon Historical Quarterly,* 44 (1943): 377.

claimed that local Democrats were overwhelmingly opposed to the enactment of a suffrage law. But across town, Mrs. John B. Allen, wife of the Republican leader who was soon to unseat Voorhees as delegate to Congress, pleaded the cause of her sex in a letter to Semple in which she claimed that Voorhees himself was backing the suffrage crusade. At Colfax, the delegate's home town, citizens held a mass meeting and voted two to one in favor of letting women vote. On Puget Sound, where business groups seemed particularly unfriendly to the feminists, religious groups and organized labor endorsed the women's demands.[34]

From the petitions which reached his desk, Semple perceived the divisive nature of the issue and did his best to placate both sides. Not wishing to antagonize either faction, he had avoided the suffrage question in his message to the legislature the previous October. His official silence continued through mid-January 1888 as passage of a new statute became imminent and pressures on the governor from both sides intensified. The new bill granted the vote to women twenty-one years of age who had lived in the territory for six months before election day. With an eye to the courts, however, the authors of the measure inserted a clause prohibiting women from serving as jurors. The act passed its final hurdle in the upper house on January 18 and Semple signed it into law the following day.[35]

Reaction to the governor's endorsement was loud and mixed. His refusal to veto the measure was a rebuff to many businessmen, including some fellow Democrats who genuinely feared that the new law would delay and complicate Washington's admission to the Union. But Semple's choice was politically defensible. The rather swift passage of the bill by a legislature almost evenly divided between Democrats and Republicans seemed to indicate how the majority of people felt about the question. And, as former territorial delegate Orange Jacobs, a Republican, pointed out, the new law had nothing to do directly with admission; Semple had therefore done "his proper duty."[36] Another influential Republican, Allen Weir, a discerning lobbyist and

34. Burke et al. to Semple, January 16, 1888; Clarke to Semple, January 17, 1888; F. E. Curtis and A. S. Curtis to Semple, January 17, 1888; W. T. Asbury to Semple, January 17, 1888; Mrs. John B. Allen to Semple, January 17, 1888; Rev. J. Cairnes to Semple, January 16, 1888; Union Labor Party to Semple, January 17, 1888. A Vancouver petition favoring woman suffrage was sent to Semple on January 18, 1888; an antisuffrage petition from Vancouver followed it on January 19, 1888.

35. *Laws of Washington, 1887-88,* pp. 93-94.

36. Seattle *Daily Press,* January 21, 1888.

correspondent from Port Townsend who was destined soon to become Washington's first secretary of state, also supported Semple's action. Weir echoed Jacobs on the statehood question and its relation to equal suffrage. "Chief among [the] fallacious points," he said, "was that about injury to our chances for admission to Statehood. . . . Considering that Congress has power to invalidate the law, and that it can pass a Statehood enabling act so framed that we must be admitted without woman suffrage," Weir went on, "the argument falls flat and stale; unworthy of the bright minds who originated it."[37] As for Semple, the Port Townsend journalist sympathized with the governor's predicament: ". . . in the confusion and absence of any means of ascertaining the will of the majority of the people, he felt bound to regard the legislature as the proper lawmaking power and himself as merely the executive."[38]

Semple's actions elicited scores of telegrams of congratulation from suffragettes near and far, including renowned Boston feminist Lucy Stone. Temperance groups and labor organizations, including the Knights of Labor, also expressed satisfaction.[39] Semple, for his part, remained silent, perhaps not wishing to further antagonize angry Democrats, some of whom, it was rumored, had exerted considerable pressure on him to use his veto.[40]

But once again the victory of the suffragettes was short-lived. In May 1888, as if re-enacting an already overdone farce, the territorial supreme court invalidated the new law. The decision stemmed from the efforts of a dance hall girl with the unlikely name of Nevada M. Bloomer to vote in the Spokane municipal election. The election board denied her this privilege and Miss Bloomer, backed by local feminists, sued the board. She lost the suit and a subsequent appeal to the supreme court, which held that the suffrage bill was unconstitutional because the Organic Act made no explicit provision for it, and because Congress "by every possible implication" had excluded women from office.[41] As a result of the decision, Washington women did not gain the right to vote until 1910. [42]

37. Ibid.
38. Ibid., January 28, 1888.
39. Lucy Stone to Semple, January 30, 1888; William H. Galvani, Secretary of the Knights of Labor, Spokane, to Semple, January 25, 1888.
40. Seattle *Daily Press,* January 28, 1888.
41. Spokane *Review,* May 22, 1888; Seattle *Daily Press,* May 24, 1888.
42. Ault, "The Earnest Ladies," p. 137.

The suffrage fight exposed some of the limitations of the territorial government and its chief executive. For one thing, the governor was not even the leader of his own political party in the territory. And because he was appointed, not elected, he could not know the extent of his support from the voters of the territory on measures like the suffrage bill. He was also handicapped by the nearness of statehood—in spite of Weir's remarks to the contrary. Semple summarized the prevailing attitude about statehood in his reply to a Tacoma feminist who urged him to ask Congress to incorporate woman suffrage in the enabling act that would admit Washington to the Union: "There is such a strong desire on the part of all classes of our citizens . . . for admission into the Union that I consider it impolitic to complicate the situation by reference to any question upon which the friends of admission are not fully agreed." [43]

The territory's long wait for statehood was nearing an end during Semple's administration, despite the question of the annexation of northern Idaho to Washington and the delicate balance of power between Democrats and Republicans on Capitol Hill and in the territory. In the November elections of 1886 northern Idaho had voted overwhelmingly in favor of annexation to Washington and had caused Congress to re-examine the status of the two territories. [44] A few months later, shortly before Semple's inauguration, Voorhees introduced an annexation bill in the lower house. The measure passed Congress but was pocket vetoed by Cleveland. [45] Territorial party politics also hampered the progress toward statehood. Some Northwest Democrats shied away from the prospect of admission, fearing the loss of territorial patronage (which their party under Cleveland for the moment controlled) if Washington were allowed to become a state. A statehood bill introduced in Congress by Voorhees in 1886 had been openly criticized by some Democrats in the territory as an act of party betrayal. [46] Such behavior at home did nothing to help the statehood cause in Congress.

Despite the presence of opposition, the vast majority of residents of the territory favored admission. Accordingly the legislature revived the

43. Semple to Zeulda McCoy, December 26, 1888.

44. C. S. Kingston, "The North Idaho Annexation Issue," *Washington Historical Quarterly,* 21 (1930): 285; Keith A. Murray, "The Movement for Statehood in Washington," *Pacific Northwest Quarterly,* 32 (1941): 381.

45. Murray, "Movement for Statehood," p. 380.

46. Ibid., pp. 380-81.

statehood requests of previous sessions. Two memorials were passed, one urging admission with northern Idaho, one without.[47] Semple endorsed both measures in his report to the secretary of the interior: "The first thing in enumerating our needs must always be admission into the Union. We are rich and reputable and we do not require anybody to settle our bills. Give us the right to regulate our local affairs and we will not only pay our own officers, but we will render much service to the Union."[48]

Semple himself favored the admission of Washington with the prior annexation of northern Idaho, pointing to the dependence of that region on eastern Washington for farm products. The governor gave local residents what they wanted to hear during a tour of the area in the autumn of 1887. "Statehood and annexation are both certain," he told one Idaho reporter emphatically. In Spokane, citing a recent visit to the region by members of the Senate committee on the territories, he declared: "The chances for statehood are the best ever."[49] Voorhees shared these sentiments and in 1888 introduced in Congress two more statehood bills similar to those urged by the legislature. Congress declined to act on either of them mainly because Democrats were understandably fearful that admission of a territory with a majority of registered Republican voters would produce more of that party in Congress.[50]

While debate continued on the vital question of statehood, less important questions also proved vexing to Semple and the legislature. One such problem was the seemingly inconsequential though very necessary task of updating the codification of the laws of the territory. Not since 1877, before the territory had witnessed any substantial influx of settlers, had the legislature authorized a codification of the territorial statutes. This compilation, which was not completed until 1881, had become inadequate by 1887 when new demands for statutory reform were voiced.[51] Soon after, Semple asked the lawmakers to create a commission to compile the urgently needed new

47. *Laws of Washington, 1887-88,* pp. 264-65, 268-70; House Report No. 1025 (Serial 2601), 50th Cong., 1st sess., 1887-88.

48. *Report of the Governor, 1888,* p. 44.

49. Moscow (Idaho) *Star,* November 21, 1887; Spokane Falls *Chronicle,* November 10, 1887.

50. Murray, "Movement for Statehood," p. 382.

51. Arthur S. Beardsley, "The Codes and Code Makers of Washington, 1889-1937," *Pacific Northwest Quarterly,* 30 (1939): 3.

code. Acting on the governor's request the legislature authorized him to appoint a four-member bipartisan group to overhaul the statutes.[52] Semple named Democrats Henry Snively of Yakima and J. A. Wickersham of Tacoma and Republicans W. H. Doolittle of Colfax and J. F. Parks of Spokane to the commission. The appointments were well received. "The governor has appointed four of the most capable lawyers in the territory," commented the Olympia *Washington Standard.*[53]

Unfortunately the commissioners accomplished very little. Their entire project was compromised from the start by the nearness of statehood and the likelihood that a new state government would want to compile a code of its own. Almost at once, unanticipated difficulties of another nature arose. The four lawyers began their work in March 1888 only to be interrupted in May when Wickersham suddenly resigned. Then, in June, Parks, the youngest member of the group, committed suicide in Portland. Adequate replacements were hard to find. Semple offered Wickersham's post to Joseph Robinson of Olympia, who declined because of his duties as a prosecuting attorney. Not until the following April 1889, just before leaving office, did the governor manage to fill the Wickersham vacancy. In desperation he gave the job to Seattle attorney Thomas Cann, a persistent office seeker of modest qualifications. In the meantime he had appointed Alfred Isham, a Republican from Walla Walla, to fill Parks's post.[54]

Semple's growing frustration with the legal snarls arising in large measure from the outdated code was revealed in his correspondence with the undermanned commission in September 1888. In southwestern Washington, territorial fishing waters were being poached by Oregonians; elsewhere, coal mining companies were bringing in strikebreakers and private guards from outside the territory in defiance of local authority. Unsure exactly where jurisdiction lay, the governor implored the commission to "report to the legislature on this matter and make a statute enabling officers to act to uphold the dignity of the commonwealth."[55] Since the commission already lagged in its work due to the unexpected departure of Wickersham and Parks and an

52. *Laws of Washington, 1887-88,* pp. 44-45.

53. Olympia *Washington Standard,* February 24, 1888; Beardsley, "Codes, 1889-1937," p. 4.

54. Beardsley, "Codes, 1889-1937," p. 4; Beardsley, "Compiling the Territorial Codes of Washington," *Pacific Northwest Quarterly,* 28 (1937): 53; Semple to Cann, April 9, 1889.

55. Semple to the Code Commission, September 3, 1888.

apparent lack of harmony among the other members, it took no action on the request.

According to the ordinance which had created the code commission, the group was to have completed its work before the first day of the next regular legislative session in late November 1889. Long before this date arrived, however, the lawmakers had met in special session in January 1889 "to close out," as Semple phrased it, "our territorial affairs preparatory to admission into the Union."[56] In February Congress passed an enabling act in conformity with the Omnibus Bill of 1889, authorizing the admission of North and South Dakota, Montana, and Washington.[57] In November, when the first state legislature met, one of its initial acts was to codify the existing laws, taking up the uncompleted work of the luckless commission Semple had created and coaxed.[58]

More pressing than code reform was the threat to life and property generated by widespread labor unrest among coal miners, salmon fishermen, and other discontented workingmen in the territory. Semple was therefore alarmed to discover, upon entering office, the confusion of affairs within the territorial militia. The militia, or national guard, was no bulwark against anarchy, but it was expected to perform important services in times of crisis. During Seattle's anti-Chinese disturbances in 1886 it had acted as a valuable reinforcement to city and county law officers until federal troops arrived from distant Fort Vancouver.

The weaknesses of the militia were several. Although every able-bodied young man in the territory was required to serve, expenditures by the federal and territorial governments were often insufficient to maintain an adequate force. Because the cost of billeting, equipping, and training troops was prohibitive, few got called to duty. As a result, volunteers who furnished most of their own necessities formed the bulk of the approximately nine hundred officers and enlisted men in the organization. Besides financial and recruiting troubles, the guard was afflicted with a snarled chain of command which often made it more responsive to the interests of a

56. *Report of the Governor, 1888,* p. 45.
57. *Congressional Record,* 50th Cong., 2nd sess., p. 1904-16, 2095-2104, 2113-16; *United States Statutes at Large,* 25:676-84.
58. *Laws of Washington Territory, 1889-1890,* pp. 236-38; Beardsley, "Codes, 1889-1937," pp. 3-21.

semientrenched general staff of elected officers than to those of the commonwealth.[59]

Semple's doubts about the militia were confirmed during its annual encampment at Tacoma in June and early July of 1887. This particular bivouac, later dubbed the "mosquito fiasco" by the press, revealed an almost comic absence of discipline within the ranks. According to plan, the commander of the Tacoma unit, Lieutenant Sprague, was ordered to pitch camp near the city for the two regiments which were to assemble to drill for their part in the Fourth of July parade. Sprague apparently was tardy in executing his orders, for when Colonel John Haines arrived from Seattle with the first regiment, the only greeting party was a swarm of mosquitoes. With no evidence of food, bedding, or other provisions in sight, the several hundred troops settled down to make the best of a long night. Well before dawn the mosquitoes had taken their toll, precipitating a highly disorganized retreat.[60]

Civic officials, hoping to be honored by the presence of the militia in the holiday festivities, were keenly disappointed. While Colonel Haines criticized Lieutenant Sprague, their superior, Adjutant General Russell O'Brien, blamed everyone, including stingy lawmakers, for failing to provide the necessary funds to organize the militia properly.[61] Semple quickly ordered a court of inquiry which met in the Tacoma Chamber of Commerce building. The central question before the tribunal concerned the status of men under arms. Were they, as volunteers on routine maneuvers, free to break ranks at will or were they obligated to serve indefinitely once under orders? Following much unproductive discussion, Semple himself resolved the issue by pointing out that enlistees were under oath to serve the territory whether the situation involved fighting mosquitoes or quelling violence.[62]

Semple informed Secretary of the Interior Lamar of the "very defective militia laws of the Territory" under which it was "not practicable to maintain a proper degree of discipline." He also exhorted the legislators at Olympia "to amend the statutes in the interest of a

59. Adjutant General Russell G. O'Brien claimed that the territory's $2,700 share of the total $400,000 federal appropriation to the national militia units in 1887 was barely enough for supplies *(Report of the Adjutant General of Washington Territory to the Legislative Assembly, 1887-88,* p. 35); *Report of the Governor, 1887,* p. 62.

60. *Report of the Governor, 1887,* p. 62; Seattle *Post-Intelligencer,* July 3, 1887.

61. *Post-Intelligencer,* July 3, 1887.

62. Ibid.

better organization."[63] In January 1888 legislation was enacted "for the more efficient organization and discipline of the militia."[64] The governor as commander-in-chief was given explicit powers to regulate the behavior of the guard and to call upon it in time of emergency. "I am glad to be able to report," Semple told the new Secretary of the Interior, William F. Vilas, "that the last legislature passed an act placing the National Guard of the Territory upon a secure footing." He then outlined recent developments: "A tax of one-fifth of a mill was levied for military purposes, and provision was made for the enforcement of discipline. By another act the fund was made immediately available by advances from the general fund. . . . So many men offer to enlist . . . that it has become possible to establish a high standard of qualifications. . . . I think [the Guard] could be relied upon in any emergency." [65]

Despite the new laws, Semple's difficulties with his commanding officers continued. Adjutant General O'Brien, an elected officer and a Republican of some prominence in Olympia city politics, had never seen eye to eye on matters of military administration with the Democratic appointee who had become his commander-in-chief.[66] Using his authority under the new militia laws, Semple reprimanded O'Brien and members of his staff on several occasions for allocating such items as weapons, clothing, and rations without the governor's approval. He was further incensed when O'Brien and his staff ratified a new code of militia regulations without consulting him. Such squabbles, many of them trivial, continued during 1888. Semple finally appealed to Territorial Attorney General James B. Metcalfe for a ruling on the specific question of the commander-in-chief's right to review and withhold expenditures to the militia. Metcalfe, whom Semple had appointed, affirmed the governor's right to hold back military funds, even if the militia had already audited and approved them.[67] And so

63. *Report of the Governor, 1887*, p. 61; *Messages of the Governors*, p. 269.
64. *Laws of Washington, 1887-88*, p. 147.
65. *Report of the Governor, 1888*, p. 44.
66. O'Brien,. like Semple, had lived in Jersey County, Illinois. He came west to Olympia in 1870 as a tax collector with President Grant's appointee as territorial governor, Edward S. Salomon. O'Brien was elected mayor of Olympia in 1891. See Harvey K. Hines, *An Illustrated History of the State of Washington*, pp. 662-63.
67. Semple to O'Brien, July 20, 1888; Semple to James B. Metcalfe, November 9, 1888; Metcalfe to Semple, November 14, 1888.

the tug of war for control of the militia continued, even while labor disturbances challenged the agencies of law and order in the territory.

7. Labor Unrest

During 1887 and 1888 labor strife among Columbia River salmon fishermen and in the coal mines of the Cascades, as well as rumors of new anti-Chinese disturbances in Seattle, raised grave questions about the authority of the territorial governor. Semple had not long to wait for the first crisis to arise. Three days after his inauguration, William H. White, the United States Attorney for Washington Territory, wrote from Seattle to warn the new governor of potential trouble there. White was alarmed by an anonymous letter he had received from Tacoma a day earlier asserting that a new anti-Chinese disorder would engulf Seattle the following Sunday, May 1, unless drastic steps were taken. The cryptic message confirmed all of White's own fears of recent weeks. According to the letter, three unnamed agitators were preparing to lead at least fifteen hundred well-armed white workingmen from all parts of Puget Sound against the Oriental inhabitants of the city. The writer refused to divulge any more, maintaining it would be "certain death if I disclose my name."[1] White placed the matter in Semple's hands.

The situation had its ironic overtones for the governor. A year earlier Semple had publicly denounced Governor Squire for declaring martial law at Seattle to quell the anti-Chinese disorder. Now Semple was being asked to consider similar measures. He weighed the circumstances. As commander-in-chief of the territorial militia, he was being called upon to act by responsible legal authority. If he did act, charges of hypocrisy might well follow from those who remembered his censure of Squire a

1. William H. White to Semple, April 26, 1887. White enclosed the anonymous letter.

year earlier. There was also the touchy matter of Semple's own prejudice against the Chinese, a bias strong enough to appear in his annual report to the secretary of the interior: "Belonging to a non-assimilating race, and refusing to consider himself anything but a sojourner, the Chinaman is a true parasite in his relations to this country. He is useful in the same sense that a machine or a quadruped is useful, simply as a dumb instrument in the accomplishment of physical results."[2]

Despite White's concern, the strength of the Sinophobic faction in Seattle had actually diminished by 1887. A People's Party, running primarily on the racial issue and backed by various labor elements, had captured the Seattle municipal elections in 1886 and had even made a brief bid for territorial political support. But with only a handful of Chinese now brave enough to reside in the Puget Sound country, the reason for the party's existence seemed to be waning. More important for the tranquility of the community was the return of prosperity and fuller employment in the wake of renewed railroad building in 1887.[3]

After considering White's disclosures, Semple chose a course of action. On April 27 he informed White that he would if necessary call the militia to an alert and would proceed to Seattle himself if needed. Meanwhile he asked White to explain in detail the scope of the governor's legal authority for intervention. Late on Saturday afternoon, April 30, he got a reply, along with an urgent request to come to Seattle as quickly as possible. White, after consulting with leading citizens, including United States Marshal T. J. Hamilton, and noting the flurry of rumors that were sweeping the city during the day, had concluded that a mob was forming to expel the remaining Chinese the next morning—as he had predicted. Semple responded promptly, sending telegrams to Seattle Mayor George Shoudy, King County Sheriff William Cochrane, and General George Hill of the Territorial National Guard.[4] All were alerted to stand by for trouble. Hill got orders to have local militia ready to assist Sheriff Cochrane's forces and, if necessary, to garrison a company of troops at the Seattle Armory. Having given these commands, the governor boarded a steam launch for Seattle late Saturday night.

Sometime near dawn on Sunday morning, Semple arrived in the Seattle harbor. Along the waterfront of Elliott Bay hardly a soul stirred;

2. *Governor's Report, 1887*, p. 74.
3. Seattle *Daily Press*, July 14, 1886, and July 12, 1887; Nesbit, *Burke*, p. 211.
4. Semple to White, April 27, 1887; White to Semple, April 30, 1887; Semple to Hill, Shoudy, Cochrane, et al., April 30, 1887.

there was no sign of disorder. Semple had been halfway prepared for the false alarm, having received a late telegram from Cochrane before boarding the launch the night before: "Do not anticipate an expulsion of Chinese tonight or at all; can maintain peace without troops. I can and will maintain the peace of King County."[5]

Although it seemed that the sheriff had been correct, Semple felt obliged to make something of his appearance in Seattle. The executive party proceeded to the Occidental Hotel where Semple conferred with White, Cochrane, and other officials. Then the governor announced his purpose: to interview as many citizens as possible on the subject of the rumors. He summoned local reporters and read a statement in which he pledged "to spend as much time in this city as will enable me to be fully informed in regard to the situation on the Chinese question. I want to see every man who thinks he can throw any light on the subject."[6]

As Semple canvassed local opinion during the next few days, it became increasingly apparent that White's fears had aroused not only the governor but the entire community. And yet few persons, upon more careful reflection, found it possible to share White's conclusion that a riot was imminent. Former Governor Elisha Ferry scoffed at the fears of insurrection, claiming that "the laboring men are contented and prosperous." Sheriff Cochrane concurred. As far as he was concerned, there was no chance of serious trouble in the city. Other prominent citizens agreed, including Arthur A. Denny, Mayor Shoudy, and, most notably, W. E. Wilson, a leader of the strongly anti-Chinese People's Party. In Wilson's opinion the Chinese were now only a small and harmless element in the community and posed no problem for the rest of the laboring class.[7] Nevertheless, Seattle was delighted to see the new governor taking so lively an interest in its welfare. Most civic leaders agreed with White that "an ounce of prevention" had been "worth a pound of cure," and with Denny, a leading Republican, who commended Semple for bringing "what few agitators there were to their senses and [convincing] them that the laws could not be broken with impunity."[8]

While life at Seattle resumed a more normal course, new troubles arose along the Columbia River to claim Semple's attention. For several years a bitter feud had been developing between Washington and Oregon salmon

5. Cochrane to Semple, April 30, 1887.
6. Seattle *Post-Intelligencer,* May 2, 1887.
7. Ibid.
8. Ibid.

fishermen. Essentially it was a struggle involving two competing methods of catching salmon. Oregon fishermen, whose operations centered around canneries at Astoria, generally used gill nets to bring in their catch. These nets were put out from small boats and allowed fishermen to range over much of the water near the mouth of the river. By contrast, most Washington fishermen used a system of fixed gear known as pound or trap nets which were placed nearer to shore. A large number of these pound nets were used on Baker's Bay at the southwestern tip of the territory, adjacent to the main channel of the Columbia. During the eighties, as the fishing industry expanded, the two systems spread, encroaching upon each other. Gill net men from Oregon resented the fixed gear used on the Washington side of the river. In turn, Washington pound men protested the invasion of their waters by the Oregon gill netters.[9]

Besides producing rivalry over fishing methods, the two contending systems took a toll in lives, particularly among the gill netters, some of whom were swept overboard when their boats hit uncharted pound nets. Other gill netters, in search of new fishing grounds, often strayed beyond the bar or onto it and were lost. In addition, the indiscriminate methods of fishing practiced on both sides posed a hazard to navigation and to the upstream movement of the salmon. By 1887 the mouth of the river was so clogged with nets from Astoria to Baker's Bay that, as one government investigator noted, it was a miracle any fish got upstream at all.[10]

Conflict between the two rival fishing groups had reached dangerous proportions by May 1887. Pound men along the Washington side were evidently a small and not well-organized group. The Astoria faction, on the other hand, was much larger and had organized a union to contract with the canneries and, according to the Washington fishermen, to "convert" the pound men to the ways of gill netting. When this proved unsuccessful, union marauders reportedly began slashing nets along the Washington shore and refused to let pound men sell their catch at the canneries. It was said to be common knowledge around Baker's Bay that "the gill net men were out to destroy all the traps on the Washington side."[11]

9. Washington Fishermen's Association, *Washington's Salmon Fisheries on the Columbia River,* pp. 8-11; hereafter cited as *Salmon Fisheries.*

10. Captain Charles Powell and Major W. A. Jones, *Report of Salmon Fishing on the Columbia River,* Senate Executive Document No. 123 (Serial 2510), 50th Cong., 1st sess., 1888, pp. 6, 50.

11. *Salmon Fisheries,* p. 4. Admittedly this is a biased source. Nevertheless, many of the accusations against the Astoria men are sustained by the evidence in newspapers and correspondence of the governor's office.

The hostility reached a climax one Monday night in late May when several boat loads of union men, masked and under cover of darkness, sailed across to Ilwaco on Baker's Bay and began cutting nets, burning boats, and harassing the inhabitants of the fishing village. Damage was estimated at between fifteen thousand and forty thousand dollars.[12] To prevent further incursions the villagers posted an armed guard the following night. This only led to a second calamity, arising from a case of mistaken identity when three local vigilantes assigned to guard the wharf came upon an armed Indian who aroused their suspicions. The trio shouted, then opened fire, not knowing that the Indian, later identified as Tom Dalzan, was a member of their own group. Dalzan returned the fire, killing one of his pursuers, Archie Ross, and seriously wounding another.[13]

Dalzan was exonerated by a local jury but news of the tragic incident stirred interest up and down the coast. Semple, hearing what had happened, dispatched a letter to Sheriff J. H. Turner of Pacific County demanding "an immediate investigation." Whether Turner complied is not certain, but he did advise the fishermen to organize a protective union. He also told Semple he did not think it would be necessary to call out the militia. The governor agreed but ordered Turner to arrest any of the "outragers" who could be caught and promised the aid of territorial troops if they were needed.[14]

Semple himself went to the area of the trouble in August to investigate new reports (including a crisp telegram from Oregon Governor Sylvester Pennoyer) that Washington fishermen were violating the closed season on salmon. Near Astoria he watched from a boat while Washington fishermen busily worked their nets, then sold their catch to cannery buyers—all in violation of the closed season. Semple had anticipated as much and notified sheriffs in the downriver and coastal counties to enforce the law.[15] Meanwhile, canners and fishermen along the Washington shore

12. Sheriff J. H. Turner of Pacific County estimated the damage at no less than $15,000. The fishermen's association several years later placed the damage at $40,000. See Turner to Semple, June 1, 1887; *Salmon Fisheries,* p. 4.

13. Semple to Turner, May 27, 1887; Portland *Oregonian,* May 25, 1887; Astoria *Daily Astorian,* May 25, 26, 1887; *Report of the Governor, 1887,* pp. 79-80.

14. Semple to Turner, May 27, 1887; Turner to Semple, June 1, 1887; Semple to Turner, June 13, 1887.

15. Semple to George J. Moody, August 10, 1887, Governors' Papers (s.v. Semple), Washington State Archives, Olympia. Moody was the prosecuting attorney in Chehalis County (now Grays Harbor County). Semple wrote to him

complained that the territorial fishing laws were unclear, especially about the alleged closed season on the Columbia during September.[16] To clarify the matter Semple solicited the opinions of three western Washington prosecuting attorneys. According to one of the three, Joseph Robinson of Olympia, a territorial law of 1879, which allowed fishing during September, had been repealed in 1881 but through oversight had been included in the territorial code compiled in 1881. Robinson concluded therefore that the fishing industry could continue operating—at least in Washington—during September.[17] The other two attorneys concurred.

While this legal knot was being unraveled, the second skirmish of the "salmon wars" occurred at Grays Harbor in early September. With a closed season proclaimed by Oregon law on the Columbia, union gill netters from Astoria moved up the coast. One fleet of boats, loaded with gear, sailed into Grays Harbor, an important in-season fishing area for Washington pound men. Hostilities soon began. The pretext was a warning by the union group for the pound men to remove their gear from the Chehalis River by September 9, a Friday, "or else a 'committee of the union' would do it for them."[18] The ultimatum became an invitation to battle. On Friday night the union men destroyed the property of fishermen at Aberdeen with all the thoroughness of their earlier raid at Ilwaco. But as the gill netters were finishing their destruction, a force of late-arriving pound men approached by boat and fired a volley of several dozen shots into the union gang, driving the invaders away. According to Joseph Robinson, a force of about 150 union men had issued similar ultimatums for the following night at nearby Hoquiam and Cosmopolis. Robinson even feared that the upriver towns, including Montesano, were in danger, but no new incidents were reported. [19]

The violence at Aberdeen resulted in no known casualties among the inhabitants, but several union men apparently were injured.[20] Worse yet

seeking legal advice about the territorial fishing laws. See also the outgoing correspondence in the Semple Papers, August 5, 1887.

16. Semple mentioned protests from the Knapton Packing Company of Knapton, Hapgood and Company of Waterford, and the Cook Cannery of Ilwaco in his letters to Moody, August 24 and September 9, 1887, Governors' Papers.

17. Semple to Moody, August 29, 1887; Semple to Joseph Robinson, August 29, 1887; Semple to H. Dustin, September 9, 1887, Governors' Papers; Robinson to Semple, August 30, 1887, Governors' Papers.

18. Robinson to Semple, September 11, 1887, Governors' Papers. Robinson wrote from Montesano. Some of his information apparently was secondhand.

19. Ibid.

20. *Report of the Governor, 1887,* p. 80.

Eugene Semple as
governor of Wash-
ington Territory

Watson C. Squire

for the union, the defenders succeeded in identifying some fifty of the marauders. A Chehalis County grand jury, in session at the time, returned indictments against sixteen of the union ringleaders. Semple in the meantime ordered Sheriff William Bush to arrest the "depredators." Bush complied and with the aid of armed deputies seized nine of the accused men. However, most of the assault force managed to escape back to Astoria where, according to Robinson, the union was obtaining bail for the incarcerated men. [21]

Although an example had now been set for future lawbreakers, the heart of the conflict lay in an inadequate system of muddled and often unenforced fishing regulations. Semple outlined plans for correcting this situation in his message to the legislature. His remedy paralleled a series of federal proposals made during the year by Major W. A. Jones of the United States Army Corps of Engineers. Jones urged that the closed spring and fall seasons be abolished in favor of closed days each week on Saturday and Sunday. Semple's own proposals were similar, encompassing recommendations for alternate periods of open and closed seasons of from seven to ten days. Both plans aimed at allowing fish to ascend to their spawning beds. [22] In his report to Congress, Jones, whose primary concern was the Columbia River, urged federal policing of the waterway since, in his opinion, neither Oregon nor Washington had effective laws governing the use of the river. But Semple apparently hoped to make congressional action unnecessary by having territorial lawmakers pass essentially the same measures first. A weakness of this strategy, though, was that those Oregon interests which were friendly to the cause of the Astoria fishermen might persuade the state legislature to pass conflicting laws. Seeing this possibility, Semple urged the territorial legislature to name a committee to meet with Oregon representatives to study the problem together.

There the matter rested for the moment, far from resolved. Evidently the trouble at Ilwaco and Aberdeen had not set a precedent. One thing was certain, however: reckless methods of catching salmon would have to be curtailed, and quickly. From a high catch of 630,000 cases of salmon in 1883, the output by 1887 had dropped to 350,000

21. Robinson to Semple, September 11, 1887, and Moody to Semple, September 21, 1887, Governors' Papers; Semple to Bush, September 9, 19, 1887, Semple Papers.

22. *Messages of the Governors,* p. 272; Powell and Jones, *Report of Salmon Fishing,* pp. 3, 8, 43, 58.

cases.[23] By choking off the upstream spawning beds with nets, Columbia River fishermen on both sides of the water could expect to see their annual hauls reduced even further in the years ahead. Semple's warning, if not completely accurate, made the point. "If this abuse continues," he cautioned the legislature, "the fishing industry will die within the next five years."[24]

The most serious labor distrubances of Semple's administration occurred not among the salmon fishermen, but in the coal mining towns of Roslyn and Newcastle. The trouble was part of a broader pattern of industrial unrest that had already produced a decade of violence in the coal mines of Pennsylvania. By the hectic eighties, this violence had also become a familiar part of the labor movement in Washington Territory and in the West generally. The effects of rapid economic development created antagonism between capital and labor. Employees and management both used extra-legal methods to achieve objectives that seemed unattainable by legitimate means. Mining corporations in particular treated their workers callously, sometimes even ruthlessly, and occasionally usurped legal authority to do it. In the coal mines of western Washington, workingmen retaliated with mayhem reminiscent of the terrorist Molly Maguires of Pennsylvania. Most importantly for Semple, the troubles in the coal mines underscored a dangerous confusion of authority among federal, territorial, and local law enforcement agencies over the issue of industrial labor disputes.

The causes of discontent were numerous. Hours were long and wages low, and the work was arduous. Few safety precautions existed and still fewer were enforced. The territorial coal mine inspectors reported major accidents at several of the mines during 1887.[25] Besides the toll in human lives and limbs from cave-ins and faulty equipment, many workmen succumbed to the chronic illness of the coal mines, silicosis, a lung disease caused by the constant inhalation of silica dust. Management viewed the plight of the miners with indifference. Companies refused to make any significant improvements in work conditions, other than those demanded by county grand juries and mine inspectors who made occasional investigations in compliance with

23. *Report of the Governor, 1887*, p. 53.
24. Ibid., p. 54; *Messages of the Governors*, p. 272.
25. H. C. Paige to Semple, July 1, 1888, and John Sullivan to Semple, October 1, 1888, Governors' Papers. Most of the following account of the trouble at Roslyn and Newcastle appeared in the author's "The Coal Mines of Washington Territory," *Arizona and the West*, 12 (1970): 221-36.

territorial law.

A large segment of the public undoubtedly sided with the corporations in their struggles with labor. Indicative was the advice of wealthy Seattle entrepreneur Thomas Burke to business colleagues during a strike at the Gilman coal mines near Newcastle in September 1888: "The true policy, in my opinion, is to leave the mine shut down. . . . The situation is such that they [the workers] will certainly be glad to come to us at even reduced wages. In the meantime, their action has been, and is, so unjust and outrageous that an indignant public sentiment is rapidly forming against them."[26]

Caught in the middle of this unresolved conflict between capital and labor was the territorial government, and particularly the governor. Under Semple's authority as commander-in-chief were the law enforcement agencies of the territory, namely sheriffs' deputies and territorial militia. At issue was how these forces should be deployed by the governor to preserve peace in an atmosphere of impending turmoil. Also in question was whether militiamen and deputies would work for company superintendents or support union organizers—or remain scrupulously neutral.

Semple's first troubles occurred at Roslyn in the summer of 1888. Roslyn was an isolated town of approximately two thousand inhabitants, perched on the arid east slope of the Cascade Range and linked to the outside by a company spur line which ran south to Cle Elum and Ellensburg. The depressing sepia and slate tones of the surrounding landscape revealed a coal town similar to countless other company towns of the western mining frontier in the late nineteenth century. Many of the miners were family men whose wives and children lived in the community. For these people, life at Roslyn blended the monotony and drudgery of Hamlin Garland's farms of the Middle Border with the unsavory aspects of the factory towns of the urban East. The result was a rural industrial slum environment in which long hours of work, a sliding wage scale, health hazards, and minimal safety standards degraded the miner and jeopardized his life.[27]

Discontent had festered at Roslyn since the Northern Pacific Coal Company began its operations there in 1885. The Roslyn mines were among the most productive on the Pacific Coast and were a subsidiary

26. Nesbit, *Burke*, p. 296.
27. Paige to Semple, July 1, 1888, and Sullivan to Semple, October 1, 1888, Governors' Papers; and *Report of the Governor, 1888*, pp. 17-18.

interest of the Northern Pacific Railroad. Operating at full capacity, they employed more than seven hundred men who toiled six-day, ten-hour shifts for an average monthly wage of less than fifty dollars per man. By 1888 two labor groups were competing for the coal miners' support. One was a chapter of the Knights of Labor, which sought company acceptance of an eight-hour workday, better safety standards, and recognition as sole bargaining agent for the men.[28] The other was the United Miners' and Mine Laborers' Society, usually referred to as the Miners Union. At one time it had allegedly been affiliated with the International Workmen's Association, a West Coast organization established in San Francisco by the early California socialist and labor leader, Burnette Haskell, in 1882.[29] By 1888 the IWA's influence had declined and at Roslyn the Miners Union, according to its critics, had become a company union, serving as a front for professional strikebreakers brought in to intimidate the Knights of Labor. Members of the Miners Union and their supporters denied this, claiming that the union was composed of former Knights who had quit the latter organization because of internal bickering over work demands.[30]

Semple's troubles at Roslyn began in mid-August with newspaper reports that a band of about fifty Negro strikebreakers had arrived under the protection of some four dozen armed guards who were allegedly posing as deputy United States marshals.[31] The Negroes had been shipped in by the coal company from Chicago and other points in the Midwest after the Knights had threatened to strike and throw up a picket line in support of demands for an eight-hour workday. Semple reacted to the news by telegraphing Kittitas County Sheriff Samuel Packwood and Territorial Attorney General James Metcalfe for verification of the newspaper reports. Had the guards actually been

---

28. The Knights of Labor was a nonradical organization which aimed to consolidate the scattered labor groups of America. It was founded in Philadelphia in 1862 but gained its biggest membership in the early 1880s, then declined swiftly in size and influence after the Chicago Haymarket Riot of 1886. See Phillip Taft, *Organized Labor in American History*, pp. 84-88; Terence V. Powderly, *The Path I Trod, passim*, an autobiography of the Knights' leader; and Henry David, *The History of the Haymarket Affair*, pp. 132-35.

29. Walton Bean, *California, An Interpretive History*, pp. 286-87.

30. M. H. O'Conner to Semple, January 25, February 7, 1889; Seattle *Daily Press*, May 24, 1888.

31. Seattle *Post-Intelligencer*, Seattle *Daily Press*, and Portland *Oregonian*, August 21, 1888.

deputized? If so, by whom and under what authority? [32]

Packwood went to Roslyn to investigate. Two days later he informed the governor that there were indeed at least forty armed guards claiming authority as United States deputy marshals. They had in their custody some fifty Negroes who were working one of the shafts north of town where a group of white miners had recently been laid off for agitating for higher pay and shorter hours. The blacks reportedly were working an eleven-hour day for lower wages than the white miners. "There is bitter feeling against the negroes and the U.S. marshals among the miners," the sheriff told Semple. "I fear there will be bloodshed over the matter." [33]

During Packwood's visit to Roslyn a group of the guards provoked a disturbance by setting up tent living quarters near the mine on land occupied by a homesteader named Alexander Ross. Ross protested loudly but was threatened with permanent removal on a Northern Pacific boxcar if he tried to resist them. While the so-called deputies and their Negro wards occupied the land, Ross and his family fled to Ellensburg to file charges of trespassing with county authorities. This incident was pretext enough for Packwood. Deputies or not, he arrested as many of the guards as he could lay hands on. They were later released, however, and returned to their duty, pending the outcome of a grand jury hearing into the charges of usurpation of federal authority.[34]

Meanwhile, the Northern Pacific Coal Company had shut down its other shafts at Roslyn in retaliation against the Knights. As the days passed, neither side seemed willing to allow normal work to resume. As a result, scores of miners, many of whom probably had no affiliation with the Knights of Labor, found themselves out of work. Semple followed the events at Roslyn closely. His sympathy was undeniably with the workers, but he hesitated to press a case against the coal company or its hirelings until he became certain of the facts.

The crucial point of law to be determined was whether or not the corporation had actually hired the guards to impersonate federal

32. Semple to Metcalfe, August 21, 1888, and Semple to Packwood, August 21, 1888.

33. Packwood to Semple, August 23, 1888; Seattle *Daily Press,* August 21, 1888; Snively to Semple in *Report of the Governor, 1888,* pp. 46-48; and Packwood to Semple, August 23, 1888.

34. Snively to Semple, *Report of the Governor, 1888,* pp. 46-48; Packwood to Semple, August 23, 1888.

Roslyn, Washington, 1890

Miners sorting coal at Newcastle, 1902

deputies, as alleged by Packwood and some of the Knights. This point was not conclusively established, but information uncovered by Henry Snively, the prosecuting attorney for Kittitas County, seemed to indicate that the company had at least circumvented the law for its own interests. According to Snively, the firm had hired forty-one men from an outfit in Portland known as Thiel's Detective Agency to escort forty-eight Midwest Negro laborers through Washington Territory to the Roslyn mines. These "detectives" were evidently western counterparts of the Pinkerton agents and were under the supervision of a Portland man named William Sullivan. Snively claimed that Sullivan's men had rendezvoused with the Negroes at Pasco, in southeastern Washington, for the 150-mile journey across the territory to Cle Elum. They had been armed en route with Winchester rifles and small arms while aboard the Northern Pacific's regular passenger train.[35]

Such conduct was proof of an arrogant disregard for the safety of the passengers, but Snively had no evidence that Sullivan's men had actually posed as federal deputy marshals and he therefore had little hope of getting a grand jury indictment. Furthermore, the federal marshal, T. J. Hamilton, denied any knowledge of "detectives acting as deputy United States marshals, or pretending to act as such." United States Attorney William White said essentially the same thing.[36]

None the less, Semple decided to supplement the investigations of Packwood and Snively by going to Roslyn to have a look for himself. The official party, which included the governor's aide-de-camp, Lieutenant Colonel Gwin Hicks of the militia, and Attorney General Metcalfe, arrived by special train in Cle Elum on August 28 and proceeded by another car to nearby Roslyn. An orderly crowd awaited them, expecting perhaps some pronouncement from Semple that might alleviate the tension. But the governor could promise only that the militia would stand ready to quell disorder if it occurred. Otherwise, he told them, the territorial government had no power to intervene in disputes between management and labor. Barring a riot, an insurrection, or a federal order, his hands were tied.[37]

Before leaving the area, Semple's party journeyed two miles north to Ross's disputed claim at Mine Number Three, where an armed, uniformed body of men greeted them. These were the Thiel detectives,

35. Snively to Semple, *Report of the Governor, 1888,* p. 48.
36. *Report of the Governor, 1888,* pp. 46-47.
37. Ibid., pp. 47-48.

who were organized and encamped as if they represented a regular militia unit. In order to protect the mine and its Negro work crews, they had thrown up fortifications of logs and earthworks, in front of which was strung a formidable barbed wire fence.[38] Having satisfied himself that an immediate outbreak of hostilities was unlikely, Semple returned to Olympia.

In the weeks that followed, however, trouble continued. On one occasion a group of men who were reported to be Knights seized a mine superintendent and draped him across the company railroad tracks near Roslyn to await a classic fate. Before any train arrived, friends rescued the man and spirited him off to Cle Elum where Sheriff Packwood placed him in a boarding house under heavy guard.[39]

Although such incidents only served to antagonize the public, the Knights of Labor continued to press their demands. The Masterworker of their Spokane chapter, William Galvani, insisted that the fight was between all the workers and a tyrannical management. "We will to the best of our ability protect and aid any of our brothers who may suffer from the injustices of employers," he told the governor. Galvani had been a political supporter of Semple three years earlier during the latter's quest for the governorship. He now asked Semple to intervene "unofficially" in the work dispute at Roslyn in behalf of the Knights. Semple declined, telling Galvani what he had told the crowd at Roslyn—that his authority extended only to emergencies and not to labor disputes.[40]

If the governor was unwilling to become a spokesman for labor, it was not because of any sympathy for the mine owners, who demanded government protection *and* the right to employ armed guards. Before Galvani's message arrived, Semple had received an angry letter from J. M. Buckley, general manager of the Northern Pacific Coal Company at Tacoma. Buckley demanded that the governor intervene to preserve company property at Roslyn, but in the same breath insisted that the guards must stay. "I warn you," he told the governor, "if the guards are taken out the lives of the Negroes and our property will be jeopardized.... Our work should not be interfered with but our property and the lives of our employees should be protected." Then, before Semple could reply, Buckley ordered his subordinate at Roslyn,

38. Ibid. p. 48.
39. *The History of Central Washington*, p. 252.
40. William Galvani to Semple, September 2, 6, 1888.

J. W. Hoagland, to hire only nonstrikers when the mines reopened on the first Monday in September. The company would deal with individual workers but not with any union, Buckley declared, and no wage increases were to be considered.[41] Buckley's demands and subsequent orders failed to influence Semple, who took no action.

Although some of the mine shafts at Roslyn evidently were reopened, the uneasy situation continued through September with no sign of a break in the deadlock. The Knights of Labor held a bargaining position only as long as they succeeded, through threats and acts of violence, in keeping sizable numbers of workers out of the mines, thereby slowing down the company's production schedule. And the company for its part would make no concessions until the Knights called off their strike.

Despite the governor's official neutrality, his personal feelings were quite another matter. In a letter to Secretary of the Interior William Vilas he deplored the circumstances under which corporations claimed the right to maintain standing armies. Such conditions constituted "a serious menace" to free institutions, he said. As far as Semple was concerned, groups such as Sullivan's men were nothing more than "organized bodies of ruffians, offering for hire to become instruments of the rich and strong for the oppression of the poor and weak."[42]

At Ellensburg, meanwhile, a Kittitas County grand jury had found no evidence to substantiate charges that the coal company "detectives" had impersonated deputy marshals. Thus there were no grounds for prosecuting Sullivan's men or the company. Semple moved to correct this situation by pleading with the legislature to enact a law prohibiting private armies from usurping the police powers of the territorial government as Sullivan's men had done at Roslyn. But with statehood and other matters pending, the lawmakers postponed action on his recommendation. Thus, amid a climate of apprehension and distrust, the miners remained out of work while the Thiel detectives enforced an uneasy peace.[43]

41. J. M. Buckley to Semple, August 27, 1888; Buckley to J. W. Hoagland, telegram, August 31, 1888, enclosed in Semple to [Packwood?], September 3, 1888.

42. *Report of the Governor, 1888*, p. 49.

43. Ibid. *The Revised Statutes of the United States*, 1875 (2nd ed., 1878) and Vol. 1 of the *Supplement* (1874-91) contained no specific provision against this particular use of armed guards. The Washington State Constitution, Article I, Section 24, states that "nothing in this section shall be construed as authorizing

While Roslyn simmered, a volatile situation was brewing across the Cascades at Newcastle, east of Lake Washington, about fifteen miles southeast of Seattle. There the Oregon Improvement Company operated the second largest coal mining enterprise in the territory.Labor unrest and frequent work halts had highlighted the history of Newcastle since 1886, when the OIC had been forced to stop production for several months. More than 250 men were employed by the company, a Portland outfit which represented California and eastern investors. Like Roslyn, Newcastle was a company town. The miners were predominantly Welsh, Scottish, and Irish, and most of them had had experience in the coal regions of the eastern states or in their native lands before coming west. They were no strangers to the union movement either. Many of the men had brought families to Newcastle, which provided added incentive for demanding higher wages and safer working conditions.[44]

Trouble broke out at Newcastle in May 1888 when the OIC hired a member of the Miners Union, Stephen Vaughn, to replace one of its foremen, Kelly Ramsey, who belonged to the Knights of Labor. Ramsey's decision to quit may have been designed to furnish a pretext for new agitation by the Knights. The men under him were fellow Knights who refused to work for Vaughn, claiming that as a member of the Miners Union he was, *ipso facto,* a "scab." A strike began and soon men were fighting. When other Knights moved into Newcastle from the nearby mines at Franklin and Gilman to join the fracas, the company called on Semple to take action in order to protect its property.[45]

The OIC was particularly alarmed by the conduct of King County Sheriff William Cochrane. According to the company, Cochrane was affiliated with the Knights and for that reason had refused to intervene to maintain order. When the governor questioned him, the sheriff denied both allegations, stating that he had investigated the situation and saw no need to call in deputies. Besides, he said, county funds were so low that no expenditure for deputies could be made unless it were absolutely necessary. Semple concurred. Two months later, in July, Cochrane again turned a deaf ear to a company request for deputies

individuals or corporations to organize, maintain or employ an armed body of men."

44. An account of life in Newcastle is in Marilyn Tharp, "The Story of Coal at Newcastle," *Pacific Northwest Quarterly,* 48 (October 1957): 120-26.

45. Seattle *Daily Press,* May 24, 26, 1888.

following rumors that miners were threatening violence if the firm went ahead with plans to open a new shaft and bring in nonunion men to work it. As far as the sheriff was concerned, the owners' fears were groundless, and in this instance, at least, he was right.[46]

An uneasy mood prevailed during the remainder of 1888 in the coal mines of western Washington. Then, toward the end of the year, new disorders occurred, first at Roslyn, then at Newcastle. On December 30 the Northern Pacific Coal Company's assistant manager, H. C. Lytle, telegraphed Semple that two superintendents had been assaulted by striking miners (presumably Knights) and driven out of town. Lytle said he had notified Packwood first, but claimed the sheriff had done nothing.[47]

Meanwhile more serious trouble was developing at Newcastle. The conflict started when the OIC hired a group of nonunion men in defiance of the Knights. In response, the Knights gave the company an ultimatum on December 24 to dismiss the new workers or face unpleasant consequences. The company refused and on the morning of January 4 an estimated force of fifty Knights from Gilman, many of them armed, descended on the Newcastle mines. Strikers and nonstrikers quickly took sides and soon shots rang out. One member of the invading party, William Ruston, was killed and at least nine other men from both sides were injured. Acting without Semple's knowledge, Colonel John C. Haines of Seattle's First Territorial National Guard Regiment ordered two companies of troops to Newcastle to prevent more bloodshed. With the arrival of the militia, the disturbance subsided. By January 8 most of the soldiers had returned to Seattle, except for a handful who stayed on a few days more at Sheriff Cochrane's request.[48]

A coroner's jury assigned the cause of Ruston's death to "parties unknown." The Knights of Labor insisted that both the riot and the fatality were the responsibility of a leader of the Miners Union named Howell Jones. Conflicting testimony discredited that notion, however, and Jones was not indicted. Among his accusers and one of those arrested in the gun battle was Kelly Ramsey, the foreman whose departure from Newcastle the previous May had led to the earlier

46. Ibid., May 26, 1888
47. Lytle to Semple, December 30, 1888.
48. Seattle *Post-Intelligencer,* January 4, 6, 8, 1889; Semple to Haines, January 5, 12, 1889.

skirmish.[49]

While King County authorities continued an inquiry into the battle at Newcastle, the Oregon Improvement Company demanded public protection against further violence. Cochrane replied that King County could not afford to garrison a permanent guard of deputies at Newcastle at the taxpayers' expense simply to quiet the fears of the owners. In the meantime Semple directed the territorial attorney general, James Metcalfe, to investigate the activities of both the company and the workers. He especially wanted to know why the militia had been at Newcastle in the first place without his prior knowledge or consent. His concern increased when he learned that Colonel Haines, who had ordered the two companies of troops to the scene, was an attorney for the OIC.[50]

On January 16, 1889, the governor ordered Haines's superior, Brigadier General George D. Hill, to explain why Haines had been allowed to send national guardsmen to Newcastle without Semple's permission. Hill replied that the soldiers were sent at Sheriff Cochrane's request and had been transferred to his control as a *posse comitatus*—a legally authorized body of armed deputies. This did not satisfy the governor, who rebuked Hill so severely that the general resigned his commission. Hill's conduct was, in Semple's opinion, "so flagrant an act of insubordination" that nothing saved him from being called to account except his resignation. The Seattle *Post-Intelligencer* sprang to Hill's defense. The newspaper conceded that the governor was commander in chief and had final authority over the deployment of territorial militia. However, if Semple expected to exercise command, the paper admonished, he ought to stay closer to the trouble spots instead of paying "so much personal attention to his saw mill on the Columbia River."[51]

All of this squabbling among the authorities convinced the directors of the Oregon Improvement Company that they might have to act alone to protect their Newcastle property. Events on the other side of the Cascades seemed to confirm this opinion. On Saturday night, January 19, sixty miners from Roslyn invaded Cle Elum and, according to Sheriff Packwood, "attempted to clean out the town." The men

49. *Post-Intelligencer,* January 6, 1889.
50. Semple to John Haines, January 5, 1889; *Post-Intelligencer,* January 8, 17, 1889.
51. *Post-Intelligencer,* January 17, 22, 1889.

threatened a hotel proprietor and his establishment and inflicted minor property damage elsewhere but evidently injured no one. By Sunday morning the intruders had dispersed and returned to Roslyn. In the meantime an alarmed Packwood had contacted Semple, asking him to send up 150 troops. The governor refused the request, saying he would come up again to investigate instead.[52]

By now rumors of new unrest were sweeping Newcastle and adjoining communities and the new general manager of the Oregon Improvement Company, Hobart W. McNeill, was getting worried. The source of his anxiety was an unconfirmed report that a large stand of rifles had been shipped by the Knights of Labor in Seattle to some of the miners at Newcastle. As a precaution McNeill telegraphed Semple at Olympia on January 21 to ask for the protection of the National Guard. But the governor had already departed to inquire into the latest difficulties at Cle Elum and Roslyn in response to Sheriff Packwood's plea. McNeill therefore got no immediate reply. Choosing not to wait for an answer, he took matters into his own hands. On the excuse that the United States Mail and the post office at Newcastle were in danger, McNeill induced Marshal Hamilton to deputize twenty-four of the company's men to protect its property.[53] The result was an uneasy quiet for the moment.

Semple did not learn of McNeill's request until his return from the Roslyn area three days after McNeill had sent the telegram. His hasty reply was an emphatic refusal accompanied by a short lecture. "The Washington National Guard is not to be used to pacify the writers of panicy [sic] telegrams," he told him. Nor did the guardsmen exist to serve "any corporation than can pay them a per diem and furnish them with transportation and subsistence."[54] As far as the governor was concerned, McNeill's appeal was a maneuver designed to promote tension, which in turn would provide an excuse for the company to summon a private army for protection.

Semple did not learn of the use of the "deputies" at Newcastle until he read the Seattle *Post-Intelligencer* two days after his angry reply to

52. Ibid; Packwood to Semple, January 21, 1889, and Semple to Packwood, January 21, 1889.

53. Hobart McNeill to Semple, January 21, 1889. See also McNeill to Elijah Smith, January 22, 23, 1889, interoffice correspondence, Oregon Improvement Company Papers (hereafter cited as OIC Papers), University of Washington Library, Seattle.

54. Semple to McNeill, January 24, 1889.

McNeill. He promptly wired Hamilton for an explanation. The marshal confirmed the report. He insisted, however, that the deputies, although employees of the OIC, were under orders to take action only to protect the mail. Conveniently, this meant guarding not only the large company-owned building in which the post office was located, but also the corporation's railroad trestle, over which the mail passed in a company train. Hearing this, Semple concluded that McNeill had deliberately bypassed local law authorities and the governor so that company employees could be deputized by a federal marshal to protect private property. To this charge McNeill later swore that he had taken action only because Semple had not answered his telegram of January 21 "until about one week had elapsed." [55]

As the governor delved deeper into the matter he uncovered new information. In Seattle U. S. Attorney White, whose authority Marshal Hamilton had needed to deputize McNeill's guards, claimed that he had given the marshal no such power. Furthermore the guards turned out to be Sullivan "detectives" from Portland who were on the pay roll of the OIC.[56]

While these facts were coming to light Newcastle remained relatively peaceful. The question was, did the calm exist because of the presence of the Sullivan men or in spite of it? Sheriff Cochrane believed the latter was true. Neither McNeill nor Hamilton had notified him prior to the deputizing of the Sullivan agents. The agents were therefore acting illegally, he contended, and were a menace to the safety of the community. They had already allegedly halted and molested some townspeople, including several school children whose lunch baskets had been seized and searched for concealed weapons. Cochrane said many of the detectives were escaped criminals whose behavior had provoked some of the town's residents to petition Semple and President Grover Cleveland in protest over the presence of the outside force. With the testimony of White and Cochrane to sustain him, Semple wrote to United States Attorney General Augustus H. Garland on February 11 to ask for a federal investigation of Hamilton's actions—especially his refusal to inform Semple about the Sullivan detectives.[57]

55. Semple to T. J. Hamilton, January 26, 1889; and "Trouble in the Coal Mines, 1889; Documents of an Incident at Newcastle, W. T.," *Pacific Northwest Quarterly*, 37 (July 1946): 234, 246, 254-55.
56. William White to Semple, February 1, 1889; "Trouble in the Coal Mines," p. 236; McNeill to Smith, January 22, 1889, OIC Papers.
57. Cochrane to Semple, January 31, 1889; "Trouble in the Coal Mines," pp.

In the inquiry that followed, Hamilton and McNeill attempted to justify themselves by saying that Cochrane had not wanted to furnish protection against what they believed was impending trouble. McNeill had been particularly exasperated by Cochrane's behavior and seemed convinced that the sheriff was on the side of the striking workers. "The sheriff has been keeping us all in the hottest kind of water every damned day and night," he had informed Elijah Smith, president of the Oregon Improvement Company, in New York late in January. McNeill added: "His work culminated yesterday when he went to Gilman mines, swore out 26 [warrants] one by the way for me, and one for U. S. Marshal Hamilton, and started to arrest all the deputies with the intention of taking them to Gilman for trial." As he also managed the OIC's Gilman mines, McNeill had at the last minute persuaded Prosecuting Attorney Henry Snively that any arrests would lead to bloodshed. Snively in turn had prevailed on Sheriff Cochrane to postpone what McNeill referred to as a "display of power and force." McNeill was certain that Cochrane had acted under orders from "his faction," that is, the Knights of Labor, and had had "his own grand jury" waiting to indict McNeill as soon as sufficient evidence was gathered.[58]

These accusations pale in comparison with McNeill's letters to Smith, which reveal the general manager's devious use of armed detectives as well as his manipulation of Marshal Hamilton. Several days *before* informing Semple of the possibility of violence, McNeill had telegraphed Sullivan in Portland to send men to Newcastle by Saturday, January 19, and had delayed asking the governor for help until the following Monday. When the men arrived, he had six of them "made U. S. deputy marshals," without informing Semple or Cochrane. A week later, when the sheriff made an attempt to arrest the guards, McNeill, in his own words to Smith, "induced the U. S. marshal to go up on the same train, take the position that his deputies were defending trestles and a mail route and talk him out of it, which was done."[59]

Unfortunately for Semple, none of these facts were available to him when Justice Department examiner Frank Crosthwaite arrived in the territory in February to investigate the events at Newcastle in response

233-35.

58. McNeill to Smith, January 31, 1889, OIC Papers.

59. Ibid., January 26, 1889.

to the governor's letter to Garland. Neither McNeill nor Hamilton made any reference to Sullivan's imported "detectives" in their affidavits to Crosthwaite. Nor did Colonel Haines, who stated only that certain men who were on the company pay roll had been deputized, solely to guard the mail.[60]

The line between public and private interests grew even dimmer with the testimony of the acting postmaster of Newcastle, Thornton Goldsby, whose salary was paid by the OIC. Goldsby declared that he had helped persuade Hamilton to deputize the Sullivan agents and some other men loyal to the firm—but only to safeguard the mail. Hamilton, when asked by Crosthwaite why he had acted without any legal directive from U. S. Attorney White, stated that White had been absent when he tried to contact him and that White's assistant, Charles Munday, had given him verbal authorization to deputize anyone he felt might be useful at Newcastle in maintaining order.[61]

In his own statements to the Justice Department, Semple condemned the OIC for not relying on local and territorial law enforcement units, since the duty of keeping peace belonged to sheriff's officers and territorial militia, not private armies. As for the OIC's contention that federal and not local laws were involved in a rumored threat to the mail, Semple pointed out that rumors did not constitute infractions of the law. Furthermore, by Hamilton's own admission, the deputies were carried on the company pay roll—not on the pay roll of the federal government. They were therefore private employees, not public servants. The whole episode raised "a presumption of bad faith on the part of the Marshal," Semple said.[62]

Crosthwaite did not agree. "I am of the opinion that the Marshal acted in good faith in appointing the deputies," he concluded in his report to Attorney General Garland. He added, however, that on "the question as to whether the marshal did in this instance exceed his authority or not I do not pretend to pass upon."[63] On this ambivalent and inconclusive note the Justice Department dismissed Semple's charges against Hamilton and closed the inquiry.

The Oregon Improvement Company's assumption that labor constituted merely another tool of production was perhaps as prevalent

60. The testimony is contained in "Trouble in the Coal Mines," pp. 243-49, 254-57.
61. Ibid.
62. Ibid. pp. 253-54.
63. Ibid. p. 251.

an attitude in Washington Territory as elsewhere. Such a supposition often left little room for recognition of the workingman's demands. On the contrary, labor's disruptive activities made men like McNeill all the more eager to cut costs. When the Newcastle trouble at one point threatened to spread to Franklin, he urged Smith to "lease Newcastle to an outside crowd at a low price, let them install Negroes and thus put Franklin into line." He hoped thereby to unload the troublesome Newcastle enterprise, at least temporarily, and intimidate the Franklin miners with the threat of replacement by cheap black labor. "With labor as it is, I can save you my salary a good many times over," he boasted. "If I could control this labor. . . to only a reasonable extent it would reduce the net cost at the mines of all coal shipped one dollar per ton."[64] Smith balked at the idea of importing black workers; but across the Cascades at Roslyn, Negro miners remained at work for several years under strained circumstances which eventually led to their replacement by white men. [65]

Labor strife in Washington Territory reached a climax during Semple's two-year administration. By 1889 the tradition of violence which the Molly Maguires had introduced in the coal fields of Pennsylvania had become firmly rooted in the Northwest. So too had management's antidote, the Sullivan agent and the strikebreaker. In the struggles at Roslyn and Newcastle management had temporarily prevailed. But with the admission of Washington to the Union in November 1889, a new state government embraced Semple's recommendation of the previous year when it outlawed the use of armed guards by private companies.[66]

In other mining regions of the West the same pattern of industrial unrest continued through the 1890's as the Knights of Labor declined and gave way to more militant and radical organizations like the Western Federation of Miners and the Industrial Workers of the World (IWW). In Washington Territory, Semple had exercised an ineffectual, though well-intended, authority in the continuing struggle between labor and management by insisting that territorial militia and local lawmen did not exist to do the bidding of nervous corporations. By taking this position, he focused attention on the conflict between federal and local jursidictions and, more importantly, on the need for

64. McNeill to Smith, February 12, 1889, OIC Papers.
65. *History of Central Washington,* p. 252.
66. Washington State Constitution, Article I, Section 24.

better law and better law enforcement in the territory. His dilemma as governor anticipated similar problems that arose during the Homestead and Pullman strikes a few years later. At Pullman, in particular, the conflict between federal and state authorities was personified in the clash between Governor John Altgeld and President Cleveland, much as it had been at Roslyn and Newcastle by actors performing on a smaller stage. Although Semple had generally taken a narrow view of his legal powers as territorial governor, he had not compromised his office by using it for the interests of either labor or management. Given the limited powers at his disposal and the problems attending the rapid development of the territory during his governorship, perhaps few men could have done more.

8. Dabbling in State Politics

On April 9, 1889, a Walla Walla banker named Miles Moore replaced Eugene Semple as territorial governor. Moore's appointment coincided with the return of the Republican Party to power in national government. The appointment came as no great surprise, although the speed of its procurement was in marked contrast to Semple's own long-delayed nomination. The outgoing chief executive wished Moore "every success" as governor of "the great commonwealth." Moore reciprocated by expressing the hope that his administration would prove "as peaceful and successful as that of my predecessor."[1] (He was evidently ignorant of Semple's recent difficulties at the coal mines.)

The loss of the governorship did not remove Semple from the political stage. Even before Moore's inauguration Semple was mentioned as a possible Democratic candidate for *state* governor. Henry Tobin, a former Walla Walla city councilman, offered to support his candidacy with a five-hundred-dollar contribution if the governor would appoint him warden of the territorial penitentiary before leaving office. Semple indignantly rejected the proposition,[2] but Tobin had now raised the prospect of Semple's availability for the nomination. Others did too, and in spite of debts and family problems connected with the raising of his four children, which seemed to preclude any extensive campaigning, Semple consented to make his name available. "I have received so many intimations of the same sort," he told Tobin,

1. Semple to Moore, March 23, April 10, 1889; Moore to Semple, March 27, 1889, Semple Papers.
2. Tobin to Semple, February 27, March 11, 1889.

"that I suppose I will have to allow my name to be used for the Democratic nomination although I cannot enter a contest for it."[3]

In the months that followed, talk of the political candidates subsided as attention focused on the drafting of a state constitution. On February 22, 1889, Congress had passed the Omnibus Bill permitting the admission of Washington, Montana, and North and South Dakota to the Union. Shortly before Semple left office, Washington voters selected delegates to a constitutional convention which was to meet at Olympia on the Fourth of July. Most of the delegates chosen were Republicans, a fact which did nothing to cheer prospective Democratic candidates for the first state offices. Semple apparently took no part in the constitution-making that summer; newspaper accounts mention him only occasionally, and then with reference to the coming elections.[4]

Because they had dominated the constitutional convention, the Republicans looked ahead confidently to the elections on October 2. The election date left both parties little time for nominating and campaigning. The Republicans convened at Walla Walla on September 4 and chose Elisha P. Ferry of Seattle for governor on the first ballot.[5] Ferry had served eight years (1872-80) as Washington territorial governor—longer than any other western territorial chief executive. Moreover he had been out of the limelight long enough to be acceptable to the current factions within the party.

The Democrats, who gathered for their state convention a few days later, thus faced the task of finding a formidable candidate of their own. Local and county contests immediately after the constitutional convention had produced no consensus on a gubernatorial prospect, and Semple's name was just one of several mentioned. Since relinquishing the governorship in April, he had moved to Tacoma and established a small law practice, intent upon putting his financial affairs in order before openly seeking another public office. But inevitably Semple found himself being drawn back into politics. Four months after leaving office he wrote to a friend in New York: "I am doing all I can and will be on the stump whether I am nominated or not [even

3. Semple to Tobin, March 27, 1889. Part of Semple's Vancouver Sawmill was destroyed by fire on the morning of March 17, making it all the more imperative for him to devote his energies to business. (Semple to A. E. Isham, March 19, 1889).

4. Austin Mires, "Remarks on the Constitution of the State of Washington," *Washington Historical Quarterly*, 22 (1931): 276-88.

5. Seattle *Post-Intelligencer*, September 5, 1889.

though] my private affairs are in such bad shape that I ought to devote myself to them."[6]

The Tacoma Democratic primaries drew a heavy turnout. The local party favorite for governor turned out to be Hugh Wallace, who, according to the Seattle *Post-Intelligencer,* was really more interested in the nomination for Congress. As the state convention approached, Tobin's early prophecy concerning Semple's popularity began to be fulfilled. He won the endorsement of the large Lewis County delegation handily and might have carried Pierce County as well, had he not (inexplicably) alienated its representatives by failing to attend their convention.[7]

By the time the Democrats met at Ellensburg for their state convention, Semple was one of three leading contenders for the gubernatorial nomination. The other two were eastern Washington men: Chester H. Warner of Colfax, and J. J. Browne of Spokane. Warner, the chairman of the party central committee, had been an important participant in the constitutional convention. Browne was a banker and rancher. Neither man appeared to want the nomination. Rumors circulated that Browne was holding himself in readiness for the United States Senate should the Democrats somehow win control of the legislature. Warner, also looking to the future, simply had no interest in being associated with what looked like a losing ticket and did not even appear for the opening of the convention.[8] That seemed to leave the field to Semple, who was hardly the party favorite. Several Pierce County men flatly refused to support him, and the King County contingent endorsed first Browne and then former Tacoma mayor S. C. Wheelwright, rather than deliver the nomination to Semple

Eastern Washington Democrats felt differently about the former governor and pointed out, moreover, that no other prominent figure had yet emerged. Eventually this point prevailed with the majority, who awarded Semple the nomination. The *Post-Intelligencer* hastened to publicize the fact that he had received the party nod more or less by default. The front page headline declared: INTENSE NAUSEA

6. Semple to Floyd King, August 6, 1889.

7. *Post-Intelligencer,* September 6, 9, 1889.

8. Ibid., September 9, 1889. On Browne, see Clinton A. Snowden, *History of Washington: The Rise and Progress of an American State,* 4:295, 387. On Warner, see Bancroft, *Washington, Idaho, Montana,* p. 310; and Harvey K. Hines, *History of Washington,* pp. 760-61.

PRODUCED BY THE NOMINATIONS–THEY CAN'T STAND SEMPLE.[9]

Despite their lack of enthusiasm for the candidate, the Democrats adopted a campaign platform which articulated many of the sentiments Semple himself had espoused over the years. It included a resolution against Chinese labor, a demand for "swift and comprehensive" navigation improvements on the Columbia River, and a denunciation of the Republican Party "for its duplicity and violence toward the laboring masses. . . ." Other resolutions urged enactment of state laws "to serve and preserve the rights of the laborers," and to enforce the regular inspection of mines to insure the safety of workers.[10]

With its slate of officers picked and its platform drawn, the Democrats entered the abbreviated three-week election campaign with slight hope of victory. Republican optimism was correspondingly high. John F. Gowey, the state party committee chairman, confidently predicted a majority of ten thousand votes for Ferry. The *Post-Intelligencer* was just as confident. It circulated a story that one of the delegates at Ellensburg had offered a one-thousand-dollar wager that Semple would not carry a single county on Puget Sound. There were no takers![11] The Republican hopes stemmed from the commanding 43 to 29 margin in delegates the party had enjoyed in the constitutional convention. This majority was not insurmountable, however, and the Democrats, led by Semple and congressional aspirant Thomas Griffitts of Spokane, campaigned vigorously.

On the inauspicious date of Friday the 13th of September, Semple delivered his first speech of the campaign in Vancouver. It was a short, mildly worded oration keyed to local interests: a tariff high enough to protect the local lumber industry and federal money for navigation improvements along the lower Columbia.[12] Things were more lively the next night in Chehalis. Young Griffitts was on hand and lived up to his reputation as a rousing speaker.[13] Amid the rhetoric and cider, Semple's own remarks garnered polite applause. On the following Thursday night, after accusations by the local Republican press that the

9. *Post-Intelligencer,* September 9, 10, 11, 1889.

10. Ibid., September 15, 1889.

11. Gowey to Ferry, September 1, 1889, Elisha Ferry Papers, Manuscripts Division, University of Washington Library; *Post-Intelligencer,* September 11, 1889.

12. Vancouver (Washington) *Register,* September 14, 1889.

13. *Post-Intelligencer,* September 15, 1889.

two candidates were evading the real issue (the tariff question!), Semple and Griffitts spoke in Seattle. A big, enthusiastic crowd of Democrats greeted the pair at the Armory. The unexpectedly large reception acted as a tonic on Semple, who boasted to his audience that he would win by a comfortable margin in October and that a Democratic landslide would eradicate the Republicans "like a Kansas cyclone." He concentrated most of his fire on the corporations of the territory for their unauthorized use of imported private guards as deputy marshals and their intimidation of unions. In the way of constructive reform proposals, however, he had little to offer, and the remainder of his address was a blustering but uninspired recitation of the party platform. The *Post-Intelligencer* dismissed his remarks as "the twaddle of a demagogue" and reserved its measured approval for Griffitts, a young man whose oratorical talents had earned the newspaper's respect.[14]

As the contest moved into its final days Semple's campaign itinerary led him into eastern Washington. Meanwhile his fitness for office was called into question during a heated political debate in Seattle the Saturday before election day. Ostensibly the debate was to allow leaders and candidates of the two major parties to discuss issues. Instead it quickly degenerated into a session of name-calling. During one exchange, Democrats charged that the Republican nominee for the state supreme court, Theodore Stiles, had evaded military service during the Civil War. Here, John Haines (whose part in the Newcastle disturbances has been noted) hopped to his feet to assert that Semple too had been guilty of "packing up" and leaving Missouri for the Pacific Coast during the Civil War when still an "able-bodied young man."[15] Haines's remarks drew a moment of surprised silence and then angry rebuttal. The "debate" continued in this manner until the meeting was adjourned, with Semple's honor unredeemed.

The campaign trail ended for Semple two nights later in Spokane where for once he outperformed Griffitts on the rostrum by reiterating the party platform in forceful language and appealing for a heavy turnout at the polls the following day. That latter wish, at least, was granted.[16]

The election returns of October 2 confirmed Republican optimism. Party chairman John Gowey's forecast of a ten-thousand-vote majority

14. Ibid., September 20, 1889.
15. Ibid., September 29, 1889.
16. Ibid., October 2, 1889.

for Ferry was very nearly accurate. The G.O.P. swept all of the other major offices as well. Semple led the Democratic ticket, garnering 24,732 votes while holding Ferry's winning total to 33,711, the lowest of any of the many Republican victors. Even so, Semple was a badly beaten candidate. Out of a total of 34 counties, he won only three, Skamania, Franklin, and Clallam. All three were lightly populated, and in both Skamania and Clallam his margin was only ten votes. In the large counties, he lost decisively. King County voters gave Ferry forty-three hundred votes and Semple less than fourteen hundred, while Spokane County turned him down by nearly a three to two margin. His home county, Pierce, was hardly more charitable; it rejected him by nearly seven hundred votes. And in Clark County, where Semple still maintained a residence, he polled only half as many ballots as his Republican adversary. [17]

In defeat, Semple harbored no grudge nor any serious reservations about his recent opponent's capabilities as the first governor of the state. "To be the first governor of a great state like Washington is an honor which any mortal might feel proud of," he wrote Ferry two days before the latter's inauguration. "Permit me to extend my hearty congratulations to you upon your election to that high office by the vote of your fellow citizens and to wish you a peaceful and prosprous [sic] administration." [18]

On this amiable note the first gubernatorial election in the state's history came to an end. It was not, however, Semple's last foray into Washington politics. In 1892 he was again mentioned as a Democratic prospect for the governorship during the flurry of preconvention talk. Semple had moved to Seattle after his defeat in 1889 and had become an outspoken member of the state harbor line commission. In the summer of 1892, opponents of the fast-rising J. Hamilton Lewis began beating the drum for Semple in an effort to halt the Lewis drive to capture the King County delegation and with it a strong claim on the gubernatorial nomination at the state convention. Semple revealed little interest at first, insisting that he and Lewis were "good personal friends" and that the race was only a friendly contest between his supporters and those of Lewis. [19] But in the weeks that followed, his

17. Election returns, 1889, in "Abstract of Votes Polled in the Territory and State of Washington, 1865-1950," on microfilm in the Newspaper and Microcopy Division, University of Washington Library.

18. Semple to Ferry, November 16, 1889, Ferry Papers.

19. Tacoma *Daily Ledger,* July 31, 1892.

enthusiasm for the nomination increased as backers assured him he was gaining in popularity and could win the King County endorsement, and perhaps more. "If I carry King County," he told his daughter Ethel, "I will certainly get the nomination and. . . if I am nominated there is a general impression that I will be elected."[20] Actually, Semple's election was probably never seriously considered by those party regulars who supported him. Their intention was to use him to prevent Lewis from winning the King County slate, a fact to which Semple seemed strangely oblivious. His unwitting role as a counterweight to Lewis was negligible, however, for the dashing young orator with the flowing pink beard and flamboyant attire won nearly all of the 86 county delegates. It was the first big step on a.long political road that would one day lead to his election as United States Senator from Illinois.[21]

Contrary to Semple's prediction, the choice of the King County contingent did not receive the nomination in the state convention at Olympia after all. Suspicious eastern Washington delegates linked Lewis with Seattle plans for a costly federal ship canal into Lake Washington and feared the scheme might empty the pork barrel for years to come. Seeing his way blocked by strong regional opposition, Lewis reluctantly yielded and threw his support to Henry Snively of Ellensburg, who eventually received the nomination over Chester Warner, the first choice of the eastern Washington delegates.[22]

On election day many disgruntled Seattle Democrats retaliated by crossing party lines to vote for the winning Republican candidate, John McGraw, a local man who strongly endorsed the canal. McGraw's election had a bearing on Semple's own career, for it ushered in a new administration which would soon cut short the dedicated work of the first state harbor line commission, whose public interests Semple had made his own.

20. Semple to Ethel Semple, August 5, 1892.

21. *Post-Intelligencer,* August 7, 1892; *Biographical Directory of the American Congress, 1774-1961,* p. 1216; and Meany Pioneer File (s.v. Lewis), Northwest Collection, University of Washington Library.

22. *Post-Intelligencer,* August 25, 1892; and George Hazzard to Daniel H. Gilman, August 5, 1892, Daniel H. Gilman Papers, Manuscripts Division, University of Washington Library.

9. The Harbor Line Commission

Probably no other issue during the constitutional convention of 1889 attracted more attention among the business community of Puget Sound than the disposal of harbor tidelands. Long before Semple joined the new state harbor line commission, these lands had become valuable properties. Their worth continued to rise as the commerce of Seattle and Tacoma expanded during the late territorial period. By 1890 dozens of wharves and warehouses extended in an irregular manner from the mainland out over the tidal areas and into the deep waters of the Sound. Although these structures were necessary adjuncts to commerce, they cluttered the waterfronts, especially at Seattle, and were hazards to ships entering and leaving port. This situation precluded the use of much of the shore line for public streets, terminals and other facilities. It also hindered the implementation of any comprehensive public program of tideland reclamation and harbor improvement to accommodate future commercial development. The problem was complicated at Seattle by the fact that the available shore frontage offered only limited space for commercial expansion, owing to the way the local hills hugged Elliott Bay.

Various methods of land acquisition contributed to the confused situation. By gaining control of local lines like the Puget Sound Shore Line Railroad, for example, the Northern Pacific Railroad had gained access to the tidelands and claimed dubious rights as riparian owners.[1] Municipal donations to railroads like the Seattle, Lake Shore, and Eastern alienated other waterfront real estate. Still other shorelands,

1. Nesbit, *Burke*, p. 104.

such as Henry Yesler's mill property at the foot of Columbia, Cherry, and James streets, had been pre-empted during the days of earliest settlement. Another means by which settlers occupied tidelands and adjacent plots in the years before statehood was through the issuance of Valentine Scrip. These certificates, authorized by Congress in 1872, enabled persons who surrendered their land to the government at one place to relocate on unsurveyed, unreserved land elsewhere.[2]

Many delegates to the constitutional convention correctly argued that the tidelands had been misappropriated. The new state, they pointed out, had the right to control harbor areas and adjacent tidelands and ought to do so. But how? Delegates from the arid regions of the state favored permanent public ownership of all waterfront needed for general use; the remainder might be sold or leased. Riparian land users insisted, on the contrary, that the exigencies of commerce obligated the state to give initial rights of purchase or lease to those parties already in control of tideflats and harbor frontage.[3] Thus the line was drawn between private and public interests over the fate of hundreds of millions of dollars' worth of state tidelands and harbor areas.

After much debate, a compromise emerged in Article XVII of the state constitution, which declared the state's ownership of the shores of all navigable waters affected by tides up to and including the line of ordinary high tide. It also asserted state title to the shorelands of all navigable rivers and lakes up to the normal high water line. Although this satisfied the eastern Washington contingent, they were hardly delighted with the proviso added to Section 1: "This section shall not be construed so as to debar any person from asserting his claim to vested rights in the courts of the state." In short, the proviso rendered the first parts of the article ineffectual.

Having defaulted on the tideland question, the delegates turned to consider a related problem, the establishment of harbor lines. Here too there were flaws in what they wrought. Article XV of the state constitution provided that no rights could be sold or leased in the area beyond a designated outer harbor line. But within the public harbor area bounded by this line and an inner harbor line, the state could grant

2. *U.S. Statutes at Large*, Vol. 17 (1871-73), 42d Cong., 2d sess., pp. 649-50; and Thomas Donaldson, *The Public Domain: Its History with Statistics*, House Executive Document No. 47, Pt. 4, 46th Cong., 3d sess., p. 290.
    3. An account of the contest for control of the tidelands from the viewpoint of the squatter is in Nesbit, *Burke*, pp. 308-42.

leases for periods of up to thirty years, while retaining permanent ownership. These stipulations were clear enough, but it was less certain exactly where the harbor lines were to be placed. According to Article XV, Section 1, the area reserved by the state within the two harbor lines could be any width between 50 and 600 feet and might even extend in to the line of ordinary high tide. The power to locate these important lines was vested, under Article XV, in a board of harbor line commissioners.[4] Considering the use to which the tidelands had been put, this commission was in a position to expropriate much valuable waterfront for public port facilities and waterways, according to where it chose to locate the harbor lines. Whatever action its members took, the commission was certain to alienate some influential capitalists.

In 1890 the first state legislature made further provisions concerning harbor lines. After weeks of debate, the lawmakers agreed, in the closing days of the session, to allow the sale of all state tidelands except those reserved in harbor areas. Then they passed a measure which implemented Article XV by directing the governor to appoint a five-member harbor line commission. The bill was signed by Governor Ferry on March 28, 1890. The new law gave the first Washington harbor line commission broad powers.[5] It was authorized to locate lines in navigable waters of all harbors, bays, and inlets of the state that lay in front of the corporate limits of any city, and/or within one mile on either side. To accomplish this sizable task, however, the legislature appropriated a meager six hundred dollars plus five dollars per diem and a travel allowance for each member of the commission. Time as well as money was in short supply. In the first place, many tidelands could not be platted and sold until the commission determined harbor lines. Second, there was the likelihood of costly and lengthy litigation

4. Article XV, Section 1 of the Washington State Constitution defined the harbor lines and the powers of the harbor line commission as follows: "The legislature shall provide for the appointment of a commission whose duty it shall be to locate and establish harbor lines in the navigable waters of all harbors, estuaries, bays and inlets of this state, wherever such navigable waters lie within or in front of the corporate limits of any city or within one mile thereof on either side. The state shall never give, sell or lease to any private person, corporation or association any rights whatever in the waters beyond such harbor lines, nor shall any of the area lying between any harbor line and the line of ordinary high tide, and within not less than fifty feet nor more than six hundred feet of such harbor line (as the commission shall determine) be sold or granted by the state, nor its rights to control the same relinquished, but such area shall be forever reserved for landings, wharves, streets and other conveniences of navigation and commerce."

5. *Session Laws of the State of Washington* (1890), p. 240.

involving property holders whose wharves and other structures jutted beyond an inner harbor line (or, to look at it from the point of view of the landholder, whose property was cut through by an inner harbor line). Third, the commission had been given a short life span; its powers were to expire on January 5, 1893.

Governor Ferry had difficulty finding five suitable individuals to serve on the commission. Business groups who feared the presence of an overzealous public spirit on the board brought forward their own favorites. One was William Visscher, editor of the Tacoma *Globe,* an organ of the Northern Pacific Railroad, which had thousands of dollars invested in that city's waterfront.[6] Ferry rejected such persons and turned to more substantial candidates, particularly from among those who had debated the tidelands question in the constitutional convention. But the political hazards associated with an appointment to the board were apparently greater than the rewards, and many prominent figures in Washington Republican politics declined to serve. George Turner of Spokane refused in spite of his interest in the issue at the convention. According to the Seattle *Post-Intelligencer,* a term on the commission might have destroyed his chance to win a seat in the United States Senate. Two former territorial delegates, Thomas Brents of Walla Walla and Orange Jacobs of Seattle, also declined to serve when asked, as did Semple's successor as territorial governor, Miles Moore.[7] Nevertheless, by July 1890, Ferry had succeeded in making four of the five appointments. None of them were figures of statewide prominence but all appeared capable and reasonably free of strong partisan ties. Two of the appointees, Dayton banker Dennis Guernsey and Colonel William Prosser of Yakima, represented sentiment among inland residents. The other pair, D. F. Garretson of Tacoma and Frank H. Richards of Whatcom, spoke for the tidewater communities.[8] As his fifth appointment, Ferry chose Semple. His reason for doing so is not clear, since there is no evidence in Semple's correspondence to indicate he sought the position. The offer may simply have been a recognition of sorts bestowed by Ferry on his recently defeated Democratic rival.

Semple was involved at the time of his appointment in real estate promotions at Anacortes and Blaine and was enjoying no more success

6. Nelson Bennett to Ferry, January 11, 1890, Governors' Papers (s.v. Elisha Ferry), Washington State Archives, Olympia.

7. Seattle *Post-Intelligencer,* July 10, 1890.

8. Ibid., July 14, 1890; Governors' Papers (s.v. Ferry), Washington State Archives.

in land speculation there than he had had twenty years earlier in Portland. With three teen-age daughters still to support, he was in real need of cash. "The children are as brave and good as they can be," he told Lucy. "They bare [sic] our hard fare and poor quarters and stay alone while I am away on business. . . . Maude goes out a good deal but our house is so poorly furnished that she does not like to have people call on us."[9] Semple accepted the appointment and the added income that went with it.

The first Washington State Harbor Line Commission held its initial business meeting on July 25, 1890, in Seattle. Prosser, an advocate of state control of tidelands, was elected chairman.[10] He soon began correspondence with California port authorities for advice on drawing harbor lines at Seattle. The California port commissioners, basing their opinions on long experience at San Francisco, urged the Washington commission to establish the maximum 600-foot-wide harbor area authorized by the state constitution. Even this was barely adequate, they argued, for at San Francisco a harbor reserve of 850 feet was no longer considered sufficient to handle the expanding trade of the city.[11]

Opposition to the work of the commission arose in Seattle at once. Prosser soon found himself indulging in verbal combat in the editorial pages of the local newspapers with one of the leading capitalists of the city, Thomas Burke. Burke charged the board with holding secret meetings to establish harbor lines through private property, and branded Prosser "an ignorant carpetbagging office-holder." The commission's "star chamber" proceedings, Burke said, constituted a "monstrous outrage" and an attempt to "pillage and plunder Seattle and its citizens." Prosser retorted in kind, denouncing his antagonist as "a liar and a hired man of the corporations," striving to protect a million-dollar investment in water front property.[12] The fact that the board had not held any secret meetings made no difference to the Seattle press. The newspapers charged that the commission had tried to confiscate valuable property, thereby violating the intent of the legislature, which, as they saw it, was to protect those who had

9. Semple to Lucy Ames, February 13, 1890.
10. Record of the Proceedings of the Harbor Line Commission (MS copy in State Archives, Olympia), pp. 3-4.
11. Washington State Harbor Line Commission, *First Report,* p. 21.
12. *Post-Intelligencer,* October 30, November 23, 1890. There is no evidence in the commission reports or minutes to substantiate Burke's charges.

"improved" the harbor areas. The situation was no more promising in Tacoma, where the commission also had work to do. "At Tacoma," Semple warned Prosser, "the press will be more solidly against us than here because corporation influence there is farther reaching."[13]

Amid charges that the commission was determined to seize private holdings for public use, the board held several open meetings at Seattle during August, September, and October to hear testimony from all parties: city councilmen, chamber of commerce speakers, land holders, and government and private engineers. Meanwhile the commission's own engineer at Seattle, Richard Nevins, Jr., spent two and a half months surveying the six miles of city waterfront over which the harbor boundaries were to be located.[14] On October 28 the board announced its decision regarding the location of the Seattle harbor lines. Over the strenuous objections of many local businessmen, the commission decided to reserve the maximum 600-foot-wide strip for public use, placing the outer line at a 50-foot average depth at low water. This meant that the inner harbor line would fall partly along an imaginary line halfway between high and low tide and partially on the meander line of an old federal survey.[15]

These decisions had been influenced considerably by the testimony of Colonel William P. Craighill of the United States Army Corps of Engineers. According to Semple and his fellow commissioners, Craighill was "the best authority in the United States, if not in the world, on the subject of harbor lines and improvements."[16] His testimony before the commission emphasized that the inner boundary ought to be identical with either the meander line or the line of high water. Moreover, he asserted that the width between the lines should, ideally, be no less than 950 to 1,000 feet. The colonel's words were buttressed by reports solicited by Prosser, Semple, and other board members from port authorities throughout the United States and Great Britain. The consensus was that there should be as much public control over harbors as possible. San Francisco furnished perhaps the best lesson on the relative merits of lax and rigid public regulation of harbor facilities. The California city had leased its wharves and piers from 1850 to 1863. Graft, neglect, and mismanagement had resulted to such an extent that

13. Seattle *Telegraph*, October 28, 1890; *Post-Intelligencer*, October 29, 1890; Semple to Prosser, July 23, 1891
14. *First Report*, pp. 25-26.
15. Ibid.
16. Ibid., p. 24.

the state finally terminated the leases. A state board of harbor commissioners had then been created to regulate the use of the waterfront and to draw new harbor lines. Angry waterfront property holders had retaliated by preventing the state from reasserting full authority for several years through costly and lengthy litigation.[17]

Despite these arguments, many people, especially in Seattle, objected to the proposed harbor boundaries. Their alarm was understandable. If the boundaries were established and upheld by the courts, the resulting provisions of state ownership would undoubtedly disturb the pattern of commercial development. The area enclosed by the proposed lines included two miles of Railroad Avenue, a valuable artery along the waterfront, as well as 35 piers which extended from the avenue into deep water. The value of such property was immense. As an example, part of the Yesler wharf, 150 feet in width, had recently been bought by the Northern Pacific for $175,000. At a equivalent value (admittedly exaggerated) the six-mile Seattle waterfront in 1890 would have been worth approximately $37 million.[18]

Opponents of the projected harbor zone were led by Burke and John Haines, attorneys representing the Great Northern and Northern Pacific railroads, respectively. Both lines controlled substantial amounts of property along the waterfront. Backed by prominent Seattle residents like Henry Yesler, A. A. Denny, Robert Moran, and Hiram Gill, the two lawyers demanded that the width of the reserved harbor be reduced to 100 feet. As far as Semple and his colleagues on the commission were concerned, this request was an "utter absurdity," because the occupants of the areas in question were trespassers on public property in the first place.[19]

By late October the adversaries of the commission had become convinced that the board could not be dissuaded from its decision to establish the maximum harbor area. As a result, they turned to the courts for assistance, and got it. On October 29, twenty-four hours before the commission was to submit its harbor line recommendations and Nevins' accompanying survey maps to the state, King County Superior Court Judge I. J. Lichtenberg issued an injunction in behalf of the attorneys of Henry Yesler, ordering the commission to take no further action to establish the lines until the court held hearings on the

17. Ibid., pp. 21-22.
18. Ibid., p. 25.
19. Ibid., p. 13.

matter. On the following day Lichtenberg issued another injunction on behalf of the Stimson Mill Company. Enjoinders were also granted on request of the Columbia and Puget Sound Railroad, the Seattle, Lake Shore and Eastern Railroad, and Schwabacher Brothers and Company, all of which occupied waterfront property. In the case of the Columbia and Puget Sound Railroad, the company claimed that the commission's plat, if filed, would expropriate coal bunkers worth three hundred thousand dollars.[20]

The squatters based their claims on two arguments. The first was that owners of land adjacent to tideflats also owned riparian right of way through tidelands out to deep water. They were thus entitled, they said, to compensation for that right from the state. This contention seemed to challenge the traditional assumption that the state exercised jurisdiction over tidelands. The second argument advanced by the adjacent landholders was that they were entitled to first rights to purchase tidal plots under a legislative act of March 26, 1890. But this statute hardly overruled the constitutional provision for state expropriation or leasing of tidelands. Both contentions thus seemed to rest on shaky ground, and Semple in particular was eager to bring the cases before judicial review at the earliest date, confident the hearings could only strengthen the position of the commission. He counseled Prosser accordingly:

What we should do now is to assume the aggressive in the courts and move to dissolve the injunctions *at once.* What the plaintiffs want is *delay* and what we want is to have this matter heard *on its merits* as soon as possible. I have examined the question and there is not, in my opinion, a single inch of ground for them to stand on from a legal standpoint. If any man desires to come in even now in good faith to propose a reasonable modification of our line I would be in favor of hearing him, but so long as they maintain their *preposterous* position . . . I am in favor of advancing on them. Believing that further delay is dangerous to the interests of the people whom we represent, I respectfully request you to convene the board at Seattle as soon as possible.[21]

Semple's assessment of the opposition's strategy was accurate. Aided by the courts, the commission's adversaries played for time, hoping perhaps for some eventual legislative or judicial action that would nullify the board's work. Following an initial three-week delay of hearings on the harbor line cases, attorneys for the plaintiffs persuaded

20. Seattle *Telegraph,* October 30, 1890. A detailed summary of the above litigation is given in the *First Report,passim.*
21. Semple to Prosser, November 12, 1890.

state Attorney General W. C. Jones to authorize a further postponement. Judge Lichtenberg then arbitrarily announced another postponement of four weeks, resetting the hearings for December 18.[22] In the meantime Semple had asked Prosser for authority to assist Jones in presenting the case for the state. Prosser agreed.[23] Jones then filed a motion to quash the writs of injunction, but before action was taken on his motion, the hearings were held. At their conclusion, Lichtenberg took the cases under advisement. By the end of the year, as the commission prepared its first annual report to the governor and the legislature, the judge still had rendered no decision on any of the cases.[24]

Lichtenberg's actions convinced Semple that the powers of the commission would have to be broadened. At its December meeting he urged the members to request legislation empowering them to do the following: locate harbor boundaries on each side of all future waterways to be established; stop condemnation of harbor area for private use without state authorization; and reserve a 300-foot-wide zone along each side of the Duwamish River and Smith's Cove waterways in Seattle.[25] The commission approved these recommendations and made several others in its first report to the state government. The most important was a request for "a complete and comprehensive system of permanent and substantial [harbor] improvements" to be prepared and adopted by the commission after the platting of harbor lines. To finance this ambitious program, the board recommended the use of half the revenues from state tideland sales and all revenues from areas leased within harbor boundaries. It also asked for authority to eject individuals and corporations "trespassing" on areas within harbor lines, and for penalties for those violators. Finally, the board requested more state money for operating expenses and a legislative memorial to Congress for federal funds to

22. Lichtenberg had been elected the first superior court judge in King County in 1889, two years after his arrival in Seattle. He was a Democrat. He does not appear to have held property on the tidelands but no doubt had his reasons for supporting the Burke forces so consistently. See Hines, *Illustrated History of Washington,* pp. 393-94. Jones was actually in sympathy with the commission's work. He is not to be confused with Wesley Jones, later a senator from Washington state.

23. Semple to Prosser, November 12, 1890; Semple to Jones, November 19, 1890.

24. *First Report,* pp. 26-28.

25. Semple to Prosser, December 27, 1890; Prosser to Semple, December 29, 1890.

pursue the recommended program of harbor improvements.[26] Governor Ferry approved the commission report, endorsed the suggestions, and ordered one thousand copies printed.[27] In his message to the legislature he criticized the law which had created the first harbor line commission as "ambiguous, unsatisfactory and uncertain" and suggested that the statute be amended and strengthened. For guidelines, he referred the lawmakers to the board's first annual report. [28]

In January 1891 Judge Lichtenberg, who had taken the harbor line cases under advisement in December, announced that he was making his October restraining orders permanent. Seattle newspapers supported the decision. Semple did not think the ruling could stand, and told Prosser why: "Those who' desire to gobble up the people's lands must attack the whole system for it is hinged together so that it cannot be attacked in detail. I do not believe they can overthrow the whole system but we should be vigilant nevertheless. I think therefore that we should assemble at Olympia immediately . . . and take steps to see that the legislature is fully advised."[29]

Accordingly, the board shifted its attention to the legislature. On January 28 state Senator Frank Richards of Whatcom, one of the five harbor line commissioners, introduced a bill for harbor improvements. The measure incorporated the board's recommendation that it be given control over these improvements. The bill also allocated 75 percent of the funds from state tideland sales to finance the work. The measure, after being amended slightly by the lower house, passed the senate, 27-7. The house concurred by a 54-11 margin, after an unsuccessful attempt by the minority to reduce the 75 percent provision to 50 percent—which was all the commission had originally asked for anyway.[30] A second bill, introduced by Senator Henry Cooper, fared worse. It proposed to grant the board the power to begin proceedings in court to eject tideland trespassers and to levy penalties on parties who obstructed harbor areas that were under the commission's jurisdiction. Cooper, who was a member of the senate committee on harbors and harbor lines, steered the measure through the upper house but saw it die in the lower chamber. [31]

26. *First Report,* pp. 29-31.
27. Prosser to Semple, January 8, 1891.
28. Washington State Legislature, *Senate Journal* (1891), Appendix, p. 6.
29. Semple to Prosser, January 9, 1891.
30. *Senate Journal* (1891), pp. 297, 527, 533, 584, 597.
31. Ibid., pp. 432, 595; and Semple to Richards, February 28, 1891.

The net result of this legislative activity was an increase in the general power of the commission without any specific increase in its authority to deal with waterfront litigants. The closest thing to it was Section 4 of the new law, which stated that "all acts or parts of acts inconsistent with the provisions of this act are hereby repealed." But how this specifically affected individual property rights along the shore was unclear, and presumably a matter for the courts to resolve.

While the commission was prohibited by Lichtenberg's injunctions from doing more work at Seattle in the immediate future, it went ahead with surveys and harbor improvement plans at other Washington ports. Under the new harbor act, the board grouped the ports of the state into five districts and assigned to each commissioner the responsibility of supervising the survey of liens in one district. Of the nineteen harbors initially designated for survey, six, including Seattle, Ballard, and Vancouver, eventually came under Semple's jurisdiction. Except at Seattle and Ballard, his work went smoothly. Engineers hired by the board surveyed and mapped the other four harbors under his authority, at Blaine, Sidney, Vancouver, and Shelton. The work at Blaine, near the Canadian border, was completed first, on August 8, 1891. Tiny Shelton harbor, where surveys did not begin until late in September 1892, was mapped and platted in less than two weeks—in sharp contrast to the progress at Seattle.[32]

At Vancouver, in addition to supervising the location of harbor boundaries, Semple became involved in a project to improve the meager port facilities. The plan depended on federal and state assistance and was presented at the final commission meeting of 1891 by Garretson of Tacoma, who suggested that Prosser go to Washington, D. C., to obtain War Department support for the work at Vancouver and other state ports.[33] Soon thereafter, Vancouver residents also took action. "The people of this town have a plan for the improvement of their harbor and wish to have the authority of the Secretary of War to do it themselves," Semple told Richards. "They offered to send me to Washington and to pay my expenses," he added, "but . . . I suggested that they raise $500 here and that Bellingham Bay and Olympia each raise a similar amount and send Prosser to represent all three places."[34]

32. Washington State Harbor Line Commission, *First Biennial Report* (1893), Appendix, p. 107.

33. Ibid., p. 29.

34. Semple to Richards, January 14, 1892.

Vancouver, as Semple well knew, was not an easily accessible port. Shippers leaving and entering the small harbor were forced to navigate a treacherous bar. Even while local men were bemoaning their inadequate harbor, thousands of board feet of lumber destined for the Orient rotted on the wharves because the bar at that season of low water prevented deep draft vessels from reaching the town docks.[35] With this situation prevailing, Vancouver merchants quickly subscribed the money Semple had requested and in February 1892, with the authority of the commission behind him, Prosser traveled to the national capital with blueprints for the Vancouver harbor improvements in hand.[36]

The plan to renovate the port of Vancouver was largely Semple's inspiration. It called for the dredging of a channel from the main stream of the Columbia River to Vancouver harbor through the series of obstructive silt ridges which constituted the bar and which extended nearly a mile and a half below the city. These drifts of sediment reduced the depth of the only available channel into the waterfront to seven feet at low water. According to Semple's calculations, dredging would be aided by the Columbia's strong current which would carry the dislodged silt downstream and deposit it in deeper parts of the main channel some distance away.[37]

Mayor W. F. Daniels and other Vancouver residents were as sanguine about the scheme as its author. "It is beyond question that a port can be established here that will make Vancouver the most important harbor on the Columbia," a local citizens' committee informed Congress.[38] Refusing to await federal appropriations, the impatient Vancouverites collected money and began the work themselves until dredging costs and the difficulty of obtaining equipment forced them to halt.[39]

Meanwhile, Prosser was having problems with the War Department. "The pigheaded and overbearing obstinacy they... displayed was actually astounding and worthy of Burke and his confreres," he told

35. The shipping conditions at Vancouver were noted by Prosser in a letter to the War Department, January 16, 1892, in *First Biennial Report,* Appendix, p. 21.

36. Ibid., p. 112

37. Semple to Prosser, January 22, 1892; Semple to Vancouver Common Council, March 16, 1892.

38. Vancouver citizens' committee to Congress, January 26, 1892, Semple Papers.

39. Prosser to Semple, February 13, 1892.

Semple. Prosser nevertheless persevered, submitting copies of the plan to the War Department, the Corps of Engineers, and some interested congressmen.[40] Apparently his diligence paid off. In March, Secretary of War Stephen B. Elkins appointed a three-member board of army engineers (including Major Thomas Handbury, whom Semple had consulted earlier about the Vancouver port plans) to meet in Portland to examine the plans for harbor lines and improvements at Vancouver, Olympia, and Bellingham. Whether there would be any immediate financial aid from the federal government was uncertain, since the Rivers and Harbors Act of 1890 prohibited the War Department from undertaking any internal improvements without prior authorization by Congress.[41] In July, however, Congress appropriated $180,000 for federal river and harbor work in the state of Washington. It was an unexpectedly generous allocation, of which $33,000 (slightly more than the commission had requested) went for preliminary work at Vancouver.[42] Semple's plan for dredging a channel was modified substantially and incorporated in a broader scheme conceived by Major Handbury and authorized in the appropriation. Handbury's design emphasized construction of a diversion dam upstream from Vancouver to concentrate the flow of water in the main channel, thereby eroding the bar below Vancouver and opening a year-round deep water port. Semple's idea was thus relegated to secondary importance since construction of the dam would consume most of the appropriation for the next year or more.[43] After that, Handbury told Semple, it would be necessary to reassess any plans for dredging or other work.[44]

Semple cautioned Mayor Daniels that the government plan spelled long delays. Besides, he warned the mayor, the major's idea might not work; the river might not conform to human wishes that it sweep out a convenient channel for Vancouver shippers. He therefore urged the city fathers not to abandon his plan to dredge a course through the bar. He then offered his own services free of charge, exhorting local officials to proceed with the work at once, and without federal subsidies. After all, he reminded the mayor, the town would be eligible for reimbursement from state tideland revenues under the law he and the other commissioners had helped to enact the year before.[45]

40. Prosser to Semple, February 27, 1892.
41. *First Biennial Report,* Appendix, pp. 38, 39.
42. Ibid., pp. 20-21.
43. House Executive Document No. 36, 52d Cong., 2d sess.
44. Handbury to Semple, October 4, 1892.
45. Semple to Daniels, October 28, 1892.

Despite the early expectations of its supporters, Semple's plan for renovating Vancouver harbor was never carried out. His own explanation for this was that no adequate dredging machinery was available to do the work. Perhaps so, but in the long run, local apathy and government parsimony and red tape were probably more to blame. Nonetheless, in the years that followed, sporadic collaboration among federal, state and local groups did produce piecemeal improvements. By the early 1900s, the port possessed something approximating the deep water harbor Semple and the other commissioners had envisioned years earlier.

Long before the Vancouver plan was shelved, the harbor line commissioners had again become preoccupied with litigation. By March 1891, six restraining orders had been issued against the board, prohibiting it from establishing its proposed harbor lines at Seattle and elsewhere. Semple now became the commission's advocate as it sought to have the enjoinders revoked by higher courts. In March, state Attorney General Jones gave him authority to represent the state in its struggle to overthrow the injunction Judge Lichtenberg had granted in January.[46] Semple enlisted the aid of his new Seattle law partner, Julius Hale, and two other Seattle attorneys, John Wiley and W. T. Scott, and submitted an appeal to the state supreme court. In late March his position was strengthened when, in the case of *Eisenbach* v. *Hatfield,* the court upheld the right of the state to make harbor boundaries and port improvements over the claims of individual property holders. The decision abridged an 1854 territorial statute which gave squatters title to shore property for "improvements" they had made on that property. Furthermore, the court said the state was not obligated to compensate these parties when it confiscated improvements (i.e. wharves, piers, etc.) that lay beyond the high water mark.[47]

The harbor line commission's first victory against Seattle property holders came on July 5, 1891, when the state supreme court overruled Lichtenberg in the Yesler case.[48] Meanwhile, several similar disputes awaited the action of lower courts. The most important involved the Seattle, Lake Shore and Eastern Railroad, a Northern Pacific subsidiary

46. Jones to Semple, March 14, 1891.
47. Eisenbach v. Hatfield, *Washington Reports* (Kreider), 2:236.
48. Ibid. p. 530.

which had filed one of the first suits against the commission in October 1890. On this case Lichtenberg had already antagonized the commissioners by indefinitely postponing action. Accordingly, Semple asked Jones for permission to request the state supreme court to issue a writ of mandamus, ordering Lichtenberg to reach a decision.[49] Jones responded enthusiastically: "I most cheerfully authorize you to take such action as you think best and will leave management of that case entirely to you, trusting you will succeed in getting what you desire."[50] Semple took charge and presented the commission's position so forcefully that Lichtenberg issued a decision in favor of the board before the higher court could issue its writ.

This by no means ended the litigation. "I cannot see any conclusion of the suits pending except through the U.S. Supreme Court," Semple told Jones. "I do not think the U.S. Supreme Court will hear them on the merits but we will have to go there to have the appeals discussed."[51] His forecast was correct; the following year, still stalling for time until the term of the commission expired, Yesler's attorneys filed a writ of error in the United States Supreme Court. Their main contention was that the board's attempt to locate harbor lines at Seattle violated the due process clause of the Fourteenth Amendment and conflicted with the powers granted to the federal government by the Rivers and Harbors Act of 1890.[52] In the meantime, the Seattle, Lake Shore and Eastern took similar action at a lower level, appealing Lichtenberg's ruling to the state supreme court. The court decided to withhold judgment, pending the federal Supreme Court's decision in the Yesler case.

The only other major litigation at Seattle involved the Stimson Mill Company, in whose behalf Lichtenberg had granted one of his more or less permanent injunctions early in 1891. Once again, Semple asked the state supreme court to compel the judge to end the injunction, pointing out that Lichtenberg was obligated either to act on the case or yield jurisdiction.[53] Late in July the judge ruled against the board and Semple took the matter to the state supreme court on appeal. In March

---

49. Semple to Jones, July 30, 1891. Semple's old nemesis, Colonel John Haines, represented the Northern Pacific Railroad.

50. Jones to Semple, August 3, 1891.

51. Semple to Jones, July 22, 1891.

52. Washington State Harbor Line Commission, *Second and Final Report* (1893), pp. 8-10 (hereafter cited as *Second Report*).

53. Jones to Semple, July 27, 1891.

1892 the case came before the court with Semple on hand to represent the state and Burke in attendance on behalf of the company. The salient points raised by the Stimson Mill case concerned the definition of "navigable waters" in tidal bays and estuaries, and the explanation of "city" as used in the state harbor line and tidelands acts; that is, did the meaning of the word include all incorporated towns? While presenting the commission's arguments on the first point, Semple was aided by coincidence. As he talked, a large steamer entered the Olympia harbor in full view of those in the courtroom. Seizing the moment, Semple pointed out to the court what was otherwise obvious: that in a few hours, when the tide ebbed, land would be visible where the ship was now passing. No further argument was necessary; the court ruled that the commission had the right to extend its jurisdiction over land which, at high tide, becomes navigable water. The company's contention that the area in question represented "navigable waters" was declared invalid.[54] On the second question the court was emphatic. "To hold that the constitution makers and the legislature intended to draw the line strictly as between cities and towns," it stated, "would be to convict them of absurdity."[55] The court's decision in the Stimson Mill case represented a forceful endorsement of the authority of the commission. There was no appeal.

In the meantime at Tacoma, Hoquiam, and South Bend the commission encountered more litigation. Late in 1891 both the Northern Pacific Railroad and the Northwestern Lumber Company filed suits in the federal district court of Judge Cornelius H. Hanford to prevent the board from placing harbor lines over property claimed by the two corporations. At Tacoma the Northern Pacific argued that a federal land grant entitled it to a two-hundred-foot-wide strip of right of way along Commencement Bay. The area in question extended the entire length of the waterfront, with much of the company's railroad track resting on pilings built well beyond the line of high tide. As a result, the commissioners contended that the NP's claim to the property was invalid because the state constitution gave the board and not private corporations the authority to establish harbor areas and regulate seagoing commerce beyond the high tide line.[56] This did not stop Hanford from granting an injunction in behalf of the railroad, and

54. Semple related this episode to the commission in his report on April 4, 1892. See Semple Papers or *First Biennial Report*, Appendix, p. 110.

55. *Washington Reports* (Kreider), 4:6-11.

56. A summary of these cases is given in *First Biennial Report*, p. 16.

Elisha P. Ferry, ca. 1889

Colonel William F. Prosser

Will H. Parry, 1896

the commission appealed to the state supreme court. A decision was still pending when the term of the commission expired early in 1893.[57]

At Hoquiam in Chehalis County and at South Bend in Pacific County, the Northwestern Lumber Company also challenged the power of the harbor line commission in 1892. In the former area, the company argued that the Hoquiam River was not within the jurisdiction of either the town of Hoquiam or the commission because a narrow strip of land along the banks had been excluded from any legal description of the town limits. It further maintained that the commission had no right to designate harbor areas unless they were located in navigable waters of 20 feet or more at low tide.[58] Hanford issued an injunction against the commission at Hoquiam and later extended it to include a similar situation involving the company at South Bend.[59] Since both cases raised points parallel to the questions involved in the Yesler case, the litigants agreed to await the verdict of the Supreme Court before taking further action.

The long-awaited decision on the Yesler case by the high court—upon whose words Semple hoped to rest the commission's case once and for all—was delivered in December 1892. The court ruled that no federal question was presented and emphatically upheld the state supreme court on all points, as Semple had expected. The decision, delivered by Chief Justice Melville Fuller, affirmed that the state had not deprived Yesler of due process. It also asserted that no conflict existed between state and federal laws governing harbor lines, and that Yesler was entitled to no compensation since he did not own title to the land in question. Fuller's majority opinion in effect upheld the state supreme court's interpretation of the powers of the harbor line commissioners.[60]

But the decision turned out to be an empty victory for the commissioners; it came too late to offset the results of the November elections, which swept into office new men who were hostile to the board. Prosser, however, wrongly assumed that the Yesler verdict had created enough pressure to force the new legislature to renew the term of the harbor line commission. "I presume," he told Semple, "that the

57. Semple to Harbor Line Commission, January 14, 1893, Semple Papers. This was his final report to the commission.
58. Semple to Harbor Line Commission, January 6, 1892.
59. *Second Report,* pp. 13-14.
60. *U.S. Reports,* 146:646 ff. Jones presented the case of the commission before the court in October.

Yesler decision is all we require and that following that decision the other suits should be dismissed without delay." Semple was skeptical. "There is much difference of opinion here regarding the purport of the decision," he informed Prosser from Seattle.[61] That difference of opinion was manifested in the new legislature, where Seattle and Tacoma interests, backed by Republican governor-elect John McGraw, defeated Ferry's last efforts to extend the life of the commission.

Having disposed of the corpse, the lawmakers now consolidated the functions of the old commission under a new board of state land commissioners. This body consisted of three McGraw appointees and the elected commissioner of public lands, who was to serve as chairman.[62] The new commission hastily reset the harbor lines at Seattle and Tacoma, reserving only 300 feet of harbor area instead of the 600 feet recommended by the first harbor line commission.[63] This was accomplished—to the delight of many shore line property holders—by pushing the inner line far enough out into deep water to place it well beyond the end of any docks. "Human avarice and ingenuity have rarely devised a more effective method of plundering a whole people," Prosser noted bitterly.[64]

Although these concessions to private interests greatly reduced the public harbor area at Seattle and prompted property holders to drop their litigation against the state, not all of the squatters were yet appeased. As a result, the crucial inner line was pushed still further out into Elliott Bay during the mid-nineties. Moreover, McGraw's commissioners, all Puget Sound men, kept no record and made no report to the governor.[65] Such procedures stood in stark contrast to the work of the first commission, which had conducted extensive engineering studies and correspondence with other ports of the world and had evinced genuine concern for public interests.

In 1897 the struggle resumed between the advocates of strong state regulation of harbor facilities and the champions of private control. The Populist victories at the polls the previous November had brought to office many reform-minded individuals who were the political heirs of

61. Prosser to Semple, December 20, 1892; Semple to Prosser, December 22, 1892.

62. *Senate Journal* (1893), pp. 556, 745.

63. Washington State Land Commissioner, *Sixth Biennial Report* (1901), p. 18.

64. Tacoma *Daily Ledger*, February 20, 1893.

65. *Fourth Biennial Report*, p. 18.

men like Semple and Prosser on such issues as harbor use. In March the new legislators created an ex-officio board of harbor line commissioners consisting of the secretary of state, the superintendent of public instruction, and, most notably, the commissioner of public lands, Robert Bridges.[66] An ardent Populist who shared the philosophy of the original harbor line commission, Bridges sought to enforce the constitutional stipulation of a thirty-year lease on those harbor areas at Seattle which lay beyond piers but still remained within the recently redrawn inner harbor line. Uneasy claimants, fearing that the state might award this leasable area to unfriendly interests, or make the present occupants pay, raised the question of federal jurisdiction and petitioned Secretary of War Russell A. Alger. The pliant Alger responded by appointing a board of army engineers to examine the harbors of the state and reach a decision on the final location of harbor lines. The board acted by *bringing in* the inner harbor line to coincide with the pierhead line, thus thwarting Bridges' intentions by eliminating leasable harbor area between pierheads and the inner harbor line.[67] And so the same petitioners who had earlier pushed the inner line beyond their piers triumphed again by getting that same line brought back in.

In 1911, as commerce on Puget Sound increased, a need for better harbor facilities prompted the legislature belatedly to create the Seattle Port District. In order to obtain additional harbor space and facilities for public use, taxpayers compensated owners of shore line warehouses, terminals, and piers with more than six million dollars.[68] Had the advice of the first harbor line commission been heeded by public officials in 1890, much of this expenditure could have been saved.

In light of all these subsequent events, it seems remarkable that Semple and his colleagues should have failed to achieve their original objectives. Their labors in behalf of the public's interests had been endorsed by the United States Supreme Court, the first state governor, the first state legislature, the state supreme court, and the state constitution itself. Government engineers defended their work, as did port authorities in other states. On every important legal point the commission had been sustained. It had pursued an active, nonpartisan, and selfless program of harbor development and had platted harbor

66. Washington State Land Commissioner, *Fifth Biennial Report* (1898), p. 11.
67. Ibid., p. 12.
68. "The Port of Seattle, Fourth Anniversary," September 4, 1915. This is a pamphlet in the Northwest Collection, University of Washington Library.

boundaries at 19 of 23 designated ports. None of these accomplishments seemed to arouse an apathetic public. No consensus developed in support of the commission. There was no public outcry, at least not until long after the original harbor line board had ceased to exist. The First Washington State Harbor Line Commission failed, then, for a number of reasons, to protect the public's long range interests against the more immediate ambitions of private land holders. In spite of its laudable efforts, the commission constituted not an effective public regulatory board, but rather a commendable model for future state agencies charged with protecting and developing the region's great natural resources. For making it a model commission, Semple deserves much of the credit.

10. The Canal Scheme

Since the arrival of the first white settlers, the people of Seattle had been tantalized by the vision of a ship canal connecting Puget Sound with Lake Washington. In 1853, ten years before Semple's arrival in the Northwest, federal surveyors had recommended construction of such a waterway to hasten the maritime development of Seattle and to provide a fresh water harbor for American naval forces.[1] From that time forward, the inhabitants embraced the idea, proposing several routes into the lake and soliciting Congress for funds. In 1871 Major Thomas Handbury of the Army Corps of Engineers made extensive surveys and then recommended three routes. One skirted Beacon Hill at the southern end of Elliott Bay. A second extended from the northern end of the downtown waterfront near Smith's Cove through Lake Union. The third led from Shilshole Bay, north of the city, through Salmon Bay and Lake Union into Lake Washington.[2] All three routes lay over sparsely settled land, however, and Congress, not sure that the area's population growth would warrant construction of a canal, therefore refused to appropriate money.

Private interests took up the project in the 1880s. One company completed a small waterway connecting Lakes Union and Washington in 1886. During that same year the Washington Improvement Company began digging a ship canal between Puget Sound and Lake Washington

1. Neil H. Purvis, "The History of the Lake Washington Canal," *Washington Historical Quarterly*, 25 (1934) : 117-19. This chapter was published in a slightly modified version in the article, "Eugene Semple's Seattle Canal Scheme," *Pacific Northwest Quarterly*, 59 (1968) : 77-87.
2. Purvis, "Lake Washington Canal," pp. 117-19.

via Lake Union.[3] A lack of funds and an abundance of litigation, arising from attempts to purchase right of way, retarded the scheme until 1890 when the federal government again became involved. Congress authorized ten thousand dollars that year for a new survey, the results of which were contained in a report issued in 1892 by a three-member board of army engineers. Their findings were very similar to those of Major Handbury two decades earlier. The trio concluded that there were only three feasible routes: (1) from Shilshole Bay, (2) from Smith's Cove through Salmon Bay, and (3) from the southern Seattle tideflats *through* (rather than around) Beacon Hill. The engineers favored the first and second routes, primarily because they required the removal of considerably less material (twenty-seven million cubic yards less, it was estimated) than a waterway through the tidelands and Beacon Hill. A redeeming feature of the Beacon Hill, or southern, route, however, was that it provided the shortest passage directly from the waterfront into Lake Washington.[4]

The canal became an important issue in the 1892 election, and John McGraw of Seattle entered the governor's mansion firmly pledged to its completion. But while the new chief executive and many of his constituents talked enthusiastically about a government-subsidized canal via Shilshole Bay, Semple's attention had already become riveted on the more challenging and less popular tideland–Beacon Hill route. He was well acquainted with the potential value of these tidal areas as a result of his experience on the harbor line commission. The fact that the southern route passed over the tideflats gave him an inspiration: why not meet the cost of excavating a ship canal by allowing a private company to dig the canal and use the material removed in the process to fill and sell tidelands?

Early in 1891 Semple had disclosed his plan to Captain Thomas Symons of the Corps of Engineers and to Philip Eastwick, a civil engineer employed by the Army at Portland.[5] The reclaimed lands, he told them, could easily be sold to industries yearning to expand beyond Seattle's hilly and congested downtown area. Furthermore, since the

3. An earlier firm, the Lake Washington Improvement Company, had been formed in 1883 to connect the two lakes, but the contractor soon struck hardpan and the project was abandoned (ibid., p. 118; and Glenn C. Quiett, *They Built the West*, p. 479).

4. Annual Report of the Chief of Engineers, United States Army (Serial 3080), 52d Cong., 2d sess., 1892-93, Appendix, pp. 27, 62; House Executive Documents, 5 (52d Cong., 2d sess., 1892-93) : 2763-65.

5. Semple to Philip Eastwick, January 3, February 19, 1891.

state owned right of way along the southern route, the legislature might be persuaded to grant access to a private construction company to create a system of public waterways. The canal, when completed, might offer numerous benefits, Semple pointed out. Sewage could be directed into Elliott Bay instead of into beautiful Lake Washington. Property values along the lake front would soar. And the Navy would gain access to a landlocked fresh-water harbor, safe from both enemy attack and the ravages of sea storms and salt water mollusks.[6]

In order to woo investors to his scheme, Semple first needed state legislative authority to undertake the project. In February 1893 two of his Seattle friends, Representatives Will R. White and L. C. Gilman, introduced a bill into the lower house to allow private companies to dig public waterways over state-owned property and charge liens on the reclaimed tidelands that were sold to finance the work. The measure passed both houses by large margins. On March 9, McGraw signed it into law,[7] evidently unaware that the new statute could be used to promote an enterprise inimical to the popular northern route via Shilshole Bay, which the governor avidly supported. Semple's part in the conception and enactment of the canal bill is not known, but Gilman and Frank Richards, who helped guide it through the legislature, were more than his casual acquaintances. The swift passage of the measure by comfortable majorities suggests that few lawmakers realized how Semple intended to use the new law. Had his intentions been anticipated, the north canal supporters probably would have organized enough opposition to defeat the bill.

The new act empowered the state to make contracts with private companies or individuals to dig waterways and canals through tideflats and to use the excavated material to fill, above the mark of high tide, any tidelands in front of incorporated cities or within a mile of such cities. The work was to be financed by liens on the filled land. The liens amounted to the cost of the fill plus 15 percent and represented first mortgages on the reclaimed land, subject, in case of default of payment, to foreclosure. They were to carry 8 percent interest and were payable to the contractor, through the state, in ten annual installments. In addition, the contractor was authorized to levy "reasonable" tolls on

6. Semple's ideas are set down in several documents in the papers of the Seattle and Lake Washington Waterway Company, which are included in the Semple Papers.

7. Washington State Legislature, *Senate Journal* (1894), pp. 561, 597; *House Journal* (1894), pp. 414, 593, 683-86, 763.

any locks or tide gates it might construct. It was also given a six-month option to buy, at locally appraised value, any lots not sold by the state within one year after they had been filled.[8]

Soon after McGraw signed the law, Semple filed plans with state Land Commissioner W. T. Forrest to dig a canal from the southern end of Elliott Bay into Lake Washington through the tideflats, Beacon Hill, and the intervening uplands of Rainier Valley.[9] The undertaking involved the excavation of two channels running from north to south and designated by Semple as the East and West Waterways. Each was to be more than a mile in length and one thousand feet in width and was to extend from deep water across the tideflats. Then, from the southern tip of the East Waterway, a one-mile canal three hundred feet wide would be dredged eastward, crossing the remaining tideflats to the mainland. The project would culminate with the construction of a main channel from the shore line through Beacon Hill and the uplands into Lake Washington. The excavations, Semple told Forrest, would provide the material with which to fill and reclaim more than fifteen hundred acres of tidelands. In conformity with the law Semple then asked the state for permission to establish toll locks on the main channel in order to maintain elevation of the lake at thirty feet.

Several Seattle property owners promptly lodged protests with Forrest against Semple's plan, claiming that the contract and the waterway act itself were unconstitutional. But the commissioner, after consulting state Attorney General W. C. Jones, rejected their petitions.[10] Subsequent rulings by the state supreme court sustained this course of action.[11]

Semple's next objective was to form a company to undertake his dual project of tideland reclamation and canal building. In June 1894 he persuaded former Governor Elisha Ferry to "take a hand with us," and in that same month the Seattle and Lake Washington Waterway Company was created with Ferry as its president and Semple as vice-president.[12] The company soon enlisted the services of another influential man, Captain Thomas Symons, who had recently conducted

8. *Session Laws of the State of Washington* (1893), pp. 241-46.

9. Semple to W. T. Forrest, June 8, 1893.

10. *The History and Advantages of the Canal and Harbor Improvement Project Now Being Executed by the Seattle and Lake Washington Waterway Company*, p. 11 (hereafter cited as *History of the South Canal*). This pamphlet was published by the waterway company and most of it was Semple's work.

11. *Pacific Reporter*, 26:971.

12. Semple to Ferry, May 26, 1894; *History of the South Canal*, pp. 12-13.

federal studies of the problems of canal construction at Seattle. "We have been over the ground with the Captain and there is no doubt his report will be very favorable for us," Semple told Forrest.[13] Another important figure Semple enticed into the scheme was Andrew Hemrich, president of the Seattle Brewing and Malting Company. Hemrich quickly became an enthusiastic sponsor of the south canal, as it was called, subscribing a thirty-thousand-dollar stock subsidy in the SLWWC and using his influence to coax support from the Seattle Chamber of Commerce.[14]

For the bulk of investment capital, however, Semple was compelled to turn to contacts in the East, where his two wealthy nephews, Henry and Edgar Ames, had connections with the Mississippi Valley Trust Company in St. Louis.[15] The Missouri financiers were attracted to Semple's scheme but would make no commitment until McGraw signed the contract completing arrangements between the waterway company and the state. McGraw now appeared to stall, however, possibly waiting until the next legislature convened in hopes that it would repeal the canal act. Whatever his reason, the governor withheld his approval, in spite of letters endorsing the project from south Seattle property holders as well as favorable reports from Forrest and Jones.[16] Angered by the delay, Semple wrote to his nephews in October 1894, urging them to exert pressure on the governor. "Make him as strong an offer as you can," he told them.[17] The nature of the "offer" is not known, but a few days later, McGraw signed the contract.

While Semple traveled to St. Louis to negotiate a contract with the trust company, Seattle residents began to get excited about the south canal scheme. D. A. McKenzie, a candidate for King County Sheriff in 1894 and a stockholder in the SLWWC, informed Semple that he was being stopped constantly on the streets and asked about the progress of talks in St. Louis. "My stereotyped answer is that everything is working nicely," he wrote. "If news got here today that you had closed the deal I have no doubt but what one half of the population of Seattle would go on a 'toot'—providing they could raise the price."[18]

13. Semple to Forrest, June 13, 1894.
14. Semple to Andrew Hemrich, May 13, 1894; *History of the South Canal*, pp. 6, 7, 12.
15. Semple to the Waterway Company, September 15, 1894.
16. *History of the South Canal*, pp. 13-14, 39-40.
17. Semple to Edgar and Henry Ames, October 16, 1894
18. D. A. McKenzie to Semple, November 27, 1894.

Tideflats below Beacon Hill, Seattle, 1900

Hydraulic land removal for south canal project, 1903

Representatives of the trust company, including its president, Julius Walsh, visited Seattle early in 1895 to inspect the proposition at first hand.[19] Colonel Henry Flad, an engineer employed by the St. Louis firm, had challenged estimates by Symons that the project would require the excavation of twenty-nine million cubic yards of material from the hill area at a cost of five and a half million dollars. According to Flad's calculations, thirty-nine million cubic yards and seven and a half million dollars were more accurate figures.[20] These and other problems were resolved during the visit. Flad and Walsh appeared before the chamber of commerce and other civic groups and were evidently satisfied that strong local support existed for Semple's scheme. As a result, the bank agreed to finance the canal if a half-million-dollar subsidy was pledged in Seattle before work started, with the money to go to the SLWWC when construction was completed. The SLWWC also guaranteed the St. Louis investors a bond on state certificates which, under the canal act, were to be issued whenever a section of tideland was filled to state specifications.[21]

On the evening of March 28, 1895, four thousand persons crowded into the Seattle Armory for a mass meeting to discuss the south canal subsidy. Mayor Byron Phelps and other civic leaders urged public support of the project, citing the numerous advantages Semple had outlined. Those present responded with a ringing endorsement of the subsidy.[22] Nor did the effects of the national depression seem to inhibit public generosity during the weeks that followed. Within seven days after the armory meeting, nearly three hundred thousand dollars was subscribed locally.[23] Pledges ranged from a twenty-thousand-dollar subscription by the banking firm of Dexter Horton and Company to a one-dollar donation from someone named Zwick.[24] Symptoms of the canal fever appeared in the pages of the local newspapers. "No man should falter," the *Post-Intelligencer* exhorted during the subsidy drive, as it prodded its readers with daily front-page banner headlines to dig deep into their pockets. "The Seattle and Lake Washington Waterway Company project is a great one, and it . . . is entirely feasible," the

19. *History of the South Canal,* pp. 14-15.
20. Henry Ames to Semple, February 28, 1895.
21. Ibid.; *History of the South Canal,* p. 14.
22. Seattle *Times,* March 28, 1895; Seattle *Post-Intelligencer,* April 6, 1895; *History of the South Canal,* p. 15.
23. *Post-Intelligencer,* April 6, 1895.
24. *History of the South Canal,* pp. 49, 65.

paper asserted. Another editorial pronounced Semple's undertaking "the greatest enterprise yet inaugurated in this city," adding that the project would usher in "one of the great epochs in the history of Seattle."[25] By May 10 the goal of half a million dollars had been surpassed. Nearly twenty-five hundred Seattle residents had contributed, including many business leaders.[26]

During the fund raising drive Semple subcontracted with the Bowers Dredging Company of San Francisco to dig and fill the tidelands.[27] Work began on Monday, July 29, 1895. Several thousand onlookers gathered at the foot of Commercial Street for the ceremonies as Mayor Phelps, City Engineer R. H. Thomson, and other dignitaries lauded the start of the project. Then Semple spoke. "The most gratifying thing any man can do is to give his friends what they most desire," he told the assemblage. "When it is finished the people of Seattle can point to it with pride and say 'we did it ourselves.' " He concluded by telling his listeners to return in five years to witness the opening of the south canal locks into Lake Washington. Then his twenty-two-year-old daughter Zoe climbed to the pilothouse of the dredge *Anaconda* and pushed a lever that started the tideland venture. A rotating blade tore loose the first mud from the flats and hurled it into a suction pipe, through which it was carried half a mile to the site of the first fill.[28]

Work proceeded smoothly in the months that followed. By May 1896, seventy acres of tideflats had been filled to state specifications. Two Bowers dredges, the *Python* and *Anaconda,* operated incessantly to meet the brisk demand for reclaimed lands. In the process, the first eighteen hundred feet of the East Waterway were dredged.[29] By June 1897 the state had issued the SLWWC more than $250,000 in certificates for salvaged offshore marshes.[30] Semple now presided over the firm, having succeeded Ferry, who had resigned before work began. Andrew Hemrich became vice-president, and Edgar Ames was installed as general manager, a position through which he exercised considerable influence in company affairs. Symons became the company's consulting engineer.

25. *Post-Intelligencer,* April 7, April 4, July 28, 1895.
26. Ibid., May 10, 1895; *History of the South Canal,* pp. 16, 44-65, *passim.*
27. *Post-Intelligencer,* July 30, 1895; Seattle *Times,* July 30, 1895.
28. Ibid.
29. Seattle *News,* July 29, 1896.
30. Washington State Land Commissioner, *Fifth Biennial Report* (1898), p. 83.

Not everyone in Seattle rejoiced at the progress of the south canal company. Property owners along the Shilshole Bay (north canal) route were especially unhappy. Many denounced Semple's venture and even the canal act itself as part of a plot to defraud the public. John J. McGilvra, a pioneer Seattle attorney and long a prominent figure in civic affairs, criticized Semple's actions from the start. The canal law of 1893 was "a vicious act" of the state legislature, McGilvra told the public. It failed to fix a price for the digging and filling and allowed the waterway company to charge whatever the traffic would bear. The canal plan, he contended, was a smoke screen to divert attention from the real purpose of the company—the reclamation and sale of tidelands. McGilvra also objected to the SLWWC refusal to lower Lake Washington and thereby end the flood danger to farmers along the Duwamish, Black, Cedar, and White rivers. Lowering the lake, McGilvra pointed out, would deprive the company of an opportunity to build locks and charge tolls. These were hard times, he lamented, and under the circumstances "many . . . are ready to endorse or engage in any wild scheme that may be presented by political demagogues or financial speculators."[31] The weekly Seattle *Argus* also expressed alarm over the south canal enterprise. It criticized local businessmen for underwriting Semple's "wildcat scheme" with a subsidy and thereby reducing the likelihood of future federal expenditures for a north canal.[32]

Champions of the old Shilshole route were particularly disturbed by reports that Semple was trying to induce the national government to help finance his project and abandon the northern route. As a result, promoters of the latter venture, including Thomas Burke, Arthur Denny, Orange Jacobs, McGraw, and McGilvra, took steps to rekindle enthusiasm for their scheme.[33] Newspapers like the fickle *Post-Intelligencer* helped by emphasizing some previously unpublicized disadvantages of the south canal, particularly the problems of excavation. In 1896 voters approved a county property levy to defray the cost of eventual acquisition of right of way along the northern

31. Copy of a speech delivered by McGilvra to the Seattle Chamber of Commerce, July 13, 1894, John J. McGilvra Papers, Manuscripts Division, University of Washington Library. McGilvra was born in 1827 and was appointed U.S. district attorney in Washington Territory where he served 1861-65. He became prominent in Seattle law and politics and was a noted opponent of the Northern Pacific Railroad. See Clarence B. Bagley, *History of Seattle from the Earliest Settlement to the Present Time*, 2:740-44.

32. Seattle *Weekly Argus*, July 13, 1895.

33. Seattle *News*, April 18, 1896.

route.[34] During the year the federal government also indicated renewed interest when Congress appropriated $150,000 for navigation improvements on Salmon Bay, which lay along the north canal route.[35]

Besides opposition from the north canal group, Semple and his colleagues faced other serious troubles. The cost of digging waterways through the tidelands consistently exceeded the income from filling charges and liens levied on reclaimed land. One reason for this was the refusal by certain property holders to pay either liens or filling assessments. Expensive and time-consuming litigation ensued. Typical was the case of W. D. Hofius, who challenged the constitutionality of the canal act and the waterway contract provisions for interest payments and deadlines. Significantly, Hofius was represented by Burke. Although the state supreme court finally decided in favor of the SLWWC in December 1898,[36] the ruling was a Pyrrhic victory for Semple. During the eighteen months preceding the decision, injunctions had been in effect, halting work on the tideflats. Partly because of this delay, the Bowers Dredging Company, faced with rising costs and no means of paying them, went into receivership. This brought about a complete cessation of activity on the waterways. As a result, the financing from St. Louis also stopped.

It now became necessary to find new investors. The leading figure in the refinancing of the south canal gamble was not Semple but the new auditor of the SLWWC, Will H. Parry, Seattle city comptroller and general manager of the Moran Brothers Shipbuilding Company. In February 1900, after months of negotiations involving Parry, Semple, and Edgar Ames, a contract was signed between the SLWWC and the Philadelphia banking firm of Morris and Whitehead.[37] In order to obtain the new backers Parry had organized a subsidiary corporation, the Seattle General Contract Company, in which Ames, not Semple, occupied the presidency. Through this firm Parry was able to get contracts with the Puget Sound Bridge and Dredging Company to resume work on the East Waterway, and with the Queen City Contract Company for the eventual start on the Beacon Hill section.[38] In order

34. Semple to Symons, October 23, 1896.

35. Seattle *Times,* April 17, 22, 28, 1896; *Post-Intelligencer,* April 19, 1896.

36. Mississippi Valley Trust Company et al. v. W. D. Hofius et al., *Pacific Reporter,* 55:54; Allen v. Commissioner of Public Lands, *Washington Reports* (Kreider), 8:700.

37. Washington State Land Commissioner, *Sixth Biennial Report* (1901), pp. 64-65. For information on Will Parry, see Bagley Scrapbook No. 5, p. 57; and Meany Pioneer File (s.v. Parry).

38. Semple to the London and San Francisco Bank, San Francisco, October 14, 1901.

Eugene Semple, ca. the time
of his tideland activities

Judge Thomas Burke

Governor John Harte McGraw,
ca. 1897

John J. McGilvra

to refinance the canal work Semple and the other original shareholders in the parent SLWWC were forced to relinquish much of their stock. But, as Semple had told Symons earlier, "something must be done at once, public opinion demanding that we 'shoot or give up the gun.' "[39]

Before agreeing to help, Morris and Whitehead insisted that the waterway company obtain an extension of its state contract, which was scheduled to expire in 1901. Semple accordingly went to Olympia to persuade state Public Land Commissioner Robert Bridges to extend the agreement. Bridges had been friendly to the south canal idea since coming into office and in May 1900 he announced a four-year extension of the contract, with the understanding that work was to resume within ninety days after the bank loan commenced.[40]

Bridges' decision created a furor in Seattle. Burke and McGilvra protested the extension of the contract, charging that the SLWWC had failed to honor its commitment to fill tidelands.[41] This was partially true. By 1900 work on the tideflats had been stopped for two years, owing to the SLWWC's financial difficulties. Moreover, under the provisions of the state contract, property owners were forbidden to allow any other firm to fill their lots and were obliged to pay sixteen cents a foot to the SLWWC for tideland fill. It was a fee fixed arbitrarily by the company and a price that landholders considered outrageous. Nevertheless, Bridges refused Burke's request for a hearing of the issue and a roar of protest followed.[42] "Seldom has a more offensive scandal originated in the administration of any state," the *Post-Intelligencer* told its readers. Bridges replied to insinuations that he had taken a bribe by pointing out that the SLWWC had shown "due diligence" by reclaiming seventy acres of tideflats and had otherwise complied with the law, thereby earning the right to an extension of the contract. This explanation did not satisfy the *Post-Intelligencer*, which excoriated the commissioner as "a poor scrap of humanity without a rag to cover his moral nakedness."[43]

Hostility subsided, however, when work on the East Waterway resumed in October 1900. In the next two months eighty-five thousand

39. Semple to Symons, February 9, 1900.
40. *Post-Intelligencer,* May 9, 1900.
41. Ibid., May 18, 20, 1900; Seattle *Times,* May 18, 1900.
42. *Post-Intelligencer,* May 24, 1900.
43. Ibid., May 25, May 26, June 2, 1900.

cubic yards of material were dredged from the East Waterway and deposited as fill over a wide area in the vicinity east of what is today Harbor Island.[44]

Shortly after activity resumed on the tidelands, the ubiquitous Burke, in his capacity as chief western legal counsel for the Great Northern Railroad, secured a new injunction to prevent the SLWWC from filling any more railroad property west of Hanford Street.[45] The writ of injunction maintained that Semple's company was not exercising "due diligence" and reopened the issue of overcharges. Both the Great Northern and the Northern Pacific claimed that unless Semple's state contract was canceled, the railroads could not gain access to land upon which to build the proposed union depot.[46] With the injunction in effect, the Great Northern took its fight to the state legislature, where a bill was introduced to discontinue the waterway project.[47] The measure was backed by the Seattle press and the chamber of commerce, and might have been enacted had not Andrew Hemrich, now a state senator as well as an SLWWC executive, marshaled enough opposition to smother the bill on the last day of the 1901 session.[48] The Seattle *Star* claimed Hemrich had persuaded Northern Pacific lobbyists to fight the bill in return for secret concessions from the waterway company, but the truth of this charge is not known.[49]

Soon after the legislature adjourned, the waterway company and the two railroads began to negotiate their differences. By this time both lines had merged their interests in what was soon to become the Northern Securities Company, a giant holding company incorporated in 1901 by J. P. Morgan, E. H. Harriman, James J. Hill, and others to control all transcontinental rail traffic west of Chicago. In May 1901 the attorneys of James J. Hill, president of the Great Northern, sat down to bargain with Semple and his colleagues, and in August an agreement was reached. The Great Northern promised to end the injunction and the waterway company consented to fill the tideland property of both lines at a cost the two railroads would be willing to pay anyone else.[50]

44. *Sixth Biennial Report,* pp. 66-67.
45. Seattle *Times,* December 22, 1900.
46. Ibid., March 11, 16, 1901.
47. House Bill 178, Washington State Legislature, *House Journal* (1901).
48. Ibid., and Semple to Symons, March 27, 1901.
49. Seattle *Star,* March 18, 1901.
50. Semple to Symons, August 18, 1901; Seattle *Times,* July 4, August 13, 1901; *Post-Intelligencer,* August 13, 1901.

The agreement proved to be of little benefit to either party. For one thing, financial and engineering problems made it difficult, if not impossible, for the SLWWC to fill property where and when the railroad wanted.[51] Furthermore, the two lines refused to sign any exclusive long term contract with the company. By June 1904, nearly three years after the entente, both railroads were filling their own property.[52] Semple made no protest and rumors circulated that he, Parry, and others in the company had been bought off.[53] It is more likely, however, that the south canal men had grown weary of contending with Hill and saw no profit in opposing the railroads by further costly court hassles.

During these years the north canal faction remained active. A narrow channel was cut from Shilshole Bay towards Salmon Bay, while the chamber of commerce endorsed a plan to lower Lake Washington to the level of Lake Union.[54] Then, in January 1902, Seattle journalist Erastus Brainerd went to Washington, D.C., to ask the House Rivers and Harbors Committee for an appropriation for a north canal. Brainerd had been the leading booster of Seattle's commercial advantages during the recent Klondike Gold Rush and enjoyed a reputation as a persuasive lobbyist. With most of the state congressional delegation reportedly favoring the north canal route, local leaders were cautiously optimistic.[55] "You have difficult tasks to perform," McGraw told Brainerd, "yet I am confident you will succeed in getting something for the ditch."[56] Once in Washington, Brainerd ran into trouble. Congressman Theodore Burton of Ohio, the committee chairman, was unimpressed by Brainerd's arguments. Burton said he saw no need for a canal at Seattle, and evidently a majority of the committee agreed.[57] But back in Seattle, Semple was uneasy. If Congress did decide to build a north canal, and in the process lowered Lake Washington, the south canal scheme as Semple had conceived it would be ruined. Consequently he went to Washington to block any plans to lower the

51. Semple to Alexander Stewart, a civil engineer employed by the Great Northern, January 12, 1904.

52. *Post-Intelligencer,* June 14, 1904.

53. Seattle *Times,* September 14, 1904.

54. Semple to Symons, October 16, 1901.

55. *Times,* January 14, 1902. For information on Brainerd, see the introductory pamphlet in the Erastus Brainerd Papers, Manuscripts Division, University of Washington Library.

56. McGraw to Brainerd, December 19, 1901, Brainerd Papers.

57. *Times,* January 15, 1902.

lake and, if the occasion presented itself, to speak favorably of his own south canal project.

McGilvra, Burke, and others back home became alarmed in turn. Although they did not believe that the completion of the south canal was possible, they knew that Semple's presence before the committee could only reinforce that group's dim view of a north canal appropriation. Burke therefore hurried after Semple to Washington to assist Brainerd, but to no avail. While telling the committee that Semple's project was impractical and that the work of the SLWWC had been confined to filling tidelands, he blundered by erroneously asserting that the state supreme court had declared parts of the south canal plan unconstitutional. Semple challenged this falsehood immediately, claiming, correctly, that no such ruling had ever been made. He branded Burke's remarks "disingenuous" and, before the full committee, demanded that Burke either specify a legal citation to substantiate his charge or retract it and apologize. The embarrassed Burke was forced to admit that he had no specific evidence to support his contention and, having thus discredited himself before the committee, he returned to Seattle.[58]

A few weeks later, in an effort to undercut the north canal plan further, Semple and his associates offered the federal government the services of the SLWWC and its affiliates to dig a one-lock toll canal between Lake Washington and Lake Union. Their price was two and a half million dollars, provided the government secured the necessary right of way.[59] Burton's committee was not interested in any Seattle canal at the moment. As a result the 1902 rivers and harbors appropriations, which totaled $60 million, allocated only $150,000 for Seattle—substantially less than the several million dollars Brainerd and his cohorts had hoped to get.[60] Undeniably, Semple's performance in Washington had helped dampen congressional enthusiasm for the northern route, at least for the present. "Damn it all," McGraw told Brainerd, "had I gone at that damned ditch with a pick and shovel when I entered the campaign in 1892, it would be nearer completion

58. SLWWC to Committee on Rivers and Harbors of the House of Representatives, January 25, 1902, Semple Papers; and Semple to M. D. Grover, January 28, 1902.

59. Semple to Symons, January 29, 1902; Semple to House Committee on Rivers and Harbors, February 24, 1902; Semple to Theodore Burton, February 22, 1902.

60. *Times,* March 10, 1902; *Post-Intelligencer,* March 13, 1902.

than it is now."[61] George Cotterill, Democratic nominee for Congress and a former assistant city engineer in Seattle, spoke for many King County residents when he told Semple and his partners to "stop knifing this community" and "attend to your business of filling tideflats."[62]

The second phase of the south canal scheme—excavation of the three-mile main canal through Beacon Hill and Rainier Valley—began in the autumn of 1901. Earlier in the year, against mounting criticism, Semple had persuaded the Seattle Board of Public Works to rent surplus water to the SLWWC at five hundred dollars a month from the new Cedar River gravity system, for the purpose of sluicing a channel through Beacon Hill. The city also agreed to rent water from the old Lake Washington pumping station.[63] In October 1901 the Queen City Contract Company began laying pipe from the Beacon Hill reservoir to the site of hydraulic operations on the west side of the hill. More than a mile of pipe and trestle was erected along the crest of the hill from the reservoir. The pipe then turned west and carried down a steep slope to the base of the hill near the east end of Hanford Street where a large hose was situated to concentrate the stream of down-rushing water into the side of the hill under tremendous pressure. According to plan, as the side of the hill crumbled it would be washed into flumes and carried to the tideflats to be used as fill.[64]

Sluicing began on November 14, 1901. In the next year the hydraulic work accounted for the removal of nearly 450,000 cubic yards of material from the side of Beacon Hill to the tideflats. In an average workday, fourteen million gallons of water were forced against the face of the hill, breaking loose two thousand yards of clay and dirt. Meanwhile the SLWWC continued to employ two dredges on the tidelands. During this time reclaimed lands sold rapidly and Semple's firm earned state tideland certificates totaling almost $580,000. By the autumn of 1902 the East Waterway was nearing completion, 175 acres had been redeemed from the sea, and the assessed value per acre of reclaimed property had increased more than ten fold from an 1894 assessed value of $2,500 an acre. Reclaimed lands sold rapidly. In August 1903 work began on the West Waterway. In the next twelve months the dredges hauled up and deposited as fill nearly a million

61. McGraw to Brainerd, January 29, 1902, Brainerd Papers.

62. Seattle *Times,* March 9, 1902.

63. Ibid., February 8, 9, 1901; Seattle *Bulletin,* August 13, 1901; Washington State Land Commissioner, *Seventh Biennial Report* (1903), pp. 55-56.

64. *Times,* October 12, 1901.

yards of material. From October 1902 to March 1904 the SLWWC filled approximately 150 acres of tidelands and earned almost $650,000 in state certificates. In 1904 the average acre of salvaged land sold for thirty thousand dollars—twenty-seven thousand more than an unredeemed acre.[65]

Despite this progress, the SLWWC continued to encounter crippling difficulties. The demand for reclaimed tideland exceeded available capital to finance filling operations. Consequently the company was forced to operate on credit, pledging anticipated revenues from state certificates against loans made through Morris and Whitehead at increasing interest rates. This situation led in 1902 to a complicated reorganization of the SLWWC, the Seattle General Contract Company, and the Queen City Contract Company. In the process, Semple was forced to surrender most of his stock in the three firms. Other company officers suffered similar losses of stock, much of which was placed in escrow in Seattle with creditors represented by Morris and Whitehead.[66] The reorganization signified, among other things, that the creative phase of the south canal scheme had passed, and with it, Semple's paramount role. Clearly, the main task now was to keep the SLWWC in business, and for this, Will Parry, not Semple, displayed greater aptitude.

Meanwhile the sluicing at the base of Beacon Hill gave critics of the south canal new ammunition. Cotterill and others charged that the SLWWC had gotten the surplus city water too cheaply, especially since the nearby city of Ballard had offered earlier to buy the Cedar River surplus for substantially more and had been turned down.[67] The fact that Parry was a member of the Seattle City Council made many doubt the honesty of the company in its dealings with the city.[68] A cartoon in the Seattle *Star* in April 1902 depicted Parry and Semple directing a stream of water from a hose onto Beacon Hill while Hemrich and others pumped it to them from the city reservoir and McGilvra stood in the background frowning. Semple, wearing the helmet of a fire chief, was saying, "Pump harder boys, pump harder . . . . We must drown out that

65. Washington State Land Commissioner, *Seventh Biennial Report,* pp. 56-64, and *Eighth Biennial Report* (1905), pp. 75-81.

66. Outlines of the reorganization plan are contained in the waterway company papers, September 10, 1902 (Semple Papers); and in the Burke Papers (Box 57), September 19, 1902.

67. *Times,* March 9, 1902.

68. Seattle *News-Letter,* March 22, 1902.

government [i.e. north] canal while Cedar River water is cheap."[69]

The implications of collusion attracted the attention of a King County grand jury which, in February 1903, began an investigation of the arrangements between the SLWWC and the city. One alleged purpose of the inquiry was to investigate a charge that the Queen City Contract Company had given Parry twenty-five hundred dollars to persuade the other city councilmen to grant the firm the use of the Lake Washington pumping plant. Parry denied any complicity when questioned before the jury. Semple followed him onto the stand and refused to surrender the records of the SLWWC. Judge Walter Bell, after warning the former governor of the consequences of this refusal, cited him for contempt and ordered his arrest.[70]

Semple was soon released on bail, but before further action could be taken on the contempt charge, the jury proceedings themselves were halted when Bell removed foreman H. C. Piggott for leaving town during the investigation. Questions concerning the jury's integrity were subsequently raised, with the eventual result that the contempt charge was dropped, Semple was not indicted, and the city of Seattle lost an opportunity to find out whether collusion had existed between the south canal promoters and the city council. The truth of the bribery charge is not known; there is no evidence to sustain it in the correspondence of Semple or other waterway company executives. According to Semple and Parry, the investigation was instigated by opponents of the south canal scheme who sought to discredit it, found they had no case, and retreated for fear of having the inquest backfire.[71]

Soon after the grand jury hearings, the city ordered the SLWWC to stop sluicing in the vicinity of 14th and Hanford streets.The enjoinder was filed by the city council street committee in March 1903 after several angry citizens protested that the company had made no provision for adequate detours around its excavations.[72] One irate Beacon Hill couple, whose house clung precariously to the edge of the company diggings, sued the firm for six thousand dollars, contending that water from the hydraulic operations had washed away the foundations of the house.[73] Semple responded to the injunction by

69. Seattle *Star,* April 5, 1902.
70. *Times,* February 17, 25, 1903.
71. Parry to Semple, March 28, 1903; Semple to Maude Semple, March 14, 1903.
72. *Times,* March 24, 1903.
73. Ibid., May 10, 1905.

petitioning the city to vacate the area in question, maintaining that his state contract and subsequent court decisions clearly affirmed the right of the SLWWC to access for construction of a public waterway.[74] This was a dubious contention, for, as McGilvra pointed out to the Chamber of Commerce, no law could justify sluicing away city streets and private property without adequate compensation—something the company was unable to provide.[75] The city council therefore rejected Semple's petition to vacate streets and then dealt the SLWWC and its subsidiaries another blow by reducing the supply of surplus water.[76]

By 1904 the tide of public opinion had turned decisively against the south canal work and financing became much more difficult. Men like City Engineer Reginald H. Thomson, who had publicly endorsed Semple's idea a decade earlier, now decried it. Thomson urged the city to terminate the water contract immediately so that the surplus might be used on other public projects.[77] His attitude was understandable, for no one could deny that the hydraulic work of the SLWWC had created local havoc—had in fact washed out a six-block area in the vicinity of 14th and Hanford which came to be known as "the big hole."[78] In May, over the protest of its president, Hiram Gill, the city council ordered the company to cease all work in the area.[79] Reluctantly Semple's outfit complied. By the end of the year weeds were growing in "the big hole."

The fate of the south canal project was ironic, for even as the SLWWC abandoned its sluicing activities inland, its work on the tidelands was proceeding at an unprecedented pace, to enthusiastic acclaim. In mid-June 1904 the *Post-Intelligencer* reported that $350,000 of reclaimed tideflats had been sold during the week ending June 18. It was, the paper claimed, the biggest real estate week in Seattle history.[80] The state supreme court also remained friendly. In June the court again ruled in favor of the waterway company, this time

74. Ibid., April 4, 1903.

75. Typescript of a speech to the Seattle City Council, April 23, 1903, John J. McGilvra Papers. See also late April editions of the *Post-Intelligencer* and the *Times* for more of McGilvra's remarks.

76. *Post-Intelligencer*, May 1, 1903; Seattle *Star*, May 5, 1903.

77. Reginald H. Thomson, *That Man Thomson*, ed. Grant H. Redford, p. 55; Seattle *Times*, May 8, 1904.

78. *Times*, May 8, 1904.

79. *Post-Intelligencer*, May 24, 1904.

80. Ibid., June 19, 1904.

on an appeal by the Seattle Dock Company which had refused to pay liens on filled property.[81] By 1905 more than three hundred acres had been reclaimed from the waters of the Sound. In the process, the dredges of the Puget Sound Bridge and Dredging Company completed the East and West Waterways, helping to form Harbor Island—the largest man made island in the world. Along First Avenue South warehouses and manufacturing firms occupied lots where only recently high tides had covered the area under many feet of water.

But Semple's dream of a great ship canal carved through the southern part of the city had meanwhile vanished. His repeated efforts to force the city of Seattle to vacate streets in the path of his proposed waterway succeeded only in angering local officials. During one of his stormy confrontations with the street committee, chairman Robert Mullen asked: "Do you imagine this committee is crazy enough to grant such a petition as this after what we have gone through?"[82] The former governor's growing unpopularity in connection with his now hopeless canal venture led to his resignation as president of the SLWWC in May 1905. The change was part of an agreement with New York investors who consented to help refinance the floundering corporation only after Parry was installed as president.[83] In the months that followed, Parry let the idea of a south canal die quietly and the project was entirely abandoned.

The aging founder of the enterprise accepted the situation philosophically, although not without some bitterness. "The fire of the opposition has always been concentrated upon me," he wrote Symons. Then he added: "I have gotten myself out of the way and abandoned hope of carrying out, to ultimate success, the glorious comprehensive project we have dreamed of so long . . . . The 'wand of Prospero' has been taken from us in our old age and we will now 'toil like Caliban' in the commonplace business of filling tideflats." Andrew Hemrich was less sentimental. "I hope that since the fight is now all settled we can go ahead and fill tidelands," he told Semple. "This ought to give us some money in time," he continued, "but at no time will it give us what we could have had by a possible straight sellout to the Northern Pacific Railroad, as I suggested."[84]

81. Ibid., July 27, 1904; *Times,* October 31, 1904; *Washington Reports* (Remington), 35:503-16.

82. *Post-Intelligencer,* August 12, 1904.

83. A typed copy of the agreement, May 26, 1905, is in the waterway company papers (Semple Papers). See also *Post-Intelligencer,* May 23, 1905.

84. Semple to Symons, June 27, 1905; Hemrich to Semple, July 24, 1905.

The era of private promotion of a Seattle ship canal ended in 1911 when the federal government assumed the task of digging a north canal from Shilshole Bay through Salmon Bay and Lake Union into Lake Washington. Major Hiram Chittenden of the Army Corps of Engineers directed the work and on June 16, 1917, the first ship passed from Puget Sound into Lake Washington.[85] The vision of a canal through Beacon Hill at the other end of the city was just a fading memory by then. Only a tree-covered scar on the side of the hill north of Spokane Street remained as evidence of the earlier hydraulic operations. But the reclamation of the tidelands continued. In 1912 the state supreme court reaffirmed the right of the SLWWC to assess the cost of reclamation under the canal act of 1893. In 1914 the waterways were turned over to the King County Port Commission which allowed the SLWWC and its affiliates to continue their work on the tidelands. Critics attacked the commission and the state in 1917 for authorizing the company to raise its price for fill from sixteen to nineteen cents a yard. The commission chairman, Semple's old friend Robert Bridges, stood firm, however, in spite of claims that fill could be had for as little as five cents a yard if the commission would allow landowners to do the work themselves.[86]

By 1917 only about 8 percent of the tidelands described in the state contract remained unfilled. Much of the vast undertaking Semple had proposed to the people of Seattle in the early 1890s was completed—except, of course, for the canal itself. The East and West Waterways were excavated and more than fourteen hundred acres of tideflats reclaimed, creating millions of dollars' worth of industrial and commercial lots. At the south end of Elliott Bay, Harbor Island, an area which had been raised above the tides largely by the dredging of the two waterways which flanked it, provided valuable space for industrial expansion. The two waterways themselves gave large ocean-going vessels access to shipyards and wharves constructed on the new land at the south end of the bay. Similar tidal areas were reclaimed south of King Street adjacent to the mainland as the north-south waterline was pushed further and further out into the bay.[87]

85. Purvis, "Lake Washington Canal," p. 211.

86. *Post-Intelligencer,* October 23, 1912, and April 15, 1914; *Times,* April 12, 1917.

87. *Times,* April 12, 1917. The SLWWC was dissolved in 1926. Its contracts were turned over to the Dexter Horton National Bank of Seattle. See R. H. Calkins, "History of the Lake Washington Ship Canal," *Marine Digest,* 30

Semple did not live to see much of this, but Edgar Ames did. Unlike Semple, who realized no tangible reward from the south canal scheme, Ames prospered handsomely by it. By the war year of 1918, Semple's nephew owned one of the largest shipbuilding yards in the Pacific Northwest, the Ames Shipbuilding and Drydocking Company, located on land salvaged by Semple's SLWWC and its affiliates. Ames was one of the chief beneficiaries of the First World War shipbuilding boom which accelerated the industrial development of Seattle tremendously. During 1917-18 his firm built no less than twenty-one large vessels for the war effort.[88] As a gesture to his uncle's memory, Ames invited Zoe Semple to christen one of the new ships, the 8,800-ton *Westford*, in May 1918. Nearly twenty-three years had elapsed since Zoe, then a young girl, had performed a similar honor to inaugurate the south canal enterprise. Ames turned the occasion into an anniversary of sorts, presenting her with a wrist watch and recalling Semple's instrumental role "in turning the tidelands from swampy wastes into sites for great industries."[89] To Zoe, it may have seemed a small consolation for her father's work.

(February 17, 1951): 2, 15; and waterway company papers and estate notes, Semple Papers.

88. Pamphlets and limited correspondence concerning the Ames Shipbuilding Company are filed under the title "Subgroups," Semple Papers.

89. *Times,* June 1, 1918.

11. A Man on the Make

The south canal scheme became the fountainhead of several related enterprises Semple promoted during the later years of his life. Each of these intriguing but unrewarding ventures was distinguished not merely by hardihood, but by Semple's characteristic imagination, which succeeded in seducing many an unwary capitalist into becoming an investor.

Semple's abiding interest in river and harbor development reached beyond Seattle to other cities in the region. Especially fascinating to him for a time were the opportunities at the port of Tacoma—Seattle's chief rival on Puget Sound. There, in 1893, he presented a plan to build bulkheads across the flats along the inner harbor line, in conformity with the canal act, in order to improve the harbor and to permit the reclamation of tidal areas between the bulkheads and the shore. The material required for salvaging these submerged areas would be quarried from the proposed Tacoma-Edison Tunnel which was to be financed by a city bond issue.[1]

As had been the case at Seattle when similar proposals were advanced, the Tacoma scheme drew criticism. Much of it came, predictably, from waterfront interests along Commencement Bay—particularly the Tacoma Land Company and the Northern Pacific Railroad. Semple cautioned one of his co-promoters, a local dentist named James Wintermute, to act with discretion. "Our policy now is not to agitate this question but rather let it die down until the publication of our notices are [sic] completed and our contracts

1. Tacoma Harbor Documents, June 8, 1893, Semple Papers.

signed," he warned Wintermute. "If a special session of the legislature should be called and the [canal] law repealed before our contracts are signed, all our rights would be lost."[2]

With eyes fixed on the pending state contracts at both Seattle and Tacoma, Semple and Wintermute organized the Tacoma Waterway and Harbor Improvement Company as an adjunct of the Seattle enterprise. At the time, the effects of the Depression of 1893 weighed heavily on Tacoma and local investment capital seemed nonexistent. Eastern speculators also shunned the project, fearing possible injunctions against the work. A group of Chicago capitalists appeared mildly interested for a while but defected late in the year when legal complications arose. According to Wintermute the difficulties of the SLWWC were largely responsible for driving away such potential backers.[3] But local apathy was most disheartening of all. "This is the damndest town I ever lived in," Wintermute told Semple. "The truth of the matter is that no one here will oppose either the land company or the N.P.R.R. They expect these companies to do everything, and do nothing themselves: and in actual fact they really stand in awe of the companies." Semple, typically at this stage of the game, took an optimistic view, telling Wintermute that the Tacoma Land Company was itself short of funds and could be bought off: "When we deal with them we can give their treasurer $5,000 in cash which they need as badly as anyone else as all their works in Tacoma are suspended for lack of cash. We are all right in official circles; all we have to do is to exercise the cardinal virtue of patience for a few weeks longer."[4]

This was little solace to Wintermute whose personal problems were also retarding the promotion of the scheme. A lawsuit had divested him of considerable income and real estate, leaving him dependent upon his small salary as a professor of anatomy at Tacoma Dental College. To add to his plight, he had also recently suffered a severe relapse from typhoid fever.[5]

As a consequence the Tacoma venture languished during 1894 while Semple devoted most of his energies to promoting the Seattle scheme. Wintermute grew impatient and hinted that he might sell his interest in

2. Semple to Wintermute, June 17, 1893.

3. Wintermute to Semple, August 22 and September 24, 1894.

4. Wintermute to Semple, February 14, 1894; Semple to Wintermute, July 18, 1894.

5. Wintermute to Semple, October 19, 1893.

the Tacoma project to the rival Tacoma Land Company.[6] When word of this reached officers of the SLWWC, D. A. McKenzie, for one, became furious. "I suggested to Andrew [Hemrich] that we go to Tacoma and punch Wintermute's head," he told Semple, "but Andrew thinks it would be bad advertising for the company." Semple was more charitable toward his wayward Tacoma partner. Wintermute was, he judged, "a good man . . . in desperate straits financially," who had probably been enticed by the land company to make a deal against his better judgment. Rather than lose Wintermute's local influence, Semple advised McKenzie to see Wintermute immediately, buy out his interest, and cut him in for a smaller share under a new arrangement. With state contracts pending, he reminded McKenzie, "we don't want to embarrass our official friends by a contest over the Tacoma proposition if we can help it."[7]

Wintermute was thus appeased, at least for the time being, and decided to stay with the troublesome enterprise, although he remained outspokenly pessimistic, and with good reason. While rumors circulated that other parties intended to file their own plans with the commissioner of public lands for improving Tacoma harbor, the state exhibited scant interest in Semple's proposal.[8] Nor did it appear likely anything would change this official attitude. Before Semple's Tacoma outfit could make a contract with the state for right of way and other concessions, the law required the company to raise a twenty-five-thousand-dollar subsidy to underwrite the work. But, as Wintermute could testify, such a subsidy was virtually impossible to obtain without the prior guarantee of a state contract as collateral for underwriters.[9] Against this obstacle Semple and Wintermute could make no headway and in 1896 they finally abandoned the Tacoma plan.

While the Seattle and Lake Washington Waterway Company battled creditors and critics during the late 1890s, Semple shifted his attention for a period to the Far North. Soon after the discovery of gold in the Klondike he persuaded a group of prominent capitalists to support a rather bizarre scheme to dredge gold from the Yukon River. His

6. McKenzie to Semple, December 6, 1894.
7. McKenzie to Semple, December 17, 1894; Semple to McKenzie, December 24, 1894.
8. McKenzie to Semple, December 17, 1894.
9. Wintermute to Semple, February 2, 1895; Semple to Wintermute, February 15, 1895.

knowledge of the dredging operations of the SLWWC, as well as the company's desperate need for fresh capital to continue the south canal work, were important considerations behind the plan. Why not employ dredges, Semple argued, to mine gold on the Yukon and its tributaries and utilize the profits—assuming there were any—to finance work on the Seattle tidelands?

In August of 1897 he negotiated with the south canal subcontractors, the Bowers Dredging Company, for permission to lease a patented Bowers gold dredging process on the Yukon.[10] He then helped to organize the Bowers Yukon Gold Dredging Company to do the work. Semple became vice-president and general manager of the firm and Robert Moran, a former Seattle mayor and owner of the Moran Shipbuilding Company, became president. The roster of major stockholders was impressive. It included E. W. Andrews, president of the Seattle National Bank; John Campbell, general manager of the giant Port Blakely Lumber Company; S. G. Simpson, one of the wealthiest timber owners in the Pacific Northwest; and James O. Hestwood, a rich Klondike mine owner who had helped Semple conceive the enterprise.[11]

Late in 1897 Semple and Hestwood reached an agreement with a New York syndicate to help finance the scheme, and the headquarters of the company were moved to New York City. The Bowers Yukon Gold Dredging Company was then capitalized at one million dollars with ten thousand shares at one hundred dollars each. A prospectus issued early in 1898 informed the public that the company expected to have at least two dredges operating in the Yukon by the late summer of 1899. Ultimately the firm hoped to employ twenty dredges, each capable of handling two thousand cubic yards of sediment a day at an anticipated daily profit of ten thousand dollars per dredge. Semple was placed in charge of this ambitious enterprise in the distant North.[12]

Like his other ventures, the Yukon gold dredging scheme encountered serious difficulties from the beginning. One was Alphonso Bowers of San Francisco, owner of the dredging patent. Bowers had been granted a large number of shares in the company in return for the

10. A copy of Alphonso Bowers' contract with the gold dredging company is in the Seattle-Yukon Gold Dredging Company Papers, August 25, 1897, Semple Papers.

11. "Gold Dredging on the Yukon," (Seattle, 1898), *passim.* This was a prospectus published by the gold dredging firm.

12. Ibid.

use of his patent, but refused to yield his stock when the eastern syndicate, headed by New York financier James Truman, demanded it as collateral.[13] Meanwhile, some of the investors had developed doubts about the Bowers dredging process. It might be adequate for scooping mud from Elliott Bay, they admitted, but its merits on the allegedly gold-laden river beds of the Yukon were untested.[14]

A substantial loss of confidence among the investors in 1898 forced Semple to abandon the original design. For a while he and Hestwood contemplated combining the gold dredging idea with a passenger and freight service from Seattle to Dawson, Yukon Territory, in order to salvage the operation.[15] But the long Arctic winter and Truman's withdrawal from the enterprise scuttled the plan, even though Semple tried briefly to revive interest by promoting another type of dredge.[16]

The Yukon setback did not dampen the former governor's enthusiasm as an entrepreneur and developer. As his Seattle canal project faltered after 1900, his attention turned to a similar undertaking at Astoria, Oregon, the principal port at the mouth of the Columbia River. In September 1903 he began promoting a plan to grade the steep hills of the city with water pressure and flume the tailings (a la Beacon Hill) to the waterfront for use as fill to create valuable edgewater real estate. Early in 1904, John Adair, an Astoria businessman, canvassed local opinion on the idea at Semple's request and got an enthusiastic response.[17] In February Semple met with business and civic leaders to discuss his proposal in detail. He reminded them that a similar program had been taken up by the Oregon legislature in 1891 only to be abandoned two years later when the lawmakers failed to appropriate enough money. Now, Semple urged, it was time for the people of Astoria themselves to seize the initiative.[18]

A committee was formed to study his proposition while Semple returned to Seattle to persuade Charles E. Fowler, president of the Puget Sound Bridge and Dredging Company, to lend assistance. Semple hoped to use the firm's resources not only to grade the hills but to

13. Bowers contract, August 25, 1897, in Semple Papers; and Semple to Robert Moran, January 19, 1898. The Bowers-Yukon Gold Dredging Company was evidently the legal parent of the Seattle-Yukon Gold Dredging Company, whose papers I used.

14. Semple to Bowers, January 31, 1898.

15. Semple to Hestwood, February 19, 1898.

16. Semple to M. R. Straight, May 20, 1898.

17. John Adair to Semple, January 10, 1904.

18. Semple to Charles E. Fowler, February 20, 1904.

pump sand from the bed of the Columbia to utilize as waterfront fill. Despite Semple's entreaties, Fowler refused to commit his company to such an adventure unless a subsidy was raised at Astoria.[19] In the meantime the committee had reported to the Astoria Chamber of Commerce that a majority of the people who had been polled on Semple's idea favored it.[20] The committee said nothing, however, about pledging a subsidy, evidently assuming that Semple would be able to bring in all the outside money needed. Consequently, when he proposed the organization of a local corporation of waterfront property owners to finance the work, the suggestion got an icy reception. And that ended Semple's Astoria improvement scheme.[21]

The failure of the Astoria promotion did not diminish Semple's interest in the area at the entrance to the Columbia as a field of enterprise. He had long been fascinated by the formidable obstacles to navigation posed by the dangerous current and bar at the mouth of the great river. From the time of earliest recorded voyages along the Pacific Northwest coast, navigators had contended with these hazards. Ocean storms and the tremendous strength of the Columbia's current ceaselessly conspired to shift enormous amounts of sand to and fro across the entrance of the river. Channels thirty feet deep were often formed and then erased within a few seasons as tens of millions of cubic yards of sediment were moved into a given area and out again. These natural forces seriously hampered maritime commerce and took a heavy toll of ships and human life. During the nineteenth and early twentieth centuries at least 143 vessels of twenty-five tons or more had foundered or been demolished at or near the mouth of the river. The number of smaller craft—mostly tiny fishing boats—that perished has never been determined.[22]

Early in 1906 Semple unfolded his own solution to these awesome problems before the Portland Chamber of Commerce. His answer was to bypass the mouth of the river entirely by digging a fifteen-mile canal from Astoria to coastal Seaside through the intervening low, lake-dotted terrain.[23] He estimated the cost of such a waterway at approximately two million dollars, as contrasted to an estimated five

19. Semple to Adair, June 22, 1904.
20. Astoria *Daily Budget,* June 22, 1904.
21. Semple to Adair, June 22, 1904. This was apparently the last correspondence between the two men about the plan.
22. James A. Gibbs, *Pacific Graveyard,* pp. 23-24, 143-73, *passim.*
23. Semple to R. R. Hoge, January 19, 1906.

million dollars for government construction of a south jetty to facilitate navigation past the bar. Traffic on the proposed canal was to be regulated by one lock near Seaside, with a railroad trestle spanning the channel further inland. The work would take only two years, Semple told potential boosters, and could be completed without government funds. There was precedent for the scheme, too, he pointed out. At the Falls of the Willamette private money had already built a six-lock passage in two years for half a million dollars. The idea was "worth serious consideration," commented the Portland *Oregonian.*[24]

As usual, opposition arose. The Astoria *Budget,* which had endorsed Semple's earlier port improvement plan, referred to his canal proposal as "one of the most nonsensical schemes that could . . . be imagined." Astorians of course had a vested interest in opposing the canal, just as Seaside residents stood to gain from its completion. A Seaside editor observed that the canal, if dug, would allow ships to bypass the port of Astoria entirely enroute to or from the Pacific. The Portland *Journal* was another critic of the canal. It contended that the waterway would solve no problems since ocean currents eventually would create the same obstacles at the canal exit near Seaside that already existed at the entrance to the Columbia.[25] To this observation Semple replied that the proposed lock would prevent formation of a new bar at Seaside by eliminating the confluence of currents which helped cause the problem at the entry to the Columbia.[26] Still the idea continued to draw fire. United States Senator Charles W. Fulton of Oregon labeled it impractical, claiming that several engineers had told him it could not possibly be financed with private money. The only way the troublesome Columbia bar could be safely bypassed, said Fulton, was through federal construction of north and south jetties.[27]

While Senator Fulton advocated patient reliance on government planning and appropriations, Semple urged quick enactment of his own proposal by private groups. "What Portland merchants want is a way to get vessels of large draft freely in and out of the river—and they want that right away," he told the East Portland Improvement Association in October 1906. "Ten years from now will be too late," he warned. "This

24. Portland *Oregonian,* October 14, 1906. This issue gives a comprehensive illustrated report of Semple's plan.

25. Astoria *Budget,* December 10, 1905; Seaside *Signal,* December 2, 1905; Portland *Oregon Journal,* November 30, 1905.

26. Portland *Oregon Journal,* November 8, 1906.

27. Astoria *Budget,* November 5, 1906.

city can have the trade of the Pacific Coast if she wakes up and grasps her opportunity." As if to dramatize Semple's message, a four-masted schooner broke up near the site of the uncompleted South Jetty a few days later.[28]

In the weeks that followed, Semple continued to address Oregon civic groups in an attempt to promote the canal. But the initial enthusiasm was now dying, as the *Oregonian* indicated late in 1906 when it gave full support to the federal South Jetty project. Early in 1907 Congress allocated $750,000 for work on the jetty, putting an end to talk of a canal to Seaside once and for all.[29] For Semple, however, there was at least the consolation of knowing he had called new attention to an old and important problem. In the years ahead, the difficulties that faced government engineers at the entrance to the river may have stirred second thoughts about his proposed canal. Between 1910 and 1912, during the first two years of work on the North Jetty, more than thirty ships perished on the bar.[30]

Such disappointments did not seem to discourage Semple. There were always new ideas emerging from his varied involvements—especially from his endeavors at Seattle. His years of association with the canal scheme had familiarized him with a number of the hydraulic engineering difficulties connected with that enterprise. After 1900 one of the most pressing of these problems was the need for reliable sluicing pipe. In 1904 Semple was awarded a patent on a wood-lined steel sluicing pipe which he had already put to use on Beacon Hill.[31] The new conduit resisted the erosive force of water and gravel more effectively than other pipe because it was lined with laminated blocks of wood with the grain placed on end.

Unfortunately the patent yielded its inventor nothing but grief. Shortly after obtaining it, Semple came into conflict with the Lewis Construction Company and other Seattle outfits which he accused of pirating his invention to use on their own sluicing work on Denny Hill and elsewhere in the city. Charging an infringement of patent, he demanded twelve thousand dollars.[32] Lewis Construction refused to

28. Portland *Oregon Journal,* October 19, 25, 1906.

29. *Oregonian,* November 19, 1906, and April 9, 1907.

30. Gibbs, *Pacific Graveyard,* p. 140.

31. See Box 8, folders 31 to 33 inclusive, Semple Papers, particularly the letter from Semple's patent attorney, L. T. Turner to Philip Tindall, March 11, 1908.

32. Semple to Twyman O. Abbott, August 30, 1907, and September 16, 1907. Abbott was another of Semple's attorneys in the patent litigation.

discuss the matter, contending that it was using a different patent.[33] Semple took the matter to court, only to have Judge Cornelius Hanford reject his claim.[34] When Semple threatened to appeal the decision, however, his adversary decided to avert further court costs and unfavorable publicity by offering a private settlement of two thousand dollars in royalties and damages.[35] The offer did not satisfy Semple, and he appealed Hanford's decree to the court of patents in San Francisco in 1908. The appeal was denied.[36]

None of these schemes of Semple's later years earned the former governor a dime. As a consequence he and his family often faced economic hardship. At times his needs grew desperate. "I am willing to endure allmost [sic] anything in the shape of danger or deprivation in order to make some money," he told Lucy in 1898 during a lengthy halt in work on the south canal.[37] After failing, despite Governor John Rogers' endorsement, to receive an army commission during the Spanish-American War because of his age,[38] Semple lowered his sights. "I am a pretty good sailor and am ready to put my hand to anything," wrote the fifty-eight-year-old ex-governor, introducing himself to Captain J. B. Libby of Port Townsend in hope of finding work at sea. "I would not expect a large pay."[39] But Libby needed younger men and refused to hire him. Later he approached directors of Andrew Hemrich's Seattle Brewing and Malting Company with a proposal to introduce the firm's beer into the Philippines but was turned down.[40]

For his immediate family Semple left no tangible legacy. In his last years he mortgaged his remaining stock in the waterway company and its subsidiaries to Lucy in partial payment of the debt he had accumulated against her account over the previous thirty years.[41] The arrangement left the aging promoter in even greater need.

Semple's failure to provide more adequately for his family or himself is understandable. He was first and always a dreamer, intoxicated by the opportunities the frontier of the Pacific Northwest presented. Like many members of a young society, he was often more concerned with

33. Turner to Tindall, March 11, 1908.
34. Ibid.
35. F. E. Swanstrom to Zoe Semple, April 17, 1908.
36. Ibid.
37. Semple to Lucy Ames, June 12, 1898.
38. Semple to Senator John L. Wilson, May 27, 1898.
39. Semple to J. B. Libby, September 1, 1898.
40. Semple to Lucy Ames, August 31, 1898.
41. Semple to Zoe, Maude, and Ethel Semple, December 7, 1903.

the potential of the future than with the immediate problems of the present. "I can live very comfortably either in Seattle, Portland or Astoria for $25 a month in order to have money for an emergency," he informed one of his daughters in 1906.[42] To Semple, the "emergency" may well have been another freshly hatched promotional scheme. And so, on the borrowed money of relatives he lived out his last years in rented rooms. Inspirations like the Astoria and Seaside projects occupied his attention until the end. Ultimately these obsessions became the old man's great solace.

Eugene Semple died on August 28, 1908, in a San Diego rest home where he had been taken after suffering a heart attack the previous December. He was sixty-eight. Seattle and Portland newspapers carried front-page obituaries. In an interview in the *Post-Intelligencer* Will Parry hailed Semple as "a great creative engineer who, lacking formal training, had to step aside to let other men realize his dreams." He is, Parry proclaimed, "the father of the tideland improvements."[43] It was a handsome tribute but it was not the full measure of the man. Semple had come West in 1863 looking for something. His career indicates that he never found it, that he never even knew quite what it was he was seeking. If his intention had been to get rich, then surely his subsequent life had been a failure. But more than an acquisitive instinct had driven him through the years. Semple was an adventurer, always ready for challenges and excitement. He was also an idealist, willing to speak his mind on issues that mattered. He was by nature a restless man, goaded by an overly active imagination—an individual whose achievements could never quite match his expectations. Despite his practical talents as engineer, lawyer, and promoter, he was essentially a dreamer, as were so many other men who have moved onto America's western frontiers.

Semple's particular significance in Pacific Northwest history lies in his involvement, successfully and otherwise, in so many of the activities that shaped the development of the region. In recording the exploits of the major figures of any time or place, one must also take account of men like Semple who were present to offer the opposition and the alternatives, as inadequate as they may often have been. In this respect it is perhaps symbolic that Semple was the first losing candidate for governor of the new State of Washington; a man who, during a long, active involvement in politics, never won an important elective office.

42. February 6, 1906. It is not certain to which daughter he was writing.
43. Seattle *Post-Intelligencer,* August 29, 1898.

His career is also testimony to the notable contribution to the settlement of the West made by the peripatetic and often farsighted entrepreneur who prodded the public consciousness or enticed the private investor in order to exploit a situation or develop a natural resource. Many of these men combined in their activities a strong sense of public duty with a lively interest in the advancement of their own affairs. Semple in particular had a talent for promoting his ideas not only with conservative financiers but with the public at large. Thus, even in the midst of the severe nation-wide financial depression of the early nineties he was able to arouse Seattle residents as well as eastern investors to support construction of a canal from Elliott Bay into Lake Washington. No one before him had been able to do this. The fact that his vigorous espousal of a south canal only led to the success of a rival project is, in a sense, unimportant. One may only wonder how and when the vast program of tideland reclamation, which accelerated the commercial development of Seattle in the early twentieth century, would have unfolded without Semple's influence.

Mark Twain, who grew up not far from Semple's boyhood home in Illinois, once aptly expressed the importance to America of men like Eugene Semple:

In America nearly every man has his dream, his pet scheme, whereby he is to advance himself socially or pecuniarily. . . . It is a characteristic which is both bad and good, for both the individual and the nation. Good, because it allows neither to stand still, but drives both forever on, toward some point or other which is ahead. . . . Bad, because the chosen point is often badly chosen, and then the individual is wrecked. . . . Still, it is a trait which it is . . . better for a people to have and sometimes suffer from than to be without.[44]

44. Mark Twain and Charles D. Warner, *The Gilded Age,* Introduction, p. xvii.

Bibliography

The Eugene Semple Papers constitute the most important single source for this study and, indeed, its justification. The papers, which are deposited in the Manuscripts Division of the University of Washington Library in Seattle, comprise a varied and substantial collection of documents relating to Semple's domestic and public life. They contain approximately six thousand incoming letters and six thousand outgoing letters from or about Semple, included either in his general correspondence folders or in subgroups such as the papers of the Seattle and Lake Washington Waterway Company. The Semple Papers also contain business receipts, court briefs, contracts, news clippings, diaries, jottings for speeches and editorials, diagrams, blueprints, patents, and numerous other items, all illuminating his active career.

Nearly every phase of Semple's life is documented, from the time of his arrival in the Pacific Northwest in 1863 at the age of twenty-three until his death in 1908. The period 1889-1908 is especially well covered. For despite a restless nature and a frequently disorganized personal life, Semple was a conscientious collector and preserver of materials relating to his affairs. On the other hand, he occasionally omitted evidence (particularly family letters) when it reflected unfavorably upon his career. The collection was enhanced significantly in 1965 by the donation from his granddaughter, Mrs. Lucy Adair of Seattle, of several hundred items pertaining especially to Semple's early years in the Northwest. This contribution was particularly helpful in piecing together the details of Semple's life in Oregon politics.

The Semple Papers are well arranged and indexed in the manuscripts

section. They are supplemented by the papers of several of his contemporaries in Seattle public life and by nine scrapbooks of news clippings, compiled by Semple and others, in the Northwest Collection of
the Library.

MANUSCRIPTS AND ORIGINAL SOURCES

Abstract of Votes Polled in the Territory and State of Washington
    1865-1950 (Microcopy), University of Washington Library.
Clarence B. Bagley Scrapbooks, Northwest Collection, University of
    Washington Library.
Erastus Brainerd Papers, University of Washington Library.
Thomas Burke Papers, University of Washington Library.
Grover Cleveland Papers (Microcopy), University of Washington Li-
    brary.
Department of the Interior Appointment Files (Eugene Semple) (Micro-
    copy), University of Washington Library.
Elisha P. Ferry Papers, University of Washington Library.
Daniel H. Gilman Papers, University of Washington Library.
Governors' Papers, Washington Territory and State (s.v. Elisha Ferry;
    Eugene Semple). Washington State Archives, Olympia.
John J. McGraw Papers, University of Washington Library.
Edmond S. Meany Pioneer File, Northwest Collection, University of
    Washington Library.
Oregon Improvement Company Papers, University of Washington Li-
    brary.
Records of the Proceedings of the Harbor Line Commission. State Ar-
    chives, Olympia.
William F. Vilas Papers, Wisconsin Historical Society, Madison.

THESES

Airey, Wilfred J. "A History of the Constitution and Government of
    Washington Territory." Ph.D. dissertation, University of Washington,
    1945.
Johansen, Dorothy O. "Capitalism on the Far Western Frontier: The
    Oregon Steam Navigation Company." Ph.D. dissertation, University
    of Washington, 1941.

Wilson, Robert Arden. "A History of the Chinese Question in Early Oregon, 1850-1886." Master's thesis, University of Washington, 1942.

PRINTED DOCUMENTS

Congressional Record, 48th Cong., 1st sess., 1886, and 50th Cong., 2d sess., 1888.

Donaldson, Thomas. *The Public Domain: Its History with Statistics.* House Executive Document No. 47 (Serial 2158), 46th Cong., 3d sess., 1884.

Gates, Charles M., ed. *Messages of the Governor of Washington Territory to the Legislative Assembly, 1854-1889.* Seattle: University of Washington Press, 1940.

House Executive Documents No. 36 and No. 40, 52d Cong., 2d sess., 1892-93.

House Reports No. 1025 (Serial 2601), 50th Cong., 1st sess., 1887-88, and No. 2395, 52d Cong., 2d sess., 1892-93.

Journal of the Executive Proceedings of the Senate of the United States. Vols. 5 (1837-41), and 25 (1885-87).

Laws of Washington Territory, 1887-88, 1889-90. Olympia.

Official Proceedings of the Columbia Waterway Convention, 1st and 2d sess., 1885, 1886. Vancouver, Wash.

Oregon Laws, 1843-1872. Salem, 1874.

Pacific Reporter, Vols. 36 and 55. St. Paul, Minn.

Powell, Captain Charles, and Major W. A. Jones. *Report of Salmon Fishing on the Columbia River.* Senate Executive Document No. 123 (Serial 2510), 50th Cong., 1st sess., 1888.

Report of the Adjutant General of Washington Territory to the Legislative Assembly, 1887-88. Olympia, 1888.

Reports of the Governor of Washington Territory to the Secretary of the Interior, 1885-88. Washington, D.C.

Report of the Penitentiary Building Commissioners to the Governor and Legislative Assembly of Washington Territory. Olympia, 1887.

Report of the Surveyor General of Washington Territory to the Legislative Assembly, 1887. Olympia, 1888.

Report of the Territorial Treasurer to the Legislative Assembly of Washington, 1885-1887. Olympia, 1887.

Revised Statutes of the United States . . . 2d ed. Washington, D.C., 1878.

——— . . . Supplement, Vol. 1 (1874-91), Washington, D.C., 1891.

Senate Journal of the State of Oregon, 1870, 1872, 1874. Salem.

Session Laws of the State of Washington, 1890, 1893. Olympia.

Statutes of the Territory of Washington. Olympia, 1854.

United States Bureau of the Census. *Tenth Census (1880).* Washington, D.C., 1883.

———. *Eleventh Census* (1890). Washington, D.C., 1892.

United States Statutes at Large, Vol. 17, (1871-73), 42d Cong., 2d sess., and Vol. 25 (1888-89), 50th Cong., 2d sess. Washington, D.C.

United States Supreme Court Reports, Vol. 146.

Washington Reports, Vols. 2, 4, 8. (Kreider), and Vol. 35 (Remington).

Washington State Land Commissioners. *Biennial Reports.* 2d through 8th, 1893-1905. Olympia.

Washington State Harbor Line Commission. *First Report.* Olympia, 1891.

———. *First Biennial Report.* Olympia, 1893.

Washington State Legislature. *House Journal.* 1891, 1893, 1901. Olympia.

———. *Senate Journal,* 1891, 1893, 1901. Olympia.

NEWSPAPERS

Astoria (Oregon) *Daily Astorian,* 1887

Astoria *Daily Budget,* 1904-6

Colfax (Washington) *Palouse Gazette,* 1887

Eugene *Oregon State Journal,* 1874-75

Jacksonville *Oregon Sentinel,* 1863

Lewiston (Idaho) *Teller,* 1887

Moscow (Idaho) *Star,* 1887

Olympia (Washington) *Standard,* 1888

Portland *Daily Bulletin,* 1872

Portland *Daily Oregon Herald,* 1866, 1869-70, 1872

Portland *Oregon Journal,* 1905-6

Portland *Oregon Mercury,* 1887

Portland *Oregonian,* 1864-1907

Portland *Sunday Welcome,* 1887

St. Helens (Oregon) *Mist,* 1878

Salem *Mercury,* 1872

Salem *Oregon Statesman,* 1864-66, 1872

Seaside (Oregon) *Signal,* 1905
Seattle *Weekly Argus,* 1895
Seattle *Bulletin,* 1901
Seattle *Daily Press* 1886, 1888-89
Seattle *News,* 1896
Seattle Weekly *News-Letter,* 1902
Seattle *Post-Intelligencer,* 1885-1914
Seattle *Star,* 1901-2
Seattle *Telegraph,* 1890
Seattle *Times,* 1895
Spokane Falls *Chronicle,* 1885, 1887, 1889
Spokane *Review,* 1888
Tacoma *Daily Ledger,* 1889, 1892-93
Vancouver (Washington) *Independent,* 1883-87
Walla Walla *Statesman,* 1885-87

BOOKS, DIRECTORIES, AND PAMPHLETS

Bagley, Clarence B. *History of Seattle from the Earliest Settlement to the Present Time.* 3 vols. Chicago: S. J. Clarke Co., 1916.

Bancroft, Hubert Howe. *History of Oregon, 1848-1888.* 2 vols. San Francisco: History Co., 1890.

———. *History of Washington, Idaho, and Montana, 1845-1889.* San Francisco: History Co., 1890.

Bean, Walton. *California: An Interpretive History.* New York: McGraw-Hill, 1968.

Biographical Directory of the American Congress, 1774-1961. Washington, D.C., 1961.

Cassidy, Francis P. *Catholic College Foundations and Developments in the United States, 1677-1850.* Washington, D.C., 1924.

Coman, Edwin T., Jr., and Helen M. Gibbs. *Time, Tide, and Timber: A Century of Pope and Talbot.* Stanford, Calif.: Stanford University Press, 1949.

David, Henry. *The History of the Haymarket Affair.* New York: Russell and Russell, 1958.

Edwards, Jonathan. *Illustrated History of Spokane County.* San Francisco: W. H. Lever, 1900.

Frederick, James V. *Ben Holladay.* Glendale: Arthur H. Clark Co., 1940.

Gibbs, James A. *Pacific Graveyard: A Narrative of the Ships Lost Where the Columbia River Meets the Pacific Ocean.* Portland: Binfords and Mort, 1950.

Hill, Walter H. *Historical Sketches of St. Louis University.* St. Louis: P. Fox, 1879.

Hines, Harvey K. *An Illustrated History of the State of Washington.* Chicago: Lewis Publishing Co., 1893.

The History and Advantages of the Canal and Harbor Improvement Project Now Being Executed by the Seattle and Lake Washington Waterway Company. Seattle, 1902.

The History of Central Washington. Chicago: Interstate Publishing Company, 1904.

Hittell, John S. *The Commerce and Industries of the Pacific Coast.* San Francisco: A. L. Bancroft and Co., 1882.

Hyde, William, and Howard L. Conrad. *Encyclopaedia of the History of St. Louis.* 4 vols. New York and Louisville: The Southern History Co., 1899.

Johansen, Dorothy O., and Charles M. Gates. *Empire of the Columbia: A History of the Pacific Northwest.* New York: Harper and Row, 1967.

Kelly, Sister Mary G. *The Career of Joseph Lane, Frontier Politician.* Washington, D.C., 1942.

Kinnear, George. *The Anti-Chinese Riots at Seattle.* Seattle: Privately published, 1911.

Lucia, Ellis. *Ben Holladay.* New York: Hastings House, 1959.

McGrane, Reginald C. *The University of Cincinnati: A Success Story in Urban Education.* New York: Harper and Row, 1963.

Maddux, Percy. *City on the Willamette.* Portland: Binfords and Mort, 1952.

Meany, Edmond S. *History of the State of Washington.* New York: Macmillan Co., 1927.

Mott, Frank Luther. *American Journalism.* New York: Macmillan Co., 1941.

National Cyclopedia of Biography. Vol. 17. New York, 1937.

Nesbit, Robert C. *He Built Seattle: A Biography of Judge Thomas Burke.* Seattle: University of Washington Press, 1961.

Nevins, Allan. *Grover Cleveland: A Study in Courage.* New York: Dodd, Mead, and Co., 1934.

Oregon Historical Records Survey. *Vol. 1 Multnomah County.*Portland: Works Progress Administration, 1937.

——. *Vol. 24 Washington County.* Portland: Works Progress Administration, 1940.

Paul, Rodman W. *Mining Frontiers of the Far West, 1848-1880.* New York: Holt, Rinehart, and Winston, 1963.

Polk's Portland City Directory, 1865. Portland, n.d.

Pomeroy, Earl S. *The Territories and the United States, 1861-1890.* Philadelphia: University of Pennsylvania Press, 1947.

Powderly, Terence V. *The Path I Trod.* New York: Columbia University Press, 1940.

Prosser, William F. *A History of the Puget Sound Country.* 2 vols. New York and Chicago: Lewis Publishing Co., 1903.

Quiett, Glenn C. *They Built the West.* New York: D. Appleton and Century Co., 1934.

Samuel's Directory of Portland, 1873-74. Portland, 1874.

Scott, Harvey W. *History of Portland, Oregon.* Syracuse: D. Mason and Co., 1890.

Seattle and Environs. 4 vols. Seattle, 1924.

Semple, Eugene, *Martial Law at Seattle: An Inquiry into the Necessity Therefor.* Vancouver, Wash., 1886.

Shannon Fred A. *The Organization and Administration of the Union Army, 1861-1865.* 2 vols. Cleveland: Arthur H. Clark Co., 1928.

Snowden, Clinton A. *History of Washington: The Rise and Progress of an American State.* 6 vols. New York: Century History Co., 1909.

Taft, Phillip. *Organized Labor in American History.* New York: Harper and Row, 1964.

The Port of Seattle, Fourth Anniversary, 1915. Seattle Port Commission, 1915.

Thomson, Reginald H. *That Man Thomson,* ed. Grant H. Redford. Seattle: University of Washington Press, 1950.

Turnbull, George S. *History of Oregon Newspapers.* Portland: Binfords and Mort, 1939.

Twain, Mark, and Charles D. Warner. *The Gilded Age.* Hartford, Conn: American Publishing Co., 1874.

Villard, Henry. *Memoirs of Henry Villard, Journalist and Financier, 1835-1900.* 2 vols. Boston and New York: Houghton Mifflin Co., 1904.

Washington Fishermen's Association. *Washington's Salmon Fisheries on the Columbia River.* Ilwaco, Wash., 1894.

ARTICLES

Ault, Nelson A. "The Earnest Ladies: The Walla Walla Women's Club and the Equal Suffrage League of 1886-1889," *Pacific Northwest Quarterly,* 42 (1951): 123-37.

Beardsley, Arthur S. "Compiling the Territorial Codes of Washington," *Pacific Northwest Quarterly,* 28 (1937): 3-54.

———. "The Codes and Code Makers of Washington, 1889-1937," *Pacific Northwest Quarterly,* 30 (1939): 3-50.

Calkins, R. H. "The Lake Washington Ship Canal," *Marine Digest,* 30 (February 17, 1951): 2-15.

"Colonel Frank J. Parker," *Washington Historical Quarterly, 19 (1928): 159-60.*

Cushman, Mary S. A. "General James Semple," *Transactions of the Illinois State Historical Society,* 1905, pp. 62-74.

"Dr. Nathaniel Ostrander," Cowlitz County Historical Quarterly, August, 1959, pp. 1-3.

Ellis, David. "The Forfeiture of Railroad Land Grants, 1867-1894," *Mississippi Valley Historical Review,* 33 (1946): 26-60.

Ganoe, John Tilson, "History of the Oregon and California Railroad," *Oregon Historical Quarterly,* 25 (1924): 273-83.

Gaston, Joseph. "The Oregon Central Railroad," *Oregon Historical Quarterly,* 3 (1902): 315-26.

Gates, Paul W. "The Homestead Act in an Incongruous Land System," *American Historical Review,* 41 (1936): 652-81.

Hansen, Woodrow J. "Robert Semple: Pioneer, Promoter, Politician," *California Historical Society Quarterly,* 35 (1962): 223-35.

Hynding, Alan A. "Eugene Semple's Seattle Canal Scheme," *Pacific Northwest Quarterly,* 59 (1968): 77-87.

———. "The Coal Miners of Washington Territory," *Arizona and the West,* 12 (1970): 221-36.

"Joint Ownership of the Oregon Railway and Navigation Company," *Northwest Magazine,* 15 (March 1897): 24-25.

Karlin, Jules A. "The Anti-Chinese Outbreaks in Seattle, 1885-1886," *Pacific Northwest Quarterly,* 39 (1948): 103-30.

Kingston, C. S. "The North Idaho Annexation Issue," *Washington Historical Quarterly,* 21 (1930): 133-37, 204-17.

Ludington, Flora Belle. "The Newspapers of Oregon, 1846-1870," *Oregon Historical Quarterly,* 26 (1925): 229-62.

Mills, Randall V. "History of Transportation in the Pacific Northwest," *Oregon Historical Quarterly*, 47 (1946): 289-90.

Mires, Austin. "Remarks on the Constitution of the State of Washington," *Washington Historical Quarterly*, 22 (1931): 276-88.

Murray, Keith A. "The Movement for Statehood in Washington," *Pacific Northwest Quarterly*, 32 (1941): 349-84.

Pearce, Stella E. "Suffrage in the Pacific Northwest," *Washington Historical Quarterly*, 3 (1912): 106-14.

Purvis, Neil H. "The History of the Lake Washington Canal," *Washington Historical Quarterly*, 25 (1934): 114-27, 210-13.

Radcliffe, Zoe Green. "Robert Baylor Semple, Pioneer," *California Historical Society Quarterly*, 6 (1927): 130-58.

Robbins, Roy M. "The Federal Land System in an Embryo State," *Pacific Historical Review*, 4 (1935): 356-75.

Scott, Leslie M. "The Oregonian Newspaper in Oregon History," *Oregon Historical Quarterly*, 29 (1928): 225-41.

Stevens, Frank E. "The Life of Stephen Arnold Douglas," *Journal of the Illinois State Historical Society*, 16 (1923-24): 247-673.

Teiser, Sidney. "William Strong, Associate Judge of the Territorial Courts," *Oregon Historical Quarterly*, 64 (1963): 293-309.

Tharp, Marilyn. "The Story of Coal at Newcastle," *Pacific Northwest Quarterly*, 48 (1957): 120-26.

"Trouble in the Coal Mines, 1889: Documents of an Incident at Newcastle, W.T.," *Pacific Northwest Quarterly*, 37 (1946): 213-57.

Wilcox, W. P. "Anti-Chinese Riots in Washington," *Washington Historical Quarterly*, 20 (1929): 204-12.

Williams, George H. "Political History of Oregon, 1853-65." *Oregon Historical Quarterly*, 2 (1901): 1-35.

Woodward, Walter C. "The Rise and Early History of Political Parties in Oregon," *Oregon Historical Quarterly*, 13 (1912): 16-70.

Index

Hynding, Alan, 1938–
　　The public life of Eugene Semple, promoter and politician
of the Pacific Northwest. Seattle, University of Washington Press ₁1973₁

　　　xiv, 195 p. illus. 23 cm.

　　Originally presented as the author's thesis, University of Washington. Bibliography : p. 175–183.

　　1. Semple, Eugene, 1840–1908.　　I. Title. 2. Northwest,
Pacific—History.
285678 F891.H96 1973　　　　979.5′04′0924　 [B]　　73–9903
　　ISBN 0–295–95288–1　　　　　　　　　　　　　　　　MARC

　　Library of Congress　　　　　　74 ₁4₁